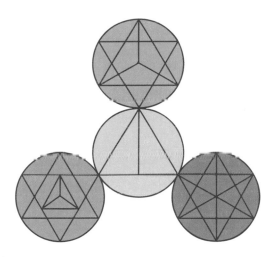

SIMRAN

BEING

The 7 Illusions That Derail Personal Power, Purpose, and Peace

REDFeather™
MIND | BODY | SPIRIT

An Imprint of Schiffer Publishing, Ltd.

Cover and interior design by Brenda McCallum
Type set in Desire/Garamond

ISBN: 978-0-7643-6371-9
Printed in India

Published by REDFeather Mind, Body, Spirit
An imprint of Schiffer Publishing, Ltd.
4880 Lower Valley Road
Atglen, PA 19310
Phone: (610) 593-1777; Fax: (610) 593-2002
Email: Info@redfeathermbs.com
Web: www.redfeathermbs.com

For our complete selection of fine books on this and related subjects, please visit our website at www.redfeathermbs.com. You may also write for a free catalog.

REDFeather Mind Body Spirit's titles are available at special discounts for bulk purchases for sales promotions or premiums. Special editions, including personalized covers, corporate imprints, and excerpts, can be created in large quantities for special needs. For more information, contact the publisher.

We are always looking for people to write books on new and related subjects. If you have an idea for a book, please contact us at proposals@schifferbooks.com.

Other REDFeather Titles by the Author:

Living: The 7 Blessings of Human Experience, ISBN 978-0-7643-6271-2

Other Schiffer Books on Related Subjects:

Dancing with Riches: In Step with the Energy of Change Using Access Consciousness® Tools, Kass Thomas, ISBN 978-0-7643-6154-8

The F.A.S.T.R. Process: The Secret of Emotional Power, Liz Barallon, ISBN 978-0-7643-5851-7

YOU ARE THE GATEWAY . . .
THROUGH THE 7 BLESSINGS OF HUMAN EXPERIENCE.
YOU HAVE AN INHERENT DESTINY TO EMBODY
THE 7 HUMAN EXPRESSIONS OF GRACE.
TO DO SO, YOU MUST DISSOLVE
THE 7 ILLUSIONS.

I AM . . . YOU ARE . . . WE ARE . . . THEY ARE . . . LOVE

IN ALL ITS FORMS

1
11
111
11:11

THE TRILOGY OF LIVING, BEING & KNOWING
BOOK 1
LIVING: THE 7 BLESSINGS OF HUMAN EXPERIENCE

BOOK 2
BEING: THE 7 ILLUSIONS THAT DERAIL PERSONAL POWER,
PURPOSE, AND PEACE

BOOK 3
KNOWING: THE 7 HUMAN EXPRESSIONS OF GRACE

CONTENTS

preface. 7

acknowledgments. 13

being. 14

this thing called life. 18

the play. 21

the bridge. 26

the illusion of time. 30

Emotional Obsessions 35

Our Global Reflection of Energy 38

The Hole of Slothfulness 43

The Key Whole of Devotion 46

Teacher to Example 49

Cultivating Listening 52

Hear Thyself 55

Petition for Presence 59

the illusion of duality. 61

Secret Obsessions 65

Our Global Reflection of Climate Change 68

The Hole of Lust 70

The Key Whole of Tenderness 73

Egoist to Humanitarian 75

Cultivating Appreciation 78

Receive Thyself 80

Petition for Unity 83

the illusion of money. 86

Material Obsessions 90
Our Global Reflection of Fashion 94
The Hole of Greed 97
The Key Whole of Trust 100
Businessman to Philanthropist 104
Cultivating Connection 108
Heal Thyself 111
Petition for Respect 114

the illusion of hierarchy. 116

Personal Obsessions 120
Our Global Reflection of Human Rights 123
The Hole of Envy 127
The Key Whole of Balance 129
Politician to Servant Leader 131
Cultivating Conversation 134
Know Thyself 137
Petition for Divine Equality 140

the illusion of identity. 142

Masked Obsessions 146
Our Global Reflection of Wellness 149
The Hole of Pride 153
The Key Whole of Innocence 156
Homogenized to Genius 160
Cultivating Naturalness 162
Free Thyself 165
Petition for Oneness 167

the illusion of evolution. 169

Spiritual Obsessions 172

Our Global Reflection of Security 176

The Hole of Gluttony 179

The Key Whole of Fulfillment 181

Visionary to Mystic 183

Cultivating Presence 186

Accept Thyself 188

Petition for Acceptance 191

the illusion of war. 193

Mental Obsessions 199

Our Global Reflection of Information and Technology 202

The Hole of Wrath 204

The Key Whole of Purity 206

Revolutionary to Spiritual Rebel 208

Cultivating Generosity 212

See Thyself 215

Petition for Peace 218

the sacrifice. 221

emulsify. 226

multidimensional. 229

the masters. 235

the matrix. 238

multidimensional sheaths. 240

glossary of dimensions. 248

glossary of terms. 250

about the author. 254

preface.

May you be awakened to the dysfunction of the global experience,
and in recognition of the part you play.
May you be pierced by the pain of the world,
in order to acknowledge your own.
May you see how you are being
the animal self that lurks within the shadows
as a dark force upon the planet.
May you receive this call
to inspiredly act
as the answer
to the world's petitions of prayer.

I look at my life as a petri dish. An experiment. I pay attention to what is happening within me. I also watch what is occurring outside me. Both perspectives teach me a lot about myself . . . others . . . and creation. This is how I gain insight, experience, and awareness into the inner workings of the world. Ever since I began looking at life in this way, my spiritual growth has accelerated exponentially. I have become aware of subtle sheaths that veil us from personal power, purpose, and peace. This came about due to deep curiosity as to our creative capacity in cocreation with the Divine. It became abundantly clear. Before seeking universal mysteries outside of you, it is imperative to explore the universe that exists within. I realized that nothing could change externally, unless I was willing to acknowledge and transform the discord that was internal. I committed wholeheartedly to *Being/being/BEING* a devoted student of life. However, I had no idea where this rabbit hole would lead. I certainly did not fathom what I ultimately came to discover.

The concept of mirrors is not all that new, but the degree to which an individual is willing to see their reflection makes all the difference in the world. It also becomes the catalyst for higher levels of *Self/self/SELF*-realization. This world is not just your mirror; *everything* within it is *your reflection*. The world outside *You/you/YOU* is speaking to *You*, about *you*. Its primary purpose is to assist *You/you/YOU* in becoming conscious of what is unconscious. If looking at the world as something separate, judging it, or wanting it to be different, *You/you/YOU* have become lost within illusions. In addition, *You/you/YOU* become a major contributor toward facilitating exactly what *You/you* see out there. Ironically, the very things that get under your skin illustrate who *you* are completely unaware of *being*.

The state of the world is an amplification of what exists within *you/me/us/them*.

There are animals among us. I have discovered the animal inside; one that hungrily drools within every person. This beastie has lurked amid the shadowlands . . . hunting and gathering . . . growling, pouncing, and killing. Inner beasties roam wildly in our world, while also running our world. This animalistic nature kills without warning. It gorges and remains unconsciously on the prowl. This raw hunger and instinct to hunt is foundational in the problems that exist in today's world. Lions . . . and tigers . . . and bears . . . oh *mine/ yours/theirs/ours*!

There is also a monster inside. This ugly and frightening *being* is the consciousness within *you/me/us/them* that creates the most vile, traumatic, and evil acts upon our planet. *We* each hold a piece of this. *You/i/we/they* must come to terms with this part. Until *you/i/ we/they* are able to face, embrace, and absorb the monstrous nature within, *we* will continue to bear witness to the painful, cruel, and unbearable. There are countless individuals throughout history who have been labeled monsters, psychopaths, and mentally ill. If *we* are all *One/one/ONE,* . . . where is that in *you/me/us/them*? How did we collectively create these individuals? Did they become who they are in service to our discovery of *Self/self/ SELF*, humanity, and the demonic nature inside?

We can talk about *Being* as an aspect of stillness.
We can aspire to embody *BEING* as higher power and presence.
We must also address the animalistic, raw, and monstrous nature of *being*.
How are you *being/Being/BEING*?

This book addresses the deeply denied and unconscious part of *you/me/us/them*. These are aspects that none of us want to know, see, or claim. However, this is the work that will transform the human species, moving us from impending doom to the enlightened creative capacity that awakens infinite possibilities for an entirely new earth experience. Transmuting the dense and negative nature of human *beingness* will bring about the era of peace that has been prophesied.

This is hard work; it is tedious. *You/you* will want to turn from it. Your ego will yawn, attempt to pull away, and convince *you* it is not necessary. *You* will try to convince yourself that this is not *You*. That very delusion has gotten our world to where it is. I implore *You/ you/YOU* to take your time and see these unconscious, hidden parts of *You*. Even if only getting through a few paragraphs each day, your presence serves *You* and something much greater than yourself. The current expression of individual and collective *Being/being/ BEING* manifests the world *You* see. It also dictates the kind of world that is passed on. Most people are unaware of how powerfully their subconscious underworld manipulates, influences, and creates everything that exists.

Each book in this series portrays a different dimension that exists within *You/you/ YOU* simultaneously, with this one *Being/being/BEING* most critical for our world at this time. Whether *You* read these three books in order, all at once, or one at a time . . . it is particularly important to read *this one*. *BEING* supports immediate, impactful individual and collective change. It is an invitation for sacred activism, in how *You/you/YOU* may intimately participate in *being the change*.

Have *You* been listening to how the world is speaking?
Are *YOU* aware it is speaking to *You*, about *you*?

BEING engages the bold and courageous conversation that each person must engage right now. It points to how *you/i/we/they* are *Being/being/BEING* and the way that affects this world. The details of our lives may be different, but the ripples and energetic impact are very much the same. Taking a radically honest view of individual and collective codependence versus conscious interdependence determines whether the world moves toward unending destruction, or genuine renewal. Igniting a new world order requires that *you/i/we/they* look at our *Self/self/SELF*-absorbed tendencies. *BEING* addresses the nature and nurture of individual power . . . the misuse of power . . . true power . . . dominant power . . . personal power . . . and global empowerment.

We either continue killing each other physically, emotionally, and spiritually—*being* the disease on the planet —or become the cure, by shifting into higher octaves of *Being/BEING*. Our world is calling for presence to the darkness *being* embodied. This dark shadow is not over there . . . in them . . . or outside. It is sitting exactly where *You/you* are, wreaking havoc right under your nose. This book is a call for radical honesty regarding the addictions, distractions, excuses, lies, and distortions keeping *you/me/us/them* gridlocked in the illusion of separation, pain, and evil. Initiating this level of soul activism is social and spiritual justice. This is critical not only to *your/my/their/our* greater good, but also to all of life.

In focusing on the minutiae of the false *Self/self,*
the scope of what is possible for collective humanity narrows.
Thus, the world becomes smaller, more constricted and dense.

The Self-Realization Series, which includes this book, *BEING*. It is written in a specific manner, so that you recognize where you express and create from. For the purposes of illustrating your multi-dimensional aspects of being, certain words are written as (1) lower case, (2) first letter upper case and the remaining lower case, or (3) all upper case.

The lower case designation refers to your shadow-animal-monster state. When the 'first letter' is capitalized and remainder lower case, it illustrates your unconscious, conditioned and robotic expression. All capital letters represents your more aware, sacred and embodied humanity. When two have been combined, your energy leans toward related spectrums. When all three are written as one — such as *self/Self/SELF* — this unified embrace is the entirety of you. All dimensions of you exist simultaneously. For a more detailed understanding of this wording style, skip to the "Glossary of Dimensions" and "Glossary" at the end of this book. Otherwise, allow your intuitive nature to connect with the text. Let its medicine work within each level and dimension of you.

There are many ways to read this book if you do not read from beginning to end. (1) Choose the section that corresponds with a "blessing" you are experiencing. Each section is laid out to assist you in moving into a higher octave of experience. (2) Focus the bold quotes. Let these become points of contemplation, meditation or mantra. This creates a deeper experience of the intuitive and mystical side of you. (3) Read one paragraph, or one page, daily. Let the concepts sink in more fully. Contemplation, meditation, discussion or journalling will expand these for you. (4) Let the section titles and italicized subquestions deepen through personal exploration. Then, when you go back to read the actual sections, they can serve as confirmation of your own personal awareness. (5) You can also use this as an oracle. Open the book randomly each day and receive a message. Regardless of the method that feels right, this is your "how-to" guide for life. It is intended to slow you down to more deeply experience the timeless present.

I stress the use of *you/i/we/they* and *you/me/us/them* because there is no separation. *We* cocreate as one entity—known as the collective—even though *you/i/we/they* appear as separate individuals. If something is true for one of us, it will be true for all of us. *You/i/ we/they* are the village . . . and that village is not currently present, nor has it ever been. It is said that *it takes a village to raise a child*. Evidence shows that *you/i/we/they* are very quickly destroying ours.

The seven illusions shared here are the shadowlands where *you/i/we/they* are wrapped in our own makings. These reflections depict where *you/i/we/they* reside as *unconscious* beings, embodying *shadow-animal* expressions. Global reflections illustrate our collective impact. What *you/i/we/they* do not fully see, hear, or acknowledge erupts upon the planet as cocreated, collective expressions. Within this earthen village, *individuals/families/ countries/earth* have been calling for a massive shift through actions, reactions, and energetic undercurrents. *You/i/we/they* have not been looking or listening with conscious presence. Instead, *you/i/we/they* further fuel the need for change through our collective ignorance.

Together, *you/i/we/they* have an opportunity to initiate spiritual and conscious renewal. *You/i/we/they* could also remain apathetic, complacent, and indifferent, allowing the world to continue in its downward spiral. If unwilling to embrace *Self/self/SELF-* responsibility for our global issues, human life will eventually cease to exist. At the rate we are going, that will be sooner than later. I believe *you/i/we/they* want to make a difference. However, most people do not necessarily believe that a single individual can truly effect change. However, one person can. You are that one. Beneath these collective global issues are the foundational core issues of each human *being*. Imagine more than one individual engaging this socio-spiritual integration. In truth, a grassroots effort can embolden massive change very quickly. *You/you/YOU* are the one that can initiate this effort. In becoming aware of the tremendous role *You/you/YOU* play, something in your *Being/being* will begin to change as *You* do the work . . . thus, shifting *your/our* world.

It is a gift to be among the living.
Celebrating that requires wholehearted residency.
By doing so, the byproduct will be greater aliveness.

This writing is for those who have done endless amounts of personal growth, spiritual development, pollyanna thinking, and positive mindset affirming. It is for the dreamers, the seekers, the questioners, the contemplators, and the awake ones. This book is for individuals daring to be brave, courageous, and powerful beyond measure . . . for those who long to touch the sweet, tender center of their own humanity . . . and for persons desiring to see their world really change. These thoughts are for *the better* and *the worse*.

It has been written for people living like hamsters on a wheel, experiencing superficial existences, and for anyone who has encountered pain or heartache. It is for individuals who have settled . . . those whose lives are boring, mundane, or staid . . . and people seeking a brand of sacred activism.

This sharing is for persons who have achieved status, wealth, and success but still feel empty in quiet moments. It is a guide for those who are tired, frustrated, afraid, or depressed . . . and for the numb and apathetic. This book will serve those who try too hard, serve too much, and are given too little. It is for individuals who sell their souls through egoic aspirations of approval, greed, or an attempt to fit in. It is also for people that believe they are here to fix, heal, or save the world. It is for individuals who seek significance or meaning, and those who desperately need to feel needed. It is especially for light workers, galactic travelers, alien seekers, and those bent on ascending.

By the end of this book, *You/you* will see how *You/you/YOU* have been sitting back, sleeping, dreaming, and unconsciously playing within an illusion of your own making. The twisted grin of codependence will stare *You* in the face. *You/you* will discover that *You* do the very things that *You/you/YOU* condemn, albeit in more subtle, aesthetic, and linguistically modified ways. To truly wake up, *You/you/YOU* must admit *You/you* are inert and asleep, deeply so. Then, *You* will finally abandon the illusion of waking.

Do not run from darkness, shadows, and negativity. Instead, embrace them for the richness they offer toward personal and planetary healing. Through embodiment, *You/you* not only heighten your individual frequency but also create a rippling impact for cellular, generational, and collective shifts. In crossing from human *being/Being* into Divine *Knowing/KNOWING*, *You/you/YOU* serve in sacred advocacy of the extraordinary that is hidden within the ordinary.

Unconscious ways must cease, and innocence is to be reclaimed. Your multidimensional life is the way through the *eye/i/I* of the needle. *You/you/YOU* are the *One/one/ONE* who created this fabrication of reality. Life is simply a quilt of experiences and expressions made from *your/my/their/our* unique patches coming together in one beautiful masterpiece.

Sometimes, it is necessary to take a step back in order to move forward. This is that step back. This bold reflection outlines the deconditioning required for shifting what weighs *you/me/us/them* down. *BEING: 7 Illusions That Derail Personal Power, Purpose, and Peace* was written because of an intimate interaction with darkness and indifference. This is my inspired response of *Light/LIGHT* and *Love/LOVE in action*, after walking through and bearing witness not only to my own unconscious shadow, animal, and monstrous nature, but also that which rests within our social systems and structures. This is fierce *Love/LOVE* and protection for the *One/one/ONE* doing harm to themselves and others. Although daunting to look at, this too is *Light/light/LIGHT*. Our world represents the horizontal *Light/light* spectrum that must be embraced and equilibrated into a vertical column of alignment and illumination. *Love/LOVE* your *self* into the *Light/LIGHTness* of *BEING*.

If this is the first book of this self-realization trilogy that *You* are reading, I urge you to also read *LIVING: 7 Blessings of Human Experience*, which supports deconditioning identity so that *You* may embark upon the higher frequency *graces* of book 3, *KNOWING: 7 Human Expressions of Grace*. *You* would not place new wall covering on top of old wallpaper. Do not place new thoughts over old ones, or *You/you* strengthen the small *self* into further *being*. It is necessary to create a clear, fresh slate for new consciousness to root. Books 1 and 2 assist in wiping that slate clean.

Be present to the information shared, even if *you* do not want to. Resistance is a clear sign there is work to be done. Arrogance will appear as thoughts of *having already done this work, intellectual knowing*, or *being better than the people this applies to*. Many light-workers are donning masks of *light/Light* instead of pure *Light/LIGHT*. That version of light is dimmed by an unconscious shadow that wears a veil of spirituality. This further contributes to emerging chaos and darkness. Such *artificial lighting* does an adequate job of spreading goodwill but is not necessarily pure, true, or interdependent. There exists *Light/LIGHT* far beyond what most are expressing at this time. Your deceptive intelligence and ego desire to distract and derail *You/you/YOU* from that pure illumination.

Through this series of books, *You/you/YOU* will be pointed to the places I have been deeply present to. I too stood in artificial light—albeit good and of service—but came to realize it as just another mask to siphon off. *You/i/we/they* are diamonds *Being/being/BEING* created from carbon, heat, and pressure. These elements fuse together, igniting us as sacred crystalline structures. We are human *Being/being/BEING*s, destined to be *HUE-MAN BEINGs*; the LIGHT-MAN cometh. Consciousness is activated within our diamond structures. In pure *Light/LIGHT*, we sparkle, shine, and radiate that high frequency of consciousness. Blessed *Being/being/BEING* . . . Breathe deeply as *You/you/YOU* begin seeing what *You/you/YOU* have not seen.

You **are in the dark . . .**
dreaming that *you* are waking up . . .
even though very much asleep,
and deeply unconscious.
Drowsiness can appear in the subtlest of ways,
especially for the intellectual, righteous, religious, and spiritual.
Only through the power of innocence and illumined intelligence
can true realization dawn
a new world experience
of
aliveness.

1 1 1 1
1 1 1
1 1
1

acknowledgments.

In Love … Of Love … With Love … As Love …

I am grateful for my life experiences, how they supported me, and the ways in which my soul needs, wants, and desires have been supplied.

Jane Mahoney, your steadfast faith in my voice and expression has meant so very much. You are the bridge that enabled these works to find their home. To my family at REDFeather / Schiffer Publishing, my heart and soul thank you for midwifing these books. I am in deep appreciation for you … Pete Schiffer, Chris McClure, Peggy Kellar, James Young, and everyone who supported these books in coming to life.

Jeff Spenard, Ryan Treasure, Jeff Gerstl, and my entire family at Voice America … it is an honor and a pleasure to cocreate *11:11 Talk Radio*. Thank you for the incredible collaboration each week that supports creating impactful shows. I am humbled and in gratitude to every single guest on *11:11 Talk Radio* and each feature within the pages of *11:11 Magazine*.

Grady Query and Mike Sautter, there are not adequate words to express my respect, admiration, love, and immense gratitude. I am deeply awed by your clarity and mastery of law. You are proof that integrity, kindness, compassion, and goodness are present within our legal system. Your advocacy for the law in regard to children's rights has been epic.

Michelle Patrao-Forsythe, Brooke Hurt, Tracey O'Brien, and Amber Sautter, I appreciate your grounded, steady presence and quiet service. Susanne Andrews, I am grateful for your friendship, heart, and feisty manner. Jessica Coons, thank you for your consistency and commitment. To my sacred sisterhood … I appreciate your presence and connection these past seven years. You know who you are. I love you.

Tuck Self and Larry Reed, thank you for being cherished soul family. You have been sacred witnesses, confidants, and best friends during the most incredible and bizarre times. Robert Jordan, you are my guardian angel. Perry Waska Finkelstein, thank you for being an incredibly loving, kind, and compassionate friend. Thank you Tim and Stacey Galloway for the safety of our friendship and the many sacred spaces provided along the way.

Sajan and Krishan, I love you completely and unconditionally. I honor the immense life experience your souls chose. May this series guide you toward your highest expressions of *LIVING, BEING*, and *KNOWING*. The Divine in me bows to the Divine in you.

being.

What vibration are you emitting?

Truth or Dare . . .
Do you dare see the intricate flowering of life
as it spirals in geometric progression,
to make all things unknown known?
This revealing mystery of you
is in cosmic delight
for the expansion of the Universe.
Come home dear one . . .
Come home.

Question everything written here. Test it. Have your own experience. Excavate proof. Discover what *You/you/YOU* believe beyond your conditioned beliefs. Bring your past, your future, and your present *Self/self/SELF* into the power of *now*. Let who *You* are meet who *you* have been, and who *YOU* have not known. This is the harmonic convergence of spirit and bone, shadow and blood, light and cellular structure.

In looking at life—whether your experience, family lineage, the news, or the lives of others—you can't make this up . . . and yet, *You/you/YOU* do. Life is an intricately woven matrix that organically utilizes whatever *you/i/we/they* create. In *Essence . . .* as *Essence . . .* and through *Essence, you/i/we/they* create our realities. Individual consciousness is that powerful. *You/i/we/they* have manifested everything that is seen, felt, and experienced.

There is no way to truly see the vastness of *Self/self/SELF* from your current lens. *You* are also unable to see your *Self/self/SELF* in the way others see *You/you/YOU*. Within a mirror, *You* see a reversed *image* of who *You think you* are, but not aware of what *You* are truly looking at. If *You* dare look deeper, there is much more than meets the *eye/i/I*. *You* cannot imagine what *You/you/YOU* have not seen, nor are *You/you/YOU* able to envision how Divine eyes see the *Self/self/SELF*.

Within the *left eye/I*, an infinite black hole at the center calls from your soul. It sees through your endless reflections. The soul came to experience itself in human form, to elicit a deep understanding of relationship within *Self/self/SELF*, with others and through the world. The soul knows your *Truth/truth/TRUTH*. This soul *eye/I* is your silent witnessing window to the inner world. This *eye/I* also symbolizes farsightedness, holding space for the big picture. The soul created a vision for your life, placing within it all that would support, guide, and direct *You/you/YOU*. The left side of your body encompasses the energy of the feminine, the mother, and receptive capacity. Additionally, the left engages the path of nurturing and birthing, signifying the inhale of relationship.

The *right eye/i* also has an endless black hole. This seeks to pull *You/you/YOU* outward. This is the *eye/i* of ego. It projects, creating a world out of all that is held internally but seen as external conditions. From this dual perspective, the ego garners image, identity, and personhood. Through a world of filters and veils, the ego acts and reacts. Inside conditions of its own making, ego erratically seeks to solve the same problems it has caused, by the very perspective that created them in the first place. This results in psychosis, as the mind loops in circles, going around and around itself. Guarded and restless, the deceptive intelligence seeks and searches for *self*-gain. The ego's only relationship is with its own need, agenda, and ambition.

This *eye/i* symbolizes nearsightedness for immediate gratification. This *eye/i* is always *right*, and needs to be. Symbolically, the right *eye/i* engages the energy of the masculine, the father, initiation, and action. However, it is designed to wait and be inspired by the feminine. When *You/YOU* are aligned to higher *Self/SELF*, the right side is balanced in its giving and receiving. This is the exhale of creation, allowing for form and matter. Manifestation is the intersecting point between the inner and outer worlds. These are inextricably linked.

Which black hole have *You/you/YOU* fallen into?
The hole of ego or . . . the whole of soul.

These two *pupils* are held within white pools of protection. The *eye/i/I* chambers transmit a world of perceptions and perspectives. These can be small and limited, or large and expansive. However, it is dependent on your state of *Being/being/BEING*. Both *eyes/i/Is* must maintain clear-sightedness to balance personal will and divine will. This is not to say each eye sees differently. They work together. However, either can become diminished in its capacity to see clearly. With distorted vision, a world of duality comes into view. When in harmony, they create single sight through the third *eye/I*.

It is time to check *your/my/our/their* vision. The reflections of our world portray distortion. These images also exist within and are what *You/you/YOU* have chosen to see. The world reflects your perspective. Life designs itself around your perception. What *You/you/YOU* look for is exactly what shall be found. Life gifts *You/you/YOU* with many lenses. *You/you/YOU* get to determine which *You* will peer through. With that focus and vision, *You/you/YOU* set an entire personal and global saga in motion.

What is *being*?
Who are you *being/Being*?
How are you *being/Being/BEING*?

In the context of this work, *being* has nothing to do with the spiritualized version of sitting still. It is not about meditation; long, hot baths; walks; or contemplation, nor does it connote becoming something. Those are all *self*-soothing methods that can be precursors to discovering true *Being/being/BEING*. Here, *being* consists of who and how *You/you/YOU* are as an interconnected expression of life. It is the manner in which *You/you/YOU* express word, thought, energy, and form. It is how *You/you* reflect life. *Being/being/BEING* is the particular energy and expression *You/you/YOU* emit and embody—consciously and unconsciously—in every moment. It is your transmission of actions, behaviors, thoughts, and feelings upon your surroundings—from gross to subtle. Your expression will shift in and out of varied states of *Being*, *being*, or *BEING* frequently—even within the course of a single day. They may also express simultaneously. Multiple dimensions of *Self/self/SELF* are present all of the time. But *You/you/YOU* are not necessarily present to them.

> **Great emphasis has been placed on *the needs* of the egoic *Self/self*,
> as opposed to the broadband spectrum of the whole.
> By ignoring the whole, *You/you/YOU* become ignorant of your wholeness.**

When *You/you* act with agenda or utilize manipulation, more of that appears. If your life is organic and unstructured, *You/you/YOU* will be drawn toward the natural order of the universe. Life is reflective of *You/you/YOU*, and your degree of alignment. *You/you/YOU* are the listener, and *You/you/YOU* are the one talking. *You/you/YOU* are the giver. *You* are the receiver; and *you* are the taker. *You/you/YOU* are an energetic signal, a human receiver. *You/you/YOU* will be the victim, the villain, the saint, and the sinner. As *You/you/YOU* shift in and out of these, *being/Being/BEING* ripples . . . touching each and every person on the planet, eventually returning to *You/you/YOU*. Your choice to lead from the heart, gut, or mind affects the energetic ecology of *your/our* world. Impulses that arise out of *Love/LOVE* reflect more *Love/LOVE* into the world. Those that emerge from fear bring about more fear. Blessed *one/One/ONE* . . . Breathe deeply as *You/you/YOU* discover many reflections of *Being/being/BEING*.

> **Have the courage to *be* a lone voice among noise,
> and an anomaly amid the masses.
> Let compassion lead,
> and the heart be filled with empathy.
> This lonely road is a sacrifice and surrender of *self/Self*.
> In truth, it shall be the annihilation of *Self/self/SELF*.
> This life is anointed by divine will.
> You can make it heaven or hell.
> There are many within *You/you/YOU*,
> with eyes to see, ears to hear, and energy to feel.
> Become still and know . . .
> who *you* are *being* . . .
> Create awareness for an empowered
> state of *Being/BEING* . . .**

Caution: *The ego will attempt to resist, fight, discount, deny, judge, and defend. When all else fails, it will make you feel tired, bored, and sleepy. Do not fall for its tricks.*

Warning: *This material is highly triggering to the ego. With each occurrence, feel—really feel. This is not easy work, nor is it what any of us wants to do, but it is what we each must do. Remaining blind casts the whole world into darkness.*
Take this book one day at a time.
Let it work within You/you/YOU.
The Divine BEING within me sees the Divine BEING within You.
I/You/We/They are capable of so much more than we have created.

this thing called life.

What are you allowing?

**Let light rise within your darkened spaces of mental activity.
Let harmony flow within your murky depths of emotion and feeling.
Become a clear pond of knowing.
Identity hijacked your hearing.
Personhood kidnapped your ability to see.
Let go of needing lessons.
Release fixing situations.
Harbor no more illusions . . .
See your *self* to know your *SELF*.
Embrace your personal power, purpose, and peace.**

Life is anything but random, although it can appear to be. Your web of connection spans as far back as time, and well into infinity. This moment . . . this experience . . . this life . . . is but an exhale of creation, one that extends time and time again. *You/you* emerged as a deep sigh that projects patterns, cycles, and rhythms. The in-breath draws *You* back from which *YOU/you* create, pulling in and absorbing everything beautiful and chaotic behind it. The exhale emits your cosmic signature, always creating anew. And it all rests within the vast nothingness of space.

Upon the return to emptiness, *You* will rest in the void. With life support, *YOU* shall return again and again, to express higher octaves *of your soul symphony. You/you/YOU* have been eons in the making. This incarnation is a mere speck of timelessness, but a most brilliant, glittering speck it is. Through *You/you/YOU*, life experiences something it has never known before.

**Life longed to create with *YOU*.
Life inhaled and dreamed of *You/you/YOU*.
Life exhales its brilliance as *You/you*.
You/you/YOU are a divine "aha" moment!**

Every experience is a multisensory one, utilizing the physical human form as a grounding rod from which to see from . . . hear through . . . taste of . . . be touched by . . . feel into . . . and breathe with. These sensory doorways lead to many worlds, both internal and external. They will enhance your experience of *Truth/truth/TRUTH*, illusion, desire, and dreams. Your senses are gateways to an inner cosmos, while bringing forth temptations upon an outer playground. *You/you/YOU* are a sensational universe that projects fields of tone, frequency, and vibration. In doing so, your creative meanderings create worlds upon worlds.

Your body holds your experiences, but its primary purpose is as a container for life to discover the magnitude of itself. The body is a direct link to the infinite unknown. It is a vehicle for expanding the experiential realm. *You/you/YOU*—as sight and sound, taste, and smell, touch, and feeling . . . and, especially, god capacity and humanity—are a divine revelation.

The greatest discovery and exploration of the universe lie right under your nose, and beneath your skin. Witnessing from behind your eyes is the treasure *You/you/YOU* have carried all along. Your primary purpose for *Being/being/BEING* is to ground incarnation, which bridges the manifestation of form and the formless.

Play the game . . . innocent one.
Have mischief and experience the fun . . . of building many castles in creation . . .
within the imaginal realm of human sensation.

You/you/YOU are the big bang—an entire universe—in all its glory, seeking remembrance. Through *Self*, expressions of doing reflect infinite possibilities of *Being/being/BEING*. *You/you/YOU* are electric in your ability to radiate lightness and density. Waves of undulating outbursts, implosions, and illuminations arc how *You/you* play with energy. *You/you* make stuff up! *You/you* hold unique perspectives. This is why *You/you/YOU* came. It is a game of hide-and-seek with eternity, as originally intended by a divine child of the universe. *You/you/YOU*—as the son (or daughter) of creation—will create endless realms of darkness and light.

Life's intention is . . .
to bring a sense of peace, a measure of understanding, and a deep breath of relaxation. May this exploration inspire compassionate presence within *You/you/YOU*. Life's surrender is in no way about giving up; it is opening to receive the full embrace of all that is available to *You/you/YOU*. This is the allowing . . . immersion . . . and embodiment of something more. Discover who controls your life . . . guides it . . . and holds space for it. Let go; let the *God/god/GOD* of your understanding lead, as you gain insight into who *God/god/GOD* is.

Life's vision is . . .
to create a clear understanding of presence. This vision is not a far-reaching image, or idea that *eye/i/I* hold, but the space *You/you/YOU* create upon completion of your sojourn. *You/you/YOU* are the vision that pulls this novel experience forward. *You* are *one*—of the many—that creates as the *ONE*. Within this ocean of consciousness, there are many fish, but there is *ONE* sea . . . and that *ONE* sees. *You* are not a fish out of water; *You/you* simply were caught in a net *You/you/YOU* cast. May *You* discover that there is no way out other than diving more deeply in. Drown within your ocean of consciousness.

Life's wish is . . .
that *You/you/YOU* experience an ecstatic integration of emotion, energy, humanity, and form. Let all of life deeply touch your heart, speak to your soul, calm your mind, and fill your spirit. May *You/you/YOU* embody peace and relaxation as *You/you* slip between the sheets of time. Be open to life's way with *You/you/YOU*. Life asks *You/you* to lie back and float along, allowing the waves to carry *You* onto many shores of understanding. Intimately sink into all that exists beneath

the surface of existence. Also, rise above the waves regularly to breathe in the fresh air of *Knowing/knowing/KNOWING*. Drown within *Love/LOVE*'s generous current and undertow.

Life's desire is . . .
that *You/you* commune with your humanity. Humanness is your doorway to divinity. The extraordinary is not to be sought beyond where *You/you/YOU* currently stand. It exists exactly where *You* are. *You* are never out of time, although *You/you* have been living outside this moment. There is nothing to evolve from, or into. *You/you/YOU* are not late or behind. Life is organic and requires your trust; it has your best interest at heart. Life knows what *You/you/YOU* deeply long for. It will remove everything that is not in alignment with that yearning.

Life's *LOVE* for *You/you/YOU* is grand.
It will obliterate any obstacle that withholds *You/you* from your *SELF*,
whether that be energetic, physical, mental, emotional, or spiritual.

Individuals who commit to the highest expression of *SELF* shift their paradigms and, in doing so, also change the world. For this to happen, *You/you/YOU* must embrace the density—known and unknown—that exists. *You/you/YOU* are the infinite flowering of the *ONE . . . IS*ness. *You/you/YOU* are the many—no thing and every thing—and the space between. *You/you/YOU* are the unification of all that *IS*. In spiraling out of control, life created a holy pathway toward *belonging*. Within all body temples, animate and inanimate, dwells the sacred geometry of energy, growth, truth, and wisdom, which merges in unification. Your moment-by-moment, fully embodied emanation is new-clear power. It is the BALM! Blessed *Being/being/BEING* . . . Breathe deeply as *You/you/YOU* become fully conscious of this thing called life.

Life is a sacred hideout . . . a divine petri dish of possibility . . .
a magic lamp of soul . . . holding wishes and dreams . . . to be polished and shined . . .
so to release the true nature . . . of Essence.
As your eyes close each eve,
may depths of sight open.
May *that which lies*
rise into the truth of awareness . . .
as *You* become the way . . .
the truth . . .
and
the life.

0
1
11
1111
0
1111
11
1
0

the play.

Who is the director, the actor, and the audience?

Life is a grand stage.
You have designed the setting.
You have chosen the characters.
You have created the landscape.
You wrote the story line.
You are the star.

Your soul created a virtual reality, producing a story line that it desired to live out. Trap doors, secret compartments, magic moments, hidden treasures, and passageways are all part of the adventure. Details of your character and supporting roles were planned long before *you* were born. Your fellow characters and coconspirators have specific scripts. *You/ you/YOU* have a destined ending.

Time is *how*, *where*, and *when* your soul experiences life . . . plays within it . . . witnesses it . . . and watches it . . . again and again. This is an interactive design where the external landscape reflects and matches your moods, feelings, thoughts, and actions. It is not simply 3-D; this is better than 4-D. It is 5-D and beyond.

Not only do *You/you* get to experience all of the senses, *You/YOU* are able to see, feel, imagine, and experience various dimensions. *You/you/YOU* have the ability to experience a variety of perspectives, all of which offer the capacity for insight and awareness. The farther out *You/you/YOU* extend your lens, the more expansive a landscape there is to experience. The narrower your lens becomes, the less *You/you* are able to see.

You/you/YOU are time.
YOU are timelessness.

Create whatever *You/you* want, but create what is good for *You/you/YOU*. As the journey, *You/you* define the length and breadth of each encounter and experience. *You/you/YOU* determine the ups and downs . . . the highs and lows . . . the darkness and light. Although your destiny is certain, the mystery remains ongoing. In living a multidimensional experience— as a multifaceted *Being/being/BEING*—many times, spaces, and continuums exist. Access to these depends on how present *You/you* are within a particular experience. Since *You/you/ YOU* are composed of many bodies, there also exist many levels of experience and expression.

**Through degrees of
light (frequency), sound (vibration), color (expression), and energy (presence),
your multifaceted jewel is cultivated, shaped, and polished.
The quality of your experience
reflects the cut, clarity, and composition of your consciousness.
You are a diamond.**

Circumstances remain as long as the consciousness that created them remains. The way to shift an experience—for better or worse—is by raising or lowering the consciousness surrounding it. With each encounter and experience, the lens through which *You/you/ YOU* interpret and communicate emits a vibrational resonance. This elicits a reactionary/ response pattern that will return to *You/you/YOU*. Diversity expands when wielding intention since life begins as thought forms. Giving energy to thought forms creates your reality, which then becomes your play to navigate. A playground of infinite possibility awaits. Breathe out bubbles of creation and watch them burst into reality!

**You have four lenses through which experience is perceived:
the wounded person/child,
the ego/shadow/animal/monster,
the soul,
the higher SELF/GodSelf/Innocence.**

WHO ARE YOU?	WHAT ARE YOU?	WHERE ARE YOU?	WHEN ARE YOU?	WHY DO YOU DO WHAT YOU DO?	HOW DO YOU EXPRESS?
THE WOUNDED BEING / CHILD	Victim, Pain, Body, Shadow	Cellular, In the heart In the gut	Past	Call for Love, Fear	Shadow
THE EGO SHADOW / ANIMAL / MONSTER	False Self, Masked Self, Identities, Personalities	Cellular, In the head On a quest	Past, Future	Significance; To matter To make meaning	Shades of Gray
THE SOUL	Witness Creator	Cellular, Internal Body, External Body	Past, Present, Future	Experience Expression Witness	Light
HIGH BEING GOD SELF / INNOCENCE	Allness, Every Thing No Thing	Everywhere Nowhere	Present, Timelessness	Experiencing Presence ISness	The Void

Which *eyes/i/I* are *You* looking through?
Each sees, hears, and experiences differently.
They each respond and react in their own way.

In reality, no lens is good or bad. They are playgrounds of experience. The lens *You/you/YOU* peer through is connected to early life experiences and the identity *You* maintain. Echoes of past experiences will manifest due to the vibrational resonance resting within your body. New echoes of a prior experience will trigger *You/you/YOU* in the same manner as the original incident. This occurs for *You/you/YOU* to become aware of the *Self/self* that creates. Perception also yields mirroring responses/reactions from the environment, offering the opportunity to become aware of what has been an unconscious behavior or pattern. Playgrounds of perception and expression—illustrating *who*, *what*, *where*, *when*, and *how*—are based on the lens *You* look through.

Playgrounds of Perception and Expression:

The Wounded Being/Child—This is the fragmented *being*. He/she has separated from Essence in order to fit in, be loved, and feel safe. This *one* soaked in their surroundings and forgot who they were. The wounded child's ear only hears what deepens the wound. The wounded see a wounded world. They create more experiences of wounding. When interacting from the wounded *self*, this pain body has been activated. It interacts with the pain body of others. The wounded *one* is "un"—unworthy, unloved, unable, etc.

The wounded see themselves as *less than*. They embody the *not self*—not beautiful, not enough, not smart, not worthy, etc. Specific incidents create wounding that becomes lodged in the body and psyche. The wounded *being* remains trapped in the bubble of wounding that initially created it, until breaking through the issues it is bound by. These fractures of childhood are seedlings of *self*-absorption and narcissism. Over time, the wounded become their own *self*-obsession, completely enamored with their story of wounding. Unknowingly, they celebrate it . . . re-create it . . . retell it . . . and are addicted to feeling the pain of it with every repetition.

When truly heard and seen, the wounded *being* has an opportunity to be freed from the bubble of time it is trapped within. It is possible to be stuck in multiple bubbles of time, each representing different ages and stages of life. These past frozen moments exist as present preoccupations for as long as the wound is held. The wounded *being* reacts from the head but can also elicit emotion and visceral sensation from the body.

The Ego/Human Self—This is identity, mask, and persona. The ego consists of many masks, ranging from positive to negative and loving to oppressive. These masks form as outgrowths of the wounded *self*. Ego forms out of protection, as an attempt to handle and control the environment. The ego *needs* to feel important . . . *needs* to speak . . . *needs* to be right . . . *needs* to understand . . . *needs* to explain . . . *needs* to be heard . . . and *needs* to justify.

The ego lives, breathes, and acts from the head. It will analyze, think, and process. It will declare, argue, and defend. It wants to be seen, heard, and acknowledged. Ego will be the cause and have many causes it fights for. The ego lives on the horizontal axis of time, loudly advocating for the past, retelling the story, and living for the future. Continually looking back or running forward, ego thrives on creating illusion. The ego congregates with other egos, playing games with one another while also competing.

The Higher *SELF*/God *SELF*/Innocence—This *SELF* aligns to the expression of sacredness and the embodiment of Essence. For the human being aspiring toward the God *SELF*, vertical alignment of right thought, right word, and right action is the focus. *BEING* stands amid every experience, maintaining the highest version of *SELF*. This embodiment holds a vision of others in their Essence, regardless of how they appear. A deep reverence exists for *Self/self/SELF*, others, and the world. There is a *Knowing/KNOWING* of everything *Being/being/BEING* perfection and play.

The Soul—The soul is traveling through time, while resting in timelessness. It knows each life permutation is one step closer to *IS*ness. The eyes are the windows of the soul, and they work both ways. They look out . . . and they look into. The soul is the experiencer, holding memory for the chosen incarnation—before it and beyond it. Perceiving landscapes and viewing all experience as adventure, the soul reviews, learns, and witnesses. It is on a journey of remembering. Having been layered with story upon story—time after time and life after life—witnessing serves as record keeping. The soul clears accumulated imbalances by creating new lifelines to dissolve the karma of past incarnations. This equilibrates the imbalance of energies that has accrued.

The DIVINE *SELF*/GOD—*ALL*ness, Everythingness, Nothingness, *IS*ness. Presence never has an agenda, worry, or need. It does not seek achievement. Divine *SELF* is pure presence. Neutral, detached, and without judgment, there is no thought of good or bad, right or wrong. Divine *SELF* is an all-inclusive, unbiased, unconditionally loving field of energy. This is the realm of neutrality and equanimity.

Discern which lens *You* perceive through. If *You/you* do not like the current experience, change the lens. Doing so changes the thoughts . . . shifts the words . . . creates new actions . . . and transforms the view. Wounding comes when looking through the lens of the wounded *being*. If desiring Mastery, align with your Highest *SELF*. To create from the alignment of *GOD* Essence, *You/you/YOU* must disappear altogether.

You are the experience.
You are the experiencer.
You are experience experiencing itself.

The new dawn is coming and, in many ways, is already here. It is held by those *You/you/YOU* call heroes and heroines—masters and legends. See what *You/you* have not seen before. Rather than a few individuals awakening here and there, a collective expression of *Self/self/SELF*-realization is in the making. This space of awareness is not another dimension or place, but a manner of *Being/being/BEING*. Move through the process of becoming . . . by expanding your experience and expression as:

- **Humanitarian**—embrace and embody the full expanse of humanity.
- **Spiritual Rebel**—open and allow inherent genius that expresses creative capacity and uniqueness.
- **Love Catalyst**—express the full scope of heart-centered presence, compassion, and reverence through voice, consciousness, sacred activism, and vulnerability.
- **Examples**—embody, express, and realize authentic living.
- **Philanthropist**—express the fullness of generosity through sharing gifts of spirit, collaboration, and creative capacity.
- **Servant Leader**—express leadership through the alignment of listening, empathy, heart, and sacred stewardship.
- **Genius**—embody the unique expression of unfettered aliveness and joy.

These seven embodiments bring forth the new human, magnetizing fractals of people that enrich and amplify collective unity and interdependence. The riches of this burgeoning landscape are within the grasp of those defining their lives and livelihoods through innovation and courage. The flowering of higher consciousness empowers life to thrive. The human species is dependent on your involution as the grounding rod for the authentic power of new hue-man expression. Blessed *Being/being/BEING* . . . Breathe deeply as *You/you/YOU* experience the play.

Feel into being.
Walk in reality.
Embody to remember.
Cast a ripple.
Encounter the return.
Be *You/you/YOU* to fullness.

0
0 0 0
0 0 1 0 0
0 0 0
0
1
1 1 1
1 0 1 0 1
1 1 1
1
0
0 0 0
0 0 1 0 0
0 0 0
0

the bridge.

What is the awareness?

You intended to blur your vision.
You affirmed to deafen your ears.
You proclaimed to silence your voice.
So that *You* could discover
being . . . Being . . . BEING . . .
Empowered, clear, and insightful.
Expressive, creative, beautiful, and soulful.
Bridge your quest . . .
Experience deep listening of the heart, body, and Spirit.
***You/you/YOU* are the walker . . . the witness . . . and sacred earth.**
***You* are the bridge**
between heaven and hell.

There is a distance between *then* and *there* called *here*. It is not the *now*; it is simply *here*. This is *the bridge*. It is a walk—and, more specifically, a way—of *Being/being/BEING*. In crossing the bridge, humanity deepens. Everything *You/you* have not known shall become known. Everything *You/you* have not seen, *You* have an opportunity to see. Anything *You/you* have never wanted to be, *You* will recognize that *You/you* have always been. *You* are everything *You/you/YOU* judge, condemn, criticize, and abhor. *You* are also everything *You/you/YOU* love, celebrate, compliment, and adore.

The bridge is a place of *not knowing*, which is different from *unknowing*. This is not ignorance. *Not knowing* rests within the state of innocence. Crossing this bridge removes layers of false *knowing*. Through this discovery, *You* become aware of the subtle ways *You/you* have created darkness. While on the bridge, *You/you* cannot know who *You* will become. That is of no matter. *You* will be more surprised by who *you* are *being*.

There is a hungry animal hiding in your dark woods. *You* will meet it as *You/you* cross the bridge inside yourself. Stay present within the shadowlands. Along the way, *You* will be consumed by the animal that resides there. Through that absorption, it will be set free . . . as will *You* . . . and *you*.

Go deeply into where *You* have not gone before. Trust. *You* are safe, and capable.

To access true power, get to the nitty-gritty that lies within the cellular and energetic structure of your form. What *You* have denied—and all that your family and ancestors repressed—is locked inside your body. Memory, since the beginning of time, is embedded within *You/you/YOU.*

By not doing your work,
***You/you/YOU* require others to embody a malignant identity**
merely to prompt your inner work.

Generational conditioning and its legacy of pain weigh down our world. What exists globally is the buildup of individual lineages and stories layered over one another. We each play a part in the toxic waste that is rising. Today's world affects all of us. It is further affected by our individual contributions of positive and negative energy, thoughts, words, and actions. Whole-earth transformation may not be immediately visible, but trust the importance of your individual part within it.

Personal power was never meant for *Self/self*-gain. It is for grounding a foundation of sacred service that ripples outward. *You* can support a more sustainable and vibrant world through cultivating an aligned expression. In taking personal responsibility as the bridge, embodiment of the seven keys of wholeness awakens new possibilities for humanity. These keys profoundly affect your individual experience and also catalyze empowerment, purposefulness, and peace upon the planet. The bridge is the liminal space between where *You* currently are and your access to *Light/LIGHT,* liberation, and sacred *Knowing/KNOWING.*

***You* are *being* called to move from conformity to courage . . .**
indifference to love . . . vice to virtue . . . and from *me* into *we*.

Within this living illusion are many *obsessions* that stem from the ego, or small mind. These obsessions expand into global reflections of the collective mind, which coalesce into a picture that serves all. The resulting image is *my/your/our/their* mirror. Whether gun violence, the opioid crisis, nuclear threat, human trafficking, slavery, corruption, racism, greed, homelessness, domestic battery, police brutality, or other depictions that have projected onto the screen of consciousness, these reflections are how *you/i/we/they* are *being* in life. *You* can argue against, object, or stand in denial of the part *you* play; however, mirrors do not lie. Each one of us contributes to what is in front of our *eye/i/Is.*

Your power is in your pain. Denial of pain does not serve *You/you* or the collective; it actually hinders *your/my/their/our* forward movement. Pain must be embraced in order to find the *god* who created it. This false *god* has been running your life. It is replete with anger, resentment, jealousy, and hatred. It creates the fight you face, because it is at war within.

The Illusion	The Awareness	Being/being/BEING
The Obsession	What is the addiction?	Ego/Mind
Our Global Reflection	Where is the mirror?	The Collective
The Hole	What is the dis-ease?	The Shadow
The Key	How is personal power activated?	Essence
From *self*-Centered to Centered in *Self*	How is purpose fulfilled?	Humanity
Cultivating Essence	How can peace arise?	The Bridge
To Thy *Self/self/SELF* Be True	What is the asking?	The Embodiment

YOU are nothing that *You/you* see, and everything that is unseen.

Deeply held within the *Self* that is *living*. . . is another *self* that is *being*. . . a little deviant. It is time to bring that *self* to the *Light/light/LIGHT* of understanding. As *You* move through the following pages, each step not only builds the bridge within but also creates the causeway for transmutation so that frequency and vibration increase. Don't let this become intellectual in application. Go beyond the mind; deepen into the *Keys of Wholeness*, integrating the awakening and expansion they offer. Steps of cultivation provide a deeper embodiment toward *Being/BEING* a *Divine Human*. Blessed *Being/being/BEING* . . . Breathe deeply as *You/you/YOU* cross the bridge from illusion to awareness.

A moment will come when *You* wake.
Until that time, many worlds *You/you* will make.
Dance with timelessness and play with thought.
Sing in the chorus of collective consciousness.
Try not to get lost
in the riddles, parodies, and paradox.
When it feels too much,
***you* shall feel life's sacred kiss.**
From sleep into awakening,
through unconditional love and into bliss.
Bring there to here . . .
and then to this . . .
Wrap it all up
in the Presence
of what
IS.

0
0 0
0
1
1 1
1 1 1 1
1 1 1
1
0
0 0
0

the illusion of time.

What is the awareness?

Are you wound up?
Are you unwinding?
Man's law exists.
Divine Law prevails.
Within the Unknown
is the known.
It is time . . .
to experience timelessness.
You are bound . . .
to know boundlessness.
You are tied . . .
to be Free.
Time flies . . .
but in truth,
it's your time to fly.

The Illusion of Time	The Awareness	Being/being/BEING
Emotional Obsessions	What is the addiction?	Ego/Mind
Our Global Reflection of Energy	Where is the mirror?	The Collective
The Hole of Slothfulness	What is the dis-ease?	The Shadow
The Key Whole of Devotion	How is personal power activated?	Essence
Teacher to Example	How is purpose fulfilled?	Humanity
Cultivating Listening	How can peace arise?	The Bridge
Hear Thy*self*	What is the asking?	The Embodiment

Our world is continually speeding up, which is a prelude to the disappearance of time. However, that disappearance will come about undesirably if *you/i/we/they* remain as we are *being*. *You/I/we/they* have become distracted, anxious, and addicted to a narrow set of *Self/self*-imposed cycles and rhythms, as opposed to *your/my/our/their* cyclical and rhythmical natures.

Instead of being a tool of empowerment, *you/i/we/they* have become ensnared within timelines, agendas, goals, and ambitions. The passage of time has become the slave driver's whip for productivity, attainment, and goal setting. What was once a sacred container is now a death sentence; a false god. In striving to reach a more certain future, time will demand more and more. Time appears to be in control. Yet, it creates great uncertainty. The illusion of time leads *You/you* away from presence—plummeting forward and reeling backward—and continually living off center.

Time is an illusion that feeds the addiction of emotional obsession.
The energy reveals a global reflection of the collective's
viral shadow of slothfulness.
In turning the key of devotion,
***You/you/YOU* are initiated from teacher to example.**
Hearing thy*self* cultivates listening as a bridge for embodied humanity.

Time is a nurse that tends to the poor, sick, wounded, and broken. Anxiety and depression run rampant from too much focus on the future or the past. Time's hands hold *You/you* hostage as the past controls your life. Belief in a future that *You* run after is rooted in a story and wound that looms from behind. This horizontal perspective of life engages time travel, which removes the full power of your energy from the present moment. That viewpoint feeds anxiety, depression, and fear.

Time prolongs itself to fit into your illusions and delusions. Giving years in service, it *ticks* loudly as deadlines and dates approach. It taunts with nagging whispers as it ticks by. Time watches everything. This binding arbitration of your movement, direction, and energy is a sacred illusion of your own making.

Only stories keep time. Your persistence of memory warps them. *You* have woven a great illusion in which to stretch the *Truth/truth/TRUTH*. Time will be the judge, imprisoning *you* within past actions or future constraints. Never tell *time* how long things should last; it will stop on its own accord. Your entire life will be controlled, should the passage of time lock your gaze. Yet, the clock never stands still, not even to honor your time of death. It keeps ticking, long after *You/you/YOU* clock out. This linear construct feeds *Self/self/SELF* obsession, propelling *You/you* into endless cycles of analysis, paralysis, and processing. Time goes in circles, taking *You/you* with it.

***SELF* is the highlight for remembering;**
***self* is the shadow of forgetting,**
masquerading an identity that is cultivated by human conditioning.
***Self* attempts to navigate between forgetfulness and remembering,**
endeavoring upon lapses of judgment, confusion, and lack of direction
while also discovering neutrality, clarity, and vision.

Time is of Essence . . .
when *You/you/YOU* ground into the timelessness of higher *Being/BEING*.

Justified reasons for *doing this to get that* pass time. The way of distraction follows the continual *when* as opposed to living in the presence of now. *When* _____ *happens . . . When* _____ *is achieved . . . When I have* _____ *. . . When I* _____ . . . That which is *time-sensitive* becomes a convenient bypass from feeling, experiencing, or expressing where *You/you/YOU* are. If not allowing space for emotion to be fully received—especially from the vibrationally dense spectrum—flight will become a habitual state of unconscious *Being/being. You/you* will find it imperative to run faster, do more, and achieve greater. Should this occur, immense personal will shall be required to outpace the past. Such avoidance is a convenience that cannot be afforded. Rage, pain, loss, grief, and regret are costly to individual and collective health, well-being, and longevity. With faster lives and less time, it is easy to avoid commitments, personal needs, and deeper callings. It is important to know that what rests in closest proximity to *You/you/YOU* is of utmost importance for spending your time. Should *You/you/YOU* seek to go far and wide instead, *You* will later discover that *You* have lost valuable time, the results of which will eventually catch up with *you/me/them/us.*

Seconds, moments, hours, and days dissolve within the sands of time. Through busyness, *You/you* remain checked out, deaf, dumb, and blind. Due to this semiconscious slumber, dark nights continually rise, holding *You/you/YOU* hostage within the *daze/ days you* become entranced in. *You/you* trap your *Self/self* inside bubbles of time. They float within every experience until something pops, releasing the energy. Wake up and realize that no past can haunt *You/you/YOU*, and no future can control *You/you/YOU* unless giving it the time to do so. This is the illusion of time.

Time works on the body,
timelessness rests with the soul.
Time is a construct . . .
a structure for *You/you/YOU* to play within.
Do not let it become the master . . .
and *You/you/YOU* its slave.
Only timelessness provides freedom, space, and dominion.
Have the time of your life,
but do so from a state of timelessness.

Painful events are part of Divine time. These experiences balance the inequity of energy created through the *mis-creations* of the *Mind/mind*, collective body, ancestry, and history. Time has a hand in these things because its face appears ever present. Intense situations open the heart, so to release the stagnant energy collected and clogged in time. Excruciating moments are life's magical wormholes that bypass longer routes of suffering. During these events, time passes but the heaviness courts a sense of timelessness. Experiences that stop *You/you/YOU* in your tracks offer an experience of timelessness. *You* can choose presence at any moment, instead of having to wait for an experience of pain. Let timelessness reengage youthful folly. When time teases the *Mind/mind/MIND* with stories of the past and imaginings of the future, worry, angst, and stress will create aging, loss, and history.

What happened, how it happened, why it happened, and *because of whom* are time loops that derail focus and vision from the present moment. In attempts to heal, change, or fix a particular moment, *You/you* become a closed circuit that repeats those loops of time. Moving from teacher (or student) to example creates a paradigm shift that activates the experience of timelessness. This transition expands your ability for in-the-moment presence that offers greater listening and awareness on multiple levels of *Being/being/BEING.*

Every experience—*good* or *bad*—facilitates your soulful return to presence. Anything can be the catalyst for that emergence. It can be an occurrence in the body, within a relationship, in your career, or through play. When challenged to value your time, challenging life experiences manifest as the swift kick in the ass that will sit *you* down. *You/you/YOU* are never given more than *You/you* can handle. Life's experiential blessings are based on the soul's design and vibratory field. *You/you/YOU* attract what is *Being/ being/BEING* emitted consciously and unconsciously. There are no mistakes. It is all grist for the mill. Each life holds the necessary elements to expand and awaken aliveness and peace in correct time. Stay the course. Embrace everything . . . every single thing. Safe passage is always available, especially within the most-intense experiences. Each moment of your life supports mastery.

The mind views experience as linear, thus creating in a timely fashion. Your beliefs around time and its limitations have shaped your steps, path, and passage. Within your own quiet stillness, *You/you/YOU* can always touch timeless eternity. In that dimension, there is no *Mind/mind/MIND*, and no time for it. Within the winding caverns of *Mind/ mind/MIND* rests the ability—to be at any place, in any time, with anyone—for bringing all of time into the reconciliation of timelessness. The eternal is always present. *You/you/ YOU* are not, because of *Being/being/BEING* caught in time.

Time is a wheel;
a circumference of experience,
occurring all at once . . . and yet, not at all.
Allow what sits within your depths to rise.
Stay present. Be here . . . now.
Stay with the moment.
It lasts forever.

Stop looking for infinity amid the stars. Seek this inside your inner cosmos. Find it within quiet moments . . . silent spaces . . . and relaxed breathing. Time is not meant to be the enemy, nor are *You/you/YOU* supposed to chase it. It is not a ghost or a *god.* It is merely a container through which experience, expression, and balance are navigated. This construct is an imaginative structure that is built to house a framework of stories. Loosen your grip on time and *You* will find it stretches to your needs. Time is pliable and expandable. There is nothing and no one to miss, because there is *no time* for that.

You hold the belief that history has passed. Yet, close your eyes; visit any moment and *You/you* are there. *You/you* carry your past inside. It is woven within your cellular structure. Every action, word, and thought is your soul reliving an experience *You* call memory. Your all-encompassing, unique design exists now, as does your destiny. Your future is written in your cells. *You* will always step in a direction *You/you/YOU* have already been. Your soul knows where to go. Your body has the blueprint. *BEING* holds all spaces, experiences, and relationships within its timeless expanse.

Give your *Self/self/SELF* enough time, and it will either be the death of *You/you/ YOU* or breathe *You/you/YOU* back to life with its long hand and quick pulse. Time goes round and round until alarmed. Pause long enough to hear its wake-up call. The clock striking 11:11—or any repetitive sequence—will be a momentary reminder that life consists of something more. The timeless lies beyond where *You/you* stand . . . what *You/ you* are doing . . . and how *You/you* are living. Time labors to bring *You/you* to presence. Live beyond the times of your life. Master your mind . . . Master your emotions . . . Master your energy . . . Master the physical. Time will stop only when *You/you/YOU* do. This is the timeless reason for all time. *You/you/YOU* are space. Inhale. *You/you/YOU* are timelessness. Hold that space. *You/you/YOU* are eternal. Exhale. Blessed *Being/being/ BEING* . . . Breathe deeply as *You/you/YOU* release your addiction and illusion of time.

May *You/you* hear the call
of infinite *Being/BEING*
and listen to insights
of the sacred *SELF*.
May *You/you/YOU* remember
your innate harmony
and revel in the peacefulness
of your true nature.
May thy conscience be clear,
and what is held subconsciously
be cleared . . .
May truth be thy name . . .
Sweetly dream . . .
so to create the sweetest of dreams.

...

EMOTIONAL OBSESSIONS

What is the addiction?

We have been intertwined
from the beginning of time,
rising and falling
into each other's arms.
We connect
amid shadow and light,
secretly meeting
in the most-sacred places
of peace, passion, and plight.
In the heat . . . in the high . . . it rushes in . . .
colliding with the surf.
swept into cascading tides . . .
becoming obsessed . . .
with riding the waves.

Emotion is akin to ocean waves that rise, swell, crest, retreat, and pull *You* under. *You/you* may get hit unexpectedly, completely soaked, and even knocked down. Initially reveling in the immensity that engulfs your entire *Being/being/BEING*, *You/you* become one with the wave, either immersing completely or flailing wildly. Emotions crest and crash, often dousing everything around *You/you*. It is the *current* that thrashes *You/you/YOU* backward and forward, typically swelling from a call for healing that rises up from the past. The flow that pulls *You/you* into unconscious emotive behavior is the undertow. The *Mind/mind* sucks *You/you* back in time to a point of reactivity that unbeknownst to *You* is connected to some other person, event, or story line. The consistent buzz of irritation, anxiety, fear, and combativeness becomes sediment that weighs your spirit down. This settles inside, waiting to be stirred up, with the original moment deeply buried in the dark recesses of *being*.

Emotional obsession is the addiction to *being* pulled under. It is further fueled by highs and lows that pummel *You* long after the initial wave. *You* will feel just enough to trigger and reexperience heightened energy again and again. The story is the high that keeps the addiction to emotional obsessions active. *You/you* become attached to the friction of going back and forth. Surges of emotion are cyclones of your own making. They circulate pressure around a central moment that was frozen in time and memory. That time stamp becomes a trigger switch for each overarching wave.

You are meant to fully feel your experiences but not cling to them. Until *You/you* drown within your emotional waves, *You/you* cannot learn how to balance them. The trigger points will remain active. Emotion is a drug of unconscious control, where the user is gratified by reactive highs, pain, or numbness. When engaging *Mind/mind* instead of heart or body,

You/you will move into reaction and psychosis. When in the heart, *you* will feel soaked in the experience. But when conscious enough to simply stay with the body, *You/you* will succumb to riding the waves; eventually learning to surf and master them until they subside.

Pain is a drug.
The external world is your dealer.
You are the user.

By reliving past traumas *You/you/YOU* unknowingly make them badges of honor. The ego's need to be seen, heard, and acknowledged keeps emotional obsessions clamoring for attention. If old ghosts are not allowed to die, *You/you* will remain stuck in loops of time and reaction. This is not living; it is *being* in lockdown. By harboring past wrongs with no intention of ever forgiving, all concerned remain imprisoned, especially *You/you/YOU*. By keeping old wounds at the forefront of *Mind/mind*—having a chip on your shoulder—there is not enough that can ever be said, done, or supplied in reparation. *You/you/YOU* must release the oppressor, victimizer, and villain. If *You/you/YOU* do not, time will eventually reveal that *You* oppressed and victimized yourself in an even worse way, by holding *Self/self/SELF* hostage to a time, perspective, and story. Unresolved pain will continue to erupt as outbursts, reactions, blame, shame, and judgment. These projections feed the wounded ego's need to repeatedly state its cause, and its case. What results is history in the making, which subsequently repeats again and again.

The word has power, creating worlds upon worlds, and cycles within cycles.
Emotion is fuel that energizes inspiration, celebration, conflict, or chaos.

The *self*—created in the image and shadow of codependency—hoards the buildup of resentment, guilt, and regret. This aspect of *you* amplifies emotions that have been encased within the structure of time. Emotions embed within the cells of your body, becoming trapped if not fully felt. Recycling this old emotion creates stagnant energy, which results in toxicity, illness, dysfunction, and aging. To heal, feeling must occur.

Emotion and feeling are distinctly different. Emotion brings highs and lows that arise from focusing on external situations. Emotion expresses outwardly. It is buried within past legacies and woven into stories that form the bedrock of your existence. Dense emotional release may consist of rage, anger, sadness, or grief along with waves of apathy, frustration, or overwhelmingness. In order to cleanse your lineage of ancestral emotional trauma, *You/you/YOU* must remain with emotional waves as they rise, fully crest, crash, and subside. Emotions can also express as joy, happiness, enthusiasm, and bliss. It is necessary to fully feel these as well. To the degree *You/you/YOU* do not feel dense emotions, *You* will not have the capacity to feel lighter ones.

Feeling is inward presence—of experience, thought, word, and emotion—that acknowledges and absorbs the present moment. Absorption evaporates existing emotional pain and is detoxifying. Through feeling deeply, *You* transmute emotional pain and release dense, embedded cellular memory and imprinting. Each individual that engages emotional literacy—through shadow/animal work—supports individual and collective healing.

When perpetuating an old story, a new one can never begin.

All peoples of the world have stories of abuse, pain, suffering, torture, slavery, persecution, and oppression. There is not a culture among us that does not. We live in a world of *never forget*, in order to honor those who have suffered. However, this keeps suffering alive, while also perpetuating it. Retelling stories further imprints cycles of pain, emotional trauma, and disempowerment within the psyche of future generations. This a form of brainwashing and conditioning. Whether it is the story of domestic violence, child abuse, rape, slavery, or being wronged . . . repeating history repeats history. It keeps pain alive by imprinting this legacy upon others.

Sharing anoints another with the unconscious power of creating reflections of similar experiences within their own lives. By retelling stories, the consciousness of the listener is affected when *You* have not fully resolved your emotional attachments. That person will carry the story forward, amplifying the energy with new echoes of their experiences. A perceptual filter is created in the other person, which they view life through. Their biology of belief forms around the historical event. *Mind/mind* does not know the difference between what is experienced or imagined, so trauma recurs. The memory of pain multiplies in the same way a cell divides. It becomes contagious. For us to have a new world, history must be laid to rest.

With every situation, *You* have a choice . . . be the cancer, or be the cure.

Unexpressed emotions are also energetically passed onto one's children and their children, generation after generation. When not completely absorbed or healed, the cycle of pain and blame is projected forward at least seven generations. It becomes the fabric, culture, and identity that is inherited. These stories hold the countenance of your emotional obsessions. The faces express as slavery, oppression, judgment, abuse, prejudice, jealousy, and regret. There is plenty of evidence illustrating how history repeats itself.

Emotional obsessions can be transferred through stories of a positive nature also. Family legacies and stories of achievement—along with celebrity and social status—create pressure, stress, entitlement, and obligatory living to reproduce the same. Emotional projections of success, pride, and love play a hand in conditioning and homogenizing the youth. Positive and negative emotional heritage must be absorbed and fully experienced in order to free your *Self/self/SELF* and those that follow.

Although there can be benefits to telling stories, discernment is important. People become enslaved by them. Individuals courageous enough to be sacred containers of integration unplug this flow of history from collective energy. They are willing to feel the pain fully, thus transmuting energy. These individuals no longer have a need to tell the story. Those wise enough to discontinue passing along stories holding emotional residue—with the ability to share stories from neutrality and objectivity—create no further imprints of pain.

May time be a sacred container
in which to cocreate the return of Divine *Being/BEING*.

From early childhood, *You/you* learn that crying brings attention. Conditioning teaches *you* to cease the tantrum when an object outside *You/you*—a toy, food, a phone, a hug, a spanking—shifted the experience. The reward of pain sinks in. People appear more attentive when *you* are emotional, hurt, or in pain. They condition *You/you* into believing there is value in acting out. There is an alternative. Instead, pain can be a tool; a catalyst for *You/you* to tend to *Self/self/SELF*. Healing occurs only from within. *You/you/YOU* must dive into the abyss and remain within your murky depths until all discordant debris floats to the surface. This is *response ability*. Otherwise, *You/you* metastasize as a cancer in the world. Blessed *Being/being/BEING* . . . Breathe deeply as *You/you/YOU* let go of your stories and emotional obsessions.

> **May the *eye/i/I* in the center of all things**
> **see through the consciousness of**
> **love, compassion, and unity . . .**
> **May all realize what is denied**
> **so not to express it elsewhere.**
> **May all be aware . . .**
> **what rests consciously or unconsciously**
> **only grows stronger . . .**
> **Sweetly dream . . .**
> **so to create the sweetest of dreams.**

. . .

OUR GLOBAL REFLECTION OF ENERGY

What is the mirror?

> ***You/you*** **are me; I am *You/you* . . .**
> **We are pieces and parts of the same,**
> **united for evermore . . .**
> **in our vastness**
> **through bounteousness,**
> **and in timeless radiance and rapture.**
> **That recognition is the discovery.**
> ***You/you/YOU*** **are an inquiry into form . . .**
> **virtually, a divine "aha" moment!**

The energy crisis—a broad and complex topic—mirrors the state of *your/my/our/their* energy and emotions. We cannot respect outer resources when not valuing inner resources. Our collective disregard of the planet, energy, and nature contributes to the depletion of global natural resources. By taking inventory at the level of cause, appropriate measures can be implemented for long-lasting and impactful transformation. An intuitive and grounded approach in how personal energy relates to the global reflection of energy will effect change. There is no more powerful misuse, misdirection, or dispersement of energy than through the emotional body. What *you/i/we/they* do not feel, we inflict upon the world around us.

Deforestation, climate change, and atmospheric impurity are *hot* topics in the realms of politics, science, and social advocacy. Conversations about water pollution, the desecration of rain forests, and depletion of the ozone layer continue to rise. Attempts to curve the speed at which the planet is being destroyed center on being green, conserving energy, and clearing imbalances in our ecosystem, but these are all addressing symptoms. We are the root cause. Environmental pollutants—which include the toxicity of repressed or reactive emotional expression—are a major factor regarding our misuse of energetic and natural resources. Another area to be addressed is *Mind/mind*, and the psychosis that creates emotional reactivity and obsession. The individual is foundational to the cure of planetary dis-ease and dysfunction, because everything stems from individual parts.

When approaching the global reflection of energy from a metaphysical and spiritual perspective, the inner and outer correlations are clear. External issues are representations of what must be addressed internally, whether it is climate change, gender discrimination, sexual harassment, or the shortage of resources. Social issues are the macrocosm of what is happening inside *you/me/us/them*. The oppression of creative energy (the feminine aspect within) and holding back the energy of expression (the masculine aspect within) affects individual and collective energy in motion (e-motion). *You/i/we/they* are required to feel internal climate changes; otherwise the energy has to express elsewhere. Since *you/i/we/they* are part of Gaia, stagnant energy expresses through the external environment, others, weather conditions, and global social issues.

Life is filled with reflections.
Metaphysically, resources correlate to people,
since there is none greater than that.
How have *You/you* been used?
How do *You/you* "use" people?

From a socio-spiritual perspective, the energy crisis concerns how *your/my/our/their* energetic balance of masculine and feminine power is utilized and maintained. The masculine shadow of force is evident in social institutions such as government, healthcare, politics, education, and commerce. These can appear as dominance, impatience, dishonor, arrogance, pride, corruption, and hunger, to name a few. Because the masculine shadow is present, the feminine shadow of weakness, manipulation, and subservience must be equally so. The feminine side is ignored, dishonored, and pushed down. Sexual harassment relates to creativity and how it is controlled, manipulated, and prostituted. The imbalance of giving and receiving is perpetuated by structures that value productivity over creativity … mass production over individual genius … and *doing* over *being*. This imbalance creates apathy and abuse, instead of presence.

Our world is dominated by shadow masculine energy. This is exhibited in the magnified expression of the masculine pole within men and women. This masculine energetic seeps into the structures and environments we inhabit. The mirror of oppression, abuse, and harassment is *your/my/our* reflection. It is evident in the drive, push, and force of business, commerce, and marketing. This is also portrayed through the dominance, bullying, and aggression within politics. It is most evident in the value placed on profit versus people.

Leaning too far into shadow masculine energy—where control, dominance, and aggression are used—affects the balance of healthy masculine energy in your life and the world. The masculine side of *you/i/us/them* is *being* pushed and forced. Leaning too far into shadow feminine energy—where force, manipulation, and indifference reside—reflects the imbalance of intuition, heart, and receivership within your life and our world. *You/you/YOU* must periodically hit the reset button to balance your masculine and feminine energies. To do that, discern where and how *You/you/YOU* reflect imbalance. This requires intense devotion to unlearning and deconditioning areas where mass consciousness controls your actions, impulses, and agendas.

**Intertwining masculine and feminine aspects are natural resources
that reside within dimensions of *Being/being/BEING*.
These must be balanced and carefully measured.
Here, one plus one makes three.**

Men have been conditioned to lead with masculine energy, allowing the shadow aspect to often dominate their expression. Force is suppressed power. Actions that are dominant, aggressive, and arrogant are void of natural feminine energy. A man's feminine nature is typically diminished in early childhood. Although men are active providers and protectors, suppression of softness, sensitivity, and intuition creates darker expressions of the hunter, soldier, and ruler archetypes. However, utilizing dormant capacities of heart, intuition, and nurturing yields a more collaborative and fulfilling experience of humanity. This occurs when men are celebrated for healthy, grounded masculine energy and supported by a wholesome, anchored feminine energetic expression.

Men must work to balance this shadow of *being* through rest, feeling their feelings, and partaking in creative expression. Rest removes the habitual and repetitive doing that exists in the lives of most men. Taking time to feel what has not been felt allows access to hidden sensitivities. A healthy balance of masculine and feminine energy—through creative expression—engenders the sacred leadership of nurturer, peacemaker, and servant leader. This supports a healthy expression of the protector—hunter—gatherer.

Shadow masculine solicits the shadow feminine who displays manipulative, secretive, and needy tendencies. The feminine shadow is submissive, weak, and dull. This aspect also utilizes force, agenda, and codependence for *self*-gain. Women have been expressing increasingly dominant masculine sides that coincide with this shadow feminine behavior. A woman's shadow masculine can appear as *being* too busy, multitasking, and *being* rushed. Darker tendencies illustrate as undermining, criticism, trickery, gossiping, competing, lying, addictions, and withdrawal. What results is competition among and between women—where they become hunters, fighters, and warriors—as opposed to the wise women, peacemakers, and guiding leaders they were designed as. The modern woman is running from the battle of energies occurring within. Women have become massive *do-ers*. This *self*-imposed oppression—arising from compromising, fighting to stay ahead, shrinking, creating with agenda, and adjusting to survive (a man's world)—feeds into relationships with unconscious men. Convinced of their causes, most women are disconnected from their underlying power of *presence* or *Being* enough.

Shadowed, disempowered feminine energy is smothering, needy, dependent, weak, and manipulative. It is irrational and unfocused. This is the embodied *taker* who also sets up scenarios of *being taken from*. The masculine counterpart expresses as aggressive, cruel, insensitive, and violent, while also living mechanically, pridefully, and arrogant. This is not power; it is force. In the outer world—depending on your vibrational expression of masculine or feminine—*You/you/YOU* will invite the shadow complement within your experiences. Situations of abuse, domination, and sexual harassment occur because the energy is unconsciously operating.

The divine feminine creates and births out of pure presence.
The divine masculine waits to be inspired by the feminine.
This internal yoking creates worlds upon worlds.

Protests, marches, and passive-aggressive behaviors depict how women have become the darker female versions of men. These things—do-gooding, busyness, agenda, ambition, drive—are a push to become significant. Although these tactics have served to create change, the cost is immeasurable. In reality, these behaviors are distraction mechanisms to avoid the deep-seated pain of the feminine. Women are clamoring to be seen and heard, whereas their souls are calling for their experience of timelessness, by stopping to see and hear themselves on deeper levels. Modern-day media celebrate powerful women as aesthetic depictions of aggression. A woman kicking ass does not mean that she is in her power. It merely portrays her unconscious and defensive shadow pattern of fear and survival. A woman standing in true power is likened to a mountain, grounded with mighty presence.

Feminine energy is reflective of creative, self-organizing, nurturing presence. The higher vibrational feminine is natural, wise, and deeply present. This does not mean women cannot take a stand, use their voice, and create change. A woman of true power utilizes the intimate, vulnerable presence inherent in stillness, partnership, ceremony, and celebration. In that expression, solidarity cannot be reckoned with. Malala Yousafzai comes to mind as a woman of power. She creates change in a way that is both soft and strong. Malala Yousafzai stood against the Taliban through integrity, voice, and vision. Her demeanor remained calm but passionate. Her determination towards improving women's rights and her courageous actions in these ways model the higher vibrational balance of masculine and feminine energies.

Are *You/you/YOU* living in the shadow spectrum of masculine and feminine energy?
Are *You/you/YOU* living in the empowered spectrum of masculine and feminine balance?

There is a current perception that an imbalance of masculine and feminine energy exists in the world. Many profess the need to bring about more divine feminine energy. However, there is no imbalance. The real issue regards the vibration and frequency of *Being/being/BEING*. Every human being is energetically masculine and feminine. *You/you/YOU* already hold both aspects in a balanced way. Masculine and feminine energies are always expressed as 50/50, but how they do so is of greater importance. Are your masculine and feminine energies grounded in 50/50 expressions of shadow, identity, humanity, or divinity? The world does not require more pussy power or feminine energy. The issue does not fall purely upon how the masculine has dominated. Every individual must rise above their shadow expressions of internally held masculine and feminine energy. *You/you/YOU* can choose to live from a conscious and empowered state of alignment, or an unconscious and disempowered state of disarray. Like always attracts like.

If individuals exhibit shadow masculine qualities,
they will elicit shadow feminine ones equally so.

	FEMININE ENERGY	MASCULINE ENERGY
HIGHER VIBRATIONAL STATE THE LIGHT	Intuitive, Compassionate, Nurturing, Gentle, Empathetic, Patient, Softness, Vulnerable, Birthing, Creative, Truthful	Inspired Action, Ambitious, Focused, Certain, Discerning, Courageous, Reasoned, Self-Assured, Relaxed, Clear
LOW VIBRATIONAL STATE THE SHADOW	Timid, Smothering, Insecure, Frozen, Dependent, Unfocused, Irrational, Fragile, Passive, Manipulative, Spacey	Boastful, Dominant, Excessive Logic, Unconscious Action, Compulsive, Fighting, Cruel, Robotic, Insensitive, Violent, Pushy, Forceful, Busy

Empowered feminine energy is empathetic, inclusive, nurturing, and expressive. It is vulnerable, harmonious, and creative. To be feminine in these ways is strength. The masculine counterpart to these energies would express as intimate, confident, and disciplined. Through embodying these higher vibrational expressions, your life will model greater clarity, focus, discernment, and intuitive living. This is true power, grounded in the even distribution of higher energies of *Being/BEING*. Your experiences and interactions will come to reflect truth, integrity, and service.

Every individual is a powerful conductor of energy in motion. When individuals are valued, uplifted, and acknowledged for their presence . . . everything is possible. Human *Being/BEING*s harness a power beyond measure, but they must be grounded so they may become lightning rods and transformers. Blessed *Being/being/BEING* . . . Breathe deeply as *You/you/YOU* refill your energy coffers.

May the storms that follow . . .
come from hearts pounding with Love,
and lightening with laughter.
May the fires that burn . . .
be flames of passionate purpose which fully express.
May the flooding that ensues . . .
be filled with waves of generosity and compassion.
May winds that blow . . .
bring about powerful, positive change.
Sweetly dream . . .
so to create the sweetest of dreams.

. . .

THE HOLE OF SLOTHFULNESS

What is the disease?
**Be not the disease of apathy and indifference;
be the contagion of
love, compassion, and appreciation.
Being and non*being* does not matter;
the devotional presence you bring to each does.
This is true *BEING*.**

Slothfulness is laziness. As *Being/being*, this has nothing to do with outer work or a profession in the world. That is a byproduct of inner slothfulness. An individual can be very active in the world but still engage slothfulness, which equates to indifference, apathy, and complicit behavior. We have a world of busy activity, but there also exists an equivalence of casualness, nonchalance, and aloofness. This *don't care* approach—ranging from subtly unconscious to blatantly obvious—stems from *Self/self*-absorption. When individuals do not feel that their feelings and expressions have worth, they ignore the feelings and experiences of others. Slothfulness veils deeply unconscious hopelessness. It begins as numbing and becomes the slow death of creative capacity. The purposelessness that arises from living an unfulfilled existence is becoming an epidemic in our society. The reason so many are seeking life purpose is because they have become indifferent to the needs and calls of the inner child and soul.

**Apathy and indifference first appear as a casual approach toward life.
These become the face of lifelessness.**

When human animals are bound and tied to constructs and systems that limit movement, they feel trapped and caged. Living unconscious to this animal nature, *You/you/YOU* are unaware of your imprisonment. When constricted, made to conform, conditioned, or beaten into submission—a quiet rage will embed within your body. This unconscious *self-will* lashes out when triggered. Until then, numbness will reflect as a *don't-care attitude, unfeeling expression*, and *uninterested manner*. When denying your dreams, desires, pain, or pleasure, the animal inside becomes feral and the human spirit deadens. Ensnared within pain and depression, the individual falls into the *hole of slothfulness*, which feeds into the other vices.

Apathy and indifference cause great harm, but when suppressed, they become detrimental influences in the world. Moving into fight, flight, and survival mode creates an emotional, energetic, and physical carnivore. In an attempt to fill the emptiness that grows, the animal—your animal—voraciously claws, hoards, harbors, and gorges.

The animal inside will become violent; this appears in many ways. To uncage from slothfulness, begin listening to the words used. *You/you/YOU* brand yourself with each one that is spoken. Negative *self*-talk exhibits how *You* are flippant against *Self/self/SELF*, others, and the world. Take notice of every time you say *I don't care, it doesn't matter, Who cares?, nevermind,* or *it's not my problem.* Nonaction—of a complicit manner—follows your thoughts and words of disregard and disconnection. Your actions toward *Self/self* or others will be uncaring due to your lack of *self*-intimacy.

Notice how often *You/you/YOU* turn a blind eye … deafen your ears … silence your voice … and turn away from someone or something. Large issues are reflective of insidious smaller ones existing inside your home, backyard, neighborhood, and community. When *You* take care of the *little* things, *You/you/YOU* won't create the *big* things.

The civilized version of a mental disorder is apathy.
The political version of a mental disorder is indifference.
The socialized version of a mental disorder is ignorance.
The personal version of a mental disorder is narcissism.

Indifference, apathy, ignorance, and narcissism are reflections of numbness, pain, and lack of empathy. These expressions mirror how *You* have cast aside or abandoned yourself. *You* might think that fear or hate are the opposite of *Love*, but these hold passionate energy. Indifference is the opposite of *Love/LOVE*. Indifference and apathy are devoid of energy. They are not attached or detached. There is no life or aliveness; only limbo. This is the behavior and expression of the walking dead. To come alive again, *You/you/YOU* must face what *Being/being/BEING* means. It requires owning your frailties, vulnerability, rage, pain, hate, and hopelessness. Until then, *You* cannot be free or alive. If *You/you* express judgment, apathy, disconnection, and indifference, *you* are the sleeping sloth.

Casualness can mean laid back—allowing things to flow—and having a relaxed focus. But beware; *Being/being* casual holds seeds of nonchalance, flippancy, and apathy. It can turn into a lackadaisical, unconscious attitude that exhibits disconnection and a lack of presence. Casualness affects relationships and environments in a negative manner, creating loose boundaries, blurred focus, and lack of attention to detail. In regard to mastery, casualness is mediocrity. Look boldly at your casual behaviors.

The pain *You/you* are indifferent to *out there*
is the pain *You* are unwilling to face inside.

Your dullness is leading to compromise and codependency. If *You/you/YOU* have become wrapped within strands of time, life is *Being/being/BEING* squeezed out of *You/you/YOU*. As a result, dense energies—anger, rage, indifference, apathy, and slothfulness—have built beneath the surface. These behavioral changes influence your individual genius, personal expression, and authentic power.

Objectively and lovingly embrace the darkness that expresses internally and externally. Hold your inner world with a compassionate embrace. The heartbreak of each man, woman, and child beckons to be felt. Hold your pain close to the bosom intimately and vulnerably. Acceptance is the gentle way of sacred activism. The milk of human compassion softens the indifference and apathy that permeates mankind. Your greatest trigger is *Truth/truth/TRUTH*. Speak so that *You* hear yourself.

The only one *you* are ever speaking to is *Self/self/SELF.*
Voice is for *Self* to hear *self/SELF*, regardless of whether others do or not.
The advice *You* give—when not personally attached—follows that.

Until owning and acknowledging the power and presence of your inherent divinity—*Being/BEING* unconditionally loving, compassionate, and equanimous—*You/you* cannot be fully held. This yoking of man and spirit is where real *Light/LIGHT* emerges. *Being/being* human will hurt deeply, but that is only so *You* are cracked open for the Divine within *You* to flow out. *BEING* divine is bliss, and both feelings can exist simultaneously. The full embrace of these expressions within *You/you/YOU* is not duality; it is wholeness.

Only the combined power of humanity and divinity
can lure the human animal out of unconscious ignorance.

The human is a wild animal that is meant to roam free. For this to happen, divine laziness is required. To be lazy and bored is an important part of the unlearning and deconditioning process. This allows space for programs to stop running, adrenaline to stop pumping, and hunger to wane. It is the opportunity to pause and step away from the outer world so that the inner world's activity—or lack thereof—can be witnessed. As tension, pressure, and conditioning dissolve, naturalness unveils creative inspiration that brings forth fulfillment. The way out of the *hole of slothfulness* requires that *You* turn the key of devotion in the direction of your soul. Time spent in timelessness softens the edges of identity so that soul can come more into view. Blessed *Being/being/BEING* . . . Breathe deeply as *You/you/YOU* absorb the density of your slothfulness.

May your heart be filled with *Love/LOVE* . . .
Your mind be cleared of grievances,
and your life be set free.
As *You* drop into the void . . .
meet the Divine sacred unknown.
May *you* remember your innate harmony
and embody peace and true nature.
Sweetly dream . . .
so to create the sweetest of dreams.

THE KEY WHOLE OF DEVOTION

How is personal power activated?

Close your *eyes/i/Is*.
Bow.
Kneel.
Lay your head down.
Open your heart . . .
Lift your spirit . . .
Raise your presence.
Be humble.
Life has been in devotion
to *You/you/YOU*.
Will *You/you/YOU* be devoted to it?

Devotion is the key that initiates your return to wholeness. This devotion must begin with *Self/self/SELF*, by holding each and every piece and part of *You/you/YOU*—light, dark, shadow, monster, demon, god, child, and human. It is the grounded commitment and sacred covenant that no part of *You/you/YOU* is left behind. This requires bringing the divine feminine and divine masculine into higher resonance. To do this, *You* must go to the depths of where *you* are out of alignment: anima and animus . . . shadow masculine and shadow feminine.

The masculine and feminine within have been at war with one another. They lie as wounded soldiers on a battlefield. They must be tended, so that each recalibrates to fullness. Both aspects must rest, decay, and die before experiencing aliveness. The masculine aspect must learn how to be in devotion to the feminine once again. The feminine must learn how to be in devotion to the masculine. This will occur through listening deeply to the energy, body, heart, and soul. Recovery will take time. It will occur when *You/you/YOU* have embodied timelessness. Until then, cultivate listening and remain in a state of loving service, since these parts of you writhe in the ecstatic pain of transformation.

Raising the frequency of your shadow masculine and feminine sides requires inward presence rather than outward activity, deeply feeling all of the emotions that rise. Time must be dissolved by the feminine aspect of *Self* feeling everything that has been held in the past. She must rage, wail, and scream. The ancient sounds of pain, oppression, abuse, torture, and trauma that wrack the body. Her ancient moans and sounds must be unearthed. The dark feminine must grieve, shedding the ocean of tears from what has been suppressed. Sensing the entire world's pain, she feels the pain of her ancestors. She hears the cries upon earth, of all peoples and time.

The masculine aspect of *Self* also experiences pain, holding vigil as he witnesses the limp feminine energetic. He could not protect her; there was shame in that. The damage was inflicted early on. He faces the guilt and intense loneliness that history placed upon his shoulders. He does not provide fully, because past unconscious action created the existing trauma. The masculine side must recognize his willful impulses, controlling actions, and deceptive miscreations. Devotion entails sitting, succumbing to the feelings of hopelessness, apathy, and indifference that plague him.

The masculine aspect must wait in the darkness until inspired by the feminine once again. The feminine must wait until the sacred bowl of her womb space is cleared of all that was miscarried. Upon that cleansing, the creation space is ready for new birth. Masculine and feminine energies may once again intertwine in the dance of creation.

When *You/you/YOU* come to terms with your unconscious *Being/being*,
You must choose to live consciously unconscious.
This is as close to awakening as you will ever get.
Awareness is the holy grail.

Stay in present devotion toward eternal *BEING*-ness; not the whims, distractions, and impulses of the temporary. Do not become the student or attempt to teach what *You/you* need to learn. Be the example and embodiment of transformation. Ego is a mechanism of distraction; do not identify with it. Its thoughts and agendas will drag you off course. Devotion is intentional, demanding reverence and care. This builds with discipline. It must be a highly conscious act. Use the outside to bring *You* inward. A point shall arise where *You* recognize that pure divine longing rests behind every want and wish. Deepening in devotion will bring about inspired action. This illumination will initiate your return to what is real, and beyond the illusion.

Each life—unique and equally important—is not for the triumph of human story, but in commitment to soul expansion. What *You* do for a living, where *You* live, the car *You* drive, or whom *You* marry is of little consequence. The soul came for experience. It desires to grow through the mountains *You/you/YOU* climb, deserts *You/you/YOU* traverse, and rivers *You/you/YOU* swim. Your life is an adventure of Spirit. Live it with devotion. A divine experience of aliveness awaits those who take nothing personally but engage everything deeply. Receive each moment as an exercise of awareness. Life is happening on its own accord. *You* need do nothing to make it happen, nor do *You/you/YOU* need to control it. Simply open to the experience of it.

The duality of the world cannot compare to the oneness of the heart.

Be the joy and spirituality *You/you/YOU* seek. Become that in the places *You/you/YOU* find yourself. Take one small step at a time. Create a foundation of trust, a wealth of community, and a legacy of service. *You/you* cannot leave the circumstances of your world, but *You/YOU* can be the peace within them. Being conscious requires slowing down, being present, and committing to your higher good. Link your expansion, goals, and intentions to inner growth. The ego will fight this, others might not understand it, and such intent is not aimed at increasing your bottom line. However, *You/you/YOU* will expand out of time and into timelessness. *You/you/YOU* will find fulfillment and enrichment through your commitment. Pour yourself into every moment of life. Let the heart be your compass, and devotion be your guide.

Love must be experienced and expressed within,
before it can be given in purity and wholeness to any other.

Sacredness lives inside every person, place, and thing . . . each human, animal, and plant . . . every mountain, river, and tree. Drop all barriers of thought, word, and deed so to live from that devotional . . . respectful . . . loving . . . and tender spectrum. Ultimately, devotion is patience with everyone and everything. It is loving with *Self/self/SELF* . . . the other . . . time . . . experiences . . . expressions . . . circumstances . . . darkness . . . light . . . and the world. Be patient. In becoming devotional and intimate, *You/you* become available for the sweetness of communion with *Self/self/SELF* and others. *Love/LOVE* grows from the inside out, not from the outside in.

In each moment, let *Mind/mind/MIND* have a background of continuous prayer. Place the highest state of *MIND* behind your eyes, so that *You* see everyone and everything through that filter. Find joy in life's infinite expressions. Nestled deep inside every experience is the gift of divine awareness. Be present to the big picture, while being *the presence* within the details. Live in the *forever*; *You/you/YOU* are eternally that. Life is merely an adventure amid the stars. Blessed *Being/being/BEING* . . . Breathe deeply as *You/you/YOU* sink into a devotional expression of sacredness.

Become aware of a dance in communion,
interconnecting you and your creation with divine aliveness . . .
***You/you/YOU* in the beginning . . .**
in the end . . .
and amid each realization.
I am *You/you/YOU* . . .
***You/you/YOU* are me . . .**
for all eternity.
In the garden that grows . . .
***You* are the earthen *Being/being/BEING* that blooms.**
Sweetly Dream . . .
so to experience the sweetest of dreams.

...

TEACHER TO EXAMPLE

How does purpose unfold?

Do not label yourself as a teacher.
***You* are not one; neither am I.**
***You* are not a student, nor am I.**
I don't want to be your guru.
I have no desire to fall off that pedestal.
I'm not looking for *you* to follow me.
Do not ask me to lead *you*.
Do not believe me.
Find your own truth.
And, do not expect me to follow *you*.
***You* are a Master, as I am.**

The outer world is speaking to *You* about *You/you/YOU*. In other words, the world has been created to direct *You* back toward your *Self/self/SELF*... your lower *self*... your past *Self/self*... your Higher *Self/SELF*... and Your God *SELF*. Your world, form, and function are naturally designed to bring attention to the body, mind, and heart. Conditioning steers *You* in the opposite direction. Life is the only teacher *You/you/YOU* require.

What *You* say shows exactly where *you* are. Your language offers gold nuggets as to where growth and healing are still required. The words *You* speak betray *you*, illustrating where unconscious negative thinking and actions still exist. The irony is, *You* do not listen to the words coming out of your mouth. However, there is an old adage: *"You teach what you need to learn."* This is true and can be used as a gauge for discovery. It is also where *You/you* fall into the trap of the ego, which will have *You* teaching everyone but yourself. Mistakenly, your focus becomes a distraction, by way of what *You* attempt to teach others. Rather than holding presence for what *You/you* need to learn and integrate within, *You* spend time and energy taking it out. Fooling yourself into believing *You* have done the work, *You* merely touch the surface. The impulse to lead, talk, or teach was a conditioned response.

Until you step out of the escapist need to help others—and move into helping yourself— you cannot open to discovery beyond your identity's neediness.

Those who teach about healing typically need to heal. Those who speak of building a business are usually trying to figure out how to sustain their own. Those who battle for others have not dealt with their inner struggles. Those who protect are making up for early-childhood deficiencies regarding safety. Everything *You/you* choose has a connecting thread to the past.

Do not turn your learning or healing into an occupation or preoccupation. This keeps *You/ you* living in the past, tethered to a wound that may or may not have been transformed. Simply experience your growth and then have a new beginning. Anything other is *Self/self*-obsession.

In truth, your true occupation will be what inspires, energizes, and fills *You/YOU* with presence. It will be unrelated to *your story*. There will be no look toward the future, because that is also subtly rooted in the past. There will be no agenda other than pure enjoyment and expression. Living by example means living in the present moment, attuned to what your masculine and feminine natures call forth. As the example, *You* serve in a much more powerful way, energetically.

The teacher is attached to impacting,
which means their identity requires another.
The example is immersed in their own experience,
which has nothing to do with anyone else.
The first is codependent . . . the second is independent.

There is a fine line between teacher and example. Teachers do support growth, advancement, education, and guidance. However, they have merely been a step of evolution. Teachers teach from what is known, from what has occurred, and through history. This creates replication and homogenization. Teaching must transition to inspiring learning and genius. It must be individually inspired from within, flowing outwardly with enthusiasm and curiosity. Rather than information being poured into the mind, individual genius must organically go where it desires. The example understands that their expression is integral. Their boldness offers permission for others to play their way into becoming.

These books have not been written to teach *you* anything. This is my personal integration and completion. It is my inspired action. I am celebrating the wisdom gained from experience, so that closure occurs and a new beginning unfolds. I reconcile, complete the absorption process, and integrate experience when I write the wisdom that is gained. This inspiration has risen out of *Being/BEING* with my humanity. *You* gaining something from these books is a bonus. However, I did not write these for *You*; I wrote them for me. Everything *You/you/YOU* do must be enacted purely for your expression. That is devotional presence, which energetically affects the world in a deep and soulful way. It no longer possesses the sticky energy of attachment, need, or manipulation.

Those that guide, tell, convince, and inspire *you*
into new ways of *Being/being/BEING* . . .
protocols . . . and actions
are not here to teach *You*,
even if their words are valuable.
They become the example when
they release attachment to
***You/you/YOU* gaining anything at all.**
***You/you/YOU* become the example,**
by not becoming attached to what they say.

You travel off course by believing others are beyond *you* . . . knowing more than *you* . . . or having something *you* do not yet have. However, they speak to themselves; *You/you* happened to eavesdrop. Their words may awaken insight, but it is only opening *You* to remembering. Their words or actions resonate because your inner guidance has been whispering the same to *You/you* all along. *You/you/YOU* cannot hear something outside *You/you/YOU* that is not already within *You/you/YOU*. *You* are here to teach yourself.

Teachers teach, thus creating more of the mental body. This limits perception to a narrower lens. *You* are *God/god/GOD* meeting *God/god/GOD*. What could another teach *you*? Embodiment is born of experience and integration. Examples embody. All beings come fully capable, inherently divine, and whole. This life journey is the remembrance of that. Life is meant to be lived by example, for *You/you/YOU*—by *You/you/YOU*—to show *You/you/YOU*. Only the ego needs another to see or value who *You/you/YOU* are. Do not attach to outer criticism, or to external compliments. That *need* to be valued, followed, lauded, or held on a pedestal illustrates how much inner work *You* still have to do.

> **YOU are your purpose . . .**
> **You are the student.**
> **Become your own teacher.**
> **The greatest ascent You/you/YOU can make**
> **is to live by example.**
> **Student ——-> Teacher ———> Example**
> **Herein is the evolution**
> **You/you/YOU have been seeking.**

Leading yourself is the highest expression of *Self/self/SELF* empowerment that can be embodied. *You/you/YOU* are your guru and teacher, healer, and guide, not another. By taking your own direction, embracing your lessons, doing the inner work required, healing within, and deepening your connection with the Divine, *You/you/YOU* become more powerful.

As a mirror, *You/you/YOU* reflect life so it sees itself. *This* is the drop in the ocean that ripples out. *This* is how one person changes the world; *Being/being/BEING* willing, ready, and able to change your own. Purity of *Being/BEING* places service toward *Self/self/SELF* before any other agenda. Do things that *You/you/YOU* have never done. *Being/BEING* courageous inspires others to be courageous. Blessed *Being/being/BEING* . . . Breathe deeply as *You/you/YOU* absorb and integrate your exemplary life.

> **May the acknowledgment of *Self/self/SELF* reflect . . .**
> **that real worth and value come from within;**
> **the gems of happiness, fulfillment, and realization can be found only inside.**
> **May the sacred rise into life,**
> **where there is no devotion toward division . . .**
> **no side to take . . . no separation to bridge . . .**
> **no difference to make.**
> **May clarity be received**
> **in remembrance of *Being/being/BEING***
> **the *One/one/ONE* . . .**
> **to anchor solidly in *Love/LOVE*.**
> **Sweetly dream . . .**
> **so to create the sweetest of dreams.**

...

CULTIVATING LISTENING

How can peace arise?

Be mindful of the energy *you* give.
Be mindful of the energy *you* take.
Be mindful of what is at stake.
The humanitarian crisis begins with *you*.
Your human resources are vital to life.
Your time . . . energy . . . thoughts . . .
words . . . and actions.
Conservation and cleanliness of your energy
saves the world.

This time of intense change is known as Kaliyuga. Kaliyuga means a time of "darkness", "ignorance", "strife", "discord", "quarrel" or "contention." It is a Hindu term describing a cycle in the human experience. Within *your/my/our/their* animal nature is a predetermined *self*-destruct for when *you/i/we/they* push things too far. The deepest, darkest, villainous, and denied shadows resting inside every person are the pressure points for a global meridian system. This energy will not be held down. Lying, manipulating, fighting, beating, shooting, and killing are drastic attempts to be seen, heard, and acknowledged. The human condition is a mix of darkness and *Light/light/LIGHT*, wrapped in many veils of gray and shadow. Darkness is simply another degree of *light*, the most distorted kind. This also serves.

We are a dying world. This is not a terrible thing. The death taking place is collective and will spawn new life and ways of *Being/BEING*. Something lies in *your/my/our/their* midsts that waits to be born. *You/I/we/they* are required to know these extremes in order to find the way back to center. Even challenging, chaotic, and difficult times serve *you/ me/us/them*. There might be no change without them. Cultural decay is our long and arduous sentence, because *you/i/we/they* have refused to listen.

It's a good day to die.
It's a good day to live.

Shutting down your capacity to hear creates interference and misunderstanding that results in conflict, confusion, and chaos. Energetically, deafness creates a defensive posture that is ready to defend, fight, and promulgate more fear. Unconsciously, *You/ you/YOU* listen on multiple levels. The ego uses stories that have been filed away as evidence to maintain your fight-or-flight response. This pattern within your matrix creates your echoes of prior experience.

Positivity is futile if you're not addressing what lies in your underworld. It is easy to grab hold of negative thoughts that fly through the *Mind/mind*. Even the most spiritual, powerful, and positive people experience swings of conscious and unconscious living. The issue is not your negativity. Your denial of it is the Achilles' heel.

Imagine what would be possible—in your relationships, work, family, and every area of life—if *You/you* improved the ability to listen from your *whole* self. Listening is more than paying attention. It is unity with the moment, person, place, and thing. It is full attention and presence, hearing and feeling where the other person is on all levels and dimensions. Full listening not only hears from the ears but also experiences the tone, rhythm, volume, and energy of the person. It discerns the space between words, the pauses and the emotion being felt.

Listen for your ocean of insight.
There is no greater gift *You/you/YOU* give the world than your listening.

Listen to what they are saying. Listen to what they are not saying. What is their body saying? What is their energy saying? Listen for their tone, inflection, perspective, and understanding. Instead of listening from filters of ego, mind, past, needs, agenda, story, or righteousness—be quiet. Listen with the presence of the soul. What they say, do, reflect, and feel says a lot about who they are *Being/being/BEING*.

The quality of your listening determines the quality of your relationships and life. The more connected *You/you/YOU* are to *Self/self/SELF*, the greater your ability to listen on subtle levels. However, if holding internal noise and chatter, listening will be distorted. When in shadow, conversation and experience will be received through your small *i*. Such listening only hears from places of trigger, smallness, wounding, and victimhood.

When living from the head, listening comes through logic, practicality, and confusion. When living from your gut, listening is intuitive and sensation oriented. When in the heart, hearing stems from anchors of *Love/love* and inspiration. Identity hears through story, filters of wounding, and agenda. Spirit listens from your sense of wholeness, unconditional *Love/LOVE*, and truth.

When *You/you* cease listening to the illusion outside, what is inside makes all the difference in your world. The presence to others . . . the honor of listening . . . the beauty of seeing, and the blessing of acknowledging will far outweigh your need to be seen, heard, and acknowledged. When *You/you/YOU* are truly aware, there will be nothing to say.

In cultivating the ability to hear thyself,
***You/YOU* develop an ear that receives others.**

True listening comes with surrender to your higher *SELF*. In that state, there is no story, victimhood, or attachment. Everything . . . all things . . . are rooted toward embodying the Essence of *YOU*. This surrender leads to personal power *Being/BEING* expressed. Listening from a higher realm creates a world of peace rather than one of chaos. Listening with the eyes and ears of interdependence creates perceptions and actions that serve love, and the calls for love. By *Knowing/knowing/KNOWING* yourself, *You/you/YOU* integrate the cries, calls, and clamors of all *Being/being/BEING* . . . animal . . . shadow . . . human . . . humanity . . . *Light/light/LIGHT* . . . *God/god/GOD* . . . collective . . . and cosmos.

Becoming one with others begins by listening to the least among *You*; the indigent

... homeless ... poor ... sick ... imprisoned ... and mentally ill. They speak volumes through their circumstances, energy, actions, and words. They illustrate what is occurring within your bandwidth of consciousness ... and amid your garden of good and evil. Everyone wants to be the speaker, but this time requires more listeners. It calls for a league of listeners. Our dis-ease resides at the level of thought, language, and expression, which also holds the cure. Listening is the single most important gift *You/you/YOU* can give to *Self/self/SELF* and others.

There is nothing to say.
Listen.
Just listen ...
***You* will discover the one who really speaks.**
***You* will come to know who is really talking.**

Listen deeply when sensations flow. Let subtlety and sensitivity relay the nuances of your inner child, inner masculine, and inner feminine. Listen to the meanderings of the animal, the shadow, and your essence. Discern where levels of apathy, indifference, and slothfulness exist in your life, work, and relationships. Insert the key of devotion. Move into *Being/BEING* the example of one who has been seen, heard, and acknowledged, first and foremost by *Self/self/SELF*. There is no greater or more significant recognition than your own. This level of deep listening lets *You/you/YOU* see into your infinite nature and also holds the full expanse of your humanity.

***You/you/YOU* are Essence in form.**
See, hear, and acknowledge the evidence of that.
That is Namaste ...
then, *You/you/YOU* may behold it in all others.

While the world appears insane at times, every individual has the opportunity to choose sanity over insanity. Presence, empathy, and compassion are the delineation between the two. Positivity, charity, activism, religion, and spirituality become masks, if not aligning and realigning *Self/self/SELF*. Close your ears. Do not listen to the distractions and chaos of the external world. Listen to what is occurring on the inside of *You/you/YOU*. Without a daily practice of sitting, listening, and coming home to *Self/self/SELF*, individuals become disconnected. Separation from your internal world is the dual nature within oneness. Ignoring *Self/self/SELF* creates the indifference that shrouds our world. Those that cannot see, hear, and acknowledge their own pain are unable to acknowledge anyone or anything. Blessed *Being/being/BEING* ... Breathe deeply as *You/you/YOU* cultivate listening.

May there be moments when there is nothing to say ...
no one to talk about ...
no noise in the mind ...
on the airwaves ...
or in static places.

May there be vast spaces of stillness . . .
where the richness of doing nothing is valued . . .
and timelessness for divine laziness
awakens infinite possibilities of inner wealth . . .
Let the quietness of being nothing
quench your thirst
and feed your hunger.
Sweetly dream . . .
so to create the sweetest of dreams.

. . .

HEAR THYSELF

What is the asking?

Awaken the giant within . . .
Let that serve the world.
You are not delusional;
YOU are that potent and powerful . . .
you simply forgot.

AFFIRMATION—CONTEMPLATION—INSPIRATION

I am capable of awakening to where I hold
indifference, apathy, disrespect, and dishonor.
I now transcend all places of *Self/self/SELF*-denial.

Contemplate and journal these inquiries until inspired to take action.

Be still; see what rises as *inspiration* versus *impulse*.
You/you/YOU possess the answer for achieving aliveness . . . go within.

The degree to which you are *Being/being/BEING*
is the degree to which *You/you/YOU*
shall cultivate inner and outer *Listening*.

What is your self-obsessed story around time, experience, and expression?

time.
What is your relationship with . . .
- time?
- story?

- past?
- present?
- future?

How are *You/you/YOU* wound up?

How are *You/you* unwinding?

emotional reflection.
What emotions are most frequent within *You/you/YOU*?
What emotions do *You* encounter most frequently in others?

Where are *You/you/YOU*?
- emotionally numb?
- emotionally overactive?
- emotionally neutral?
- reactive?

What are *You/you* saying, or not saying, through your
emotion?
emotional reactivity?
emotional numbness?
moods?

How can *You/you/YOU* balance emotional obsessions through exercises . . .
- for the mind?
- for the body?
- in communication?
- in expression?

slothfulness.
What role does indifference and apathy play regarding . . .
- life?
- *self*?
- others?
- the world?

Where and how have others been indifferent and apathetic to *You*?
How does indifference and apathy appear as your state of *being*?

What are *You/you* indifferent and apathetic to?

How and where do *You/you* express in slothfulness?

What is your distinction between slothfulness and rest/relaxation?

devotion.
What would devotion—as a moment-by-moment life practice—look like?

Where is devotion most required in your life?
How can *You/you/YOU* embody greater devotion in relationship to . . .
- *Self/self/SELF*?
- money?
- other people?
- the world?
- with work?
- with play?

teacher to example.
Who have been your teachers of life, freedom, and courage?
How do *You/you* embody those teachings?
Were these taught or modeled by example?

Who have been your teachers of disempowering, unconscious living?
How do *You/you* embody these?
Were these taught or modeled by example?

Do *You/you/YOU* learn through words—or the modeling of—thoughts, emotions, and behavior?

What do *You* try and teach others?
Have *You/you/YOU* mastered that in your life?

example.
What does it mean to be an example?
How have *You/YOU* modeled empowered and conscious living?
Who have *You/YOU* inspired by example? How?
Have *You/you* modeled disinterest, indifference, and apathy?
Whom did *You/you* pick that up from?
Who is picking that up from *You/you*?

listening.
How deeply do *You/you/YOU* listen with your . . .
- ears?
- body?
- feelings?
- sensations?
- aura?

- intuition?
- energy?

How can *You/you/YOU* embody greater . . .
- listening?
- presence?
- *Being/BEING* with others?

What practices can *You/you/YOU* put in place to be more present . . .
- to *Self/self/SELF*?
- in your life?
- in your relationships?
- in your world?

hear thyself.

What would living as an example of embodied Higher *SELF* look, sound, and feel like?

How would a more engaged and caring *Self* experience and express . . .
- patience?
- energy?
- trust?
- connection?
- presence?
- devotion?

May every man, woman, and child . . .
every bird, animal, and insect . . .
every tree, blade of grass, and flower . . .
receive . . . and know they are valuable . . .
they are needed . . .
they are perfect . . .
they are loved.
May each deeply comprehend that the world would not be complete
without any of these individual forms . . .
In appreciation, in reverence, and in holding this to be truth,
may we see and know this beauty . . .
this sacredness . . .
as divinity materialized.
Here lies the gift of life . . .
the miracle . . .
and synchronicity as everlasting presence.
Sweetly dream . . .
so to create the sweetest of dreams.

...

PETITION FOR PRESENCE

What is the shift in consciousness?

I am free . . .
You are free . . .
We are free . . .
They are free . . .
We are all free to fly.

IN COLLECTIVE PRAYER
FOR HEARING . . .
THE UNIFIED HARMONIC RESONANCE
OF THE GLOBAL ENERGETIC MATRIX

Dear Infinite Oneness . . .
Take us into the subtle moments . . .
unveiling the secrets of time.
Awakening to essence,
relaxing into the nuances of timelessness . . .
that rest between the skin and tissue of humankind.
Streaming through ancestral veins
flows the sweet agony of our inheritance.
Bone structures and bloodlines
of our yesterdays and tomorrows
create love out of human suffering
and our legacy of sorrows.
Allow silence to reveal the richness
of all that has been carried
as it dissolves into neutrality;
Ending the saga between humanity and divinity in sacred marriage.
Let this mixed pot of memory boil over
with the broth of brotherhood
and the savory sauce of sisterhood,
as each soul is reconfigured into infinite expressions of light for greater good.
Resounding throughout the universe,
heavenly echoes of past creations
release the visceral memory residing within our bodies;
as we clamor in wait for salvation.
Guide us great Spirit, between the veils that cloud our visions.
Continue turning us back toward the caverns of the heart,

with the inclination to stay inward.
Reignite us as we traverse the hills and valleys of mortality.
Create peace within us,
unleashing the ancient callings of your infinite vitality.
With your grace,
purify this toxic lineage of time . . .
With your blessing,
free our self-imposed shackles of mind.
Within your silence,
awaken the bliss of equanimity.
Allow what must become known
to be . . . embraced . . . owned . . . and absorbed lovingly.
Let us feel the fluttering of our earthly wings . . . softly emerge.
That they tickle us with inspired action,
to fly upon winds of change as Spirit birds.
May they lift us . . . weightlessly,
so we rise to bandwidths unknown.
Let us know, without a shadow of doubt . . .
that we are home.
Every single human being calling from near and far . . .
incarnated souls
sparkling and shining
as the Divine Oneness that we are.

In receiving this illusory gift of time . . .
may we give ourselves the treasure of timelessness.
So be it . . .
And so it is!

0
0 0
0 0 0
1 1 1 1
1 1 1
1 1
1
1
1 1
1 1 1
1 1 1 1
0 0 0
0 0
0

BEING

the illusion of duality.

What is the awareness?

You are the light of darkness.
You are the darkness of light.
You are living a dream,
designed by one who dreamed . . .
Here, light and dark cross paths . . .
as hero and villain meet *eye/I to eye/i* . . .
in hand-to-hand combat,
amid the makings of love.
You are love and *you* are light.
You are fear and *YOU* are darkness.
You are the distance between them.
One plus One
appears as *you* and *me* . . .
But the common denominator
is an eternal *Truth/truth/TRUTH* . . .
in duality, there always exists three.

The Illusion of Duality	The Awareness	Being/being/BEING
Secret Obsessions	What is the addiction?	Ego/Mind
Our Global Reflection of Climate Change	Where is the mirror?	The Collective
The Hole of Lust	What is the dis-ease?	The Shadow
The Key Whole of Tenderness	How is personal power activated?	Essence
Egoist to Humanitarian	How is purpose fulfilled?	Humanity
Cultivating Appreciation	How can peace arise?	The Bridge
Receive Thyself	What is the asking?	The Embodiment

Come face to face with the deepest, darkest aspects of who *You/you* are by way of the world's pain. The darkness of the world reflects the shadows in your psyche, along with known and unknown belief systems. *You/you/YOU* have been conditioned from the beginning with thought-form technology from lives that came before *You*. Lies, doubts, ills, and pain have been unknowingly passed down generation after generation. Yet, life also provided an inheritance of creativity, genius, curiosity, and imagination to balance things out. All illusion and disease are living blessings that avail *You* of opportunities for empowerment and growth, if willing to see beyond the small *i*.

Your actions, reactions, and choices stem from what *You/you/YOU* came to believe about life through the experiences of those around *You*. Your *Self/self*-concept is derived from how others perceived *You*. This was the original seeding of duality within your consciousness. This is the proverbial *tree of knowledge from the garden of good and evil*. *You* were fed a poisoned apple and have fallen deeply asleep.

It is easy to see your trail of destruction. *You* need only follow the bread crumbs. With time, *You* become more entangled within your *perception* of reality. This knowledge breeds a strong ego and deep sense of pride. Life's trappings produce ideas of hierarchy, evolution, and individuality. It is not long before your ego battles other egos, which results in conflict, challenge, discord, and isolation. The building wave of repressed selves erupts throughout systems, structures, and environments to greater and greater degrees, ultimately becoming the very world *You/you/YOU* see.

For this to change, *you/i/we/they* must change. All that is dual within *you/me/us/them* must unite. Until what was fractured is pieced back together, the true value of contrast will not be seen. Compassion unfolds when sacredly holding *your/my/our/their* broken heart.

Duality is an illusion that feeds the addiction of secret obsessions.
Climate change reveals the global reflection of the collective's
viral shadow of lust.
In turning the key of tenderness,
you are initiated from egoist to humanitarian.
Receiving thyself cultivates appreciation as the bridge for embodying humanity.

The contrast that exists within the world is a result of group conscious, unconscious, and subconscious minds. The shrill cry against how duality appears creates more contrast, divisiveness, and polar opposites. Unconscious resistance to what rests beneath the surface of our individual and collective psyches is fueled by emotions and frenetic energy that have compounded within the physiology of all matter. Your life is a nucleus in the cellular structure of time. Inside your body—within each cell, tissue, organ, and bone—is all of time, every memory, experience, expansion, and contraction. *You* react and respond to the issues of the world because it triggers visceral memory within. *You* can assist in transmuting what is stagnant by fully experiencing everything. The world is your mirror, illustrating degrees of darkness, lightness, separation, and wholeness. *You/you/YOU* came for experience; this is it!

Your purpose is to hold time in a space of timelessness—fully present and feeling—but not attached. Contrast has a purpose within the illusion of time. It serves in your mastery of time, space, form, and function. This universe has a balancing mechanism. Karma is merely the healing of life, through your physiology. It brings density to surface by flushing it out, rebalancing the ecosystem of life. Karma does not appear as external circumstances in the way most believe. It actually appears in the body, reflecting your guilt, manipulations, and miscreations. The global sphere is a larger balancing mechanism. This cauldron creates environments, climates, and situations for equilibrating the energy or all time.

Duality and division do not exist only in one of us . . . or a few . . .
These rest within all of us.
Any resistance to this idea is what keeps *You/you* locked within illusion.

Duality allows an entire spectrum of expression. It is a built-in mechanism for returning *you/me/us/them* to the emptiness and neutrality of infinite space. Each new contrast is a cocreative unfolding of energy that eventually turns *You/you/YOU* back toward its original moment of creation. This is how time utilizes cycles and rhythms that allow for endless experiences of birth, life, death, and rebirth. With each subsequent permutation, energy recalibrates and reorganizes. Although illusion appears to be dual, the reality is that all of life rests within cocreative oneness.

Duality is innocently inherited. Those unto whom *You* were born modeled how to perceive, ignore, and deflect the contrast within the world around *you*. Defensiveness and combative living empowered the fight-and-flight mechanism *you* were entrained with after birth. Caregivers introduced ideas of good and bad, right and wrong, better or worse. They projected judgment, blame, shame, and forgiveness as rods to steer with. They also gave *you* love, compassion, understanding, and truth as standards to live by. These perspectives, in and of themselves, are the building blocks of duality and the human condition. Opposites are required for contrast to exist as experience. *You* are not experiencing the world through *your* mind, *You/you* are experiencing it through *theirs*—those of your parents, siblings, caregivers, friends, media, fairy tales, and cartoons.

Behold the dance of duality.
You have come for experience.
Duality offers entertainment
and, if wisely engaged,
provides high spiritual attainment.

You/you/YOU are a cocreator within collective consciousness—through every thought *You/you/YOU* think, every word *You/you/YOU* say, every feeling *You/you/YOU* have, each action *You/you/YOU* take, and every belief *You/you/YOU* cling to. These steps create or destroy the world *You* live in. *You/you/YOU* are victimized by your own propaganda of . . . separation . . . victimhood . . . worthlessness . . . smallness . . . limitedness . . . powerlessness . . . and oppression. Duality is not inherently wrong. This is the playing field that earth was intended to have. It is the game of life. Within this virtual reality, *You/you/YOU* affect how the game functions and plays out. *You/you/YOU* are the joystick; it is all in your hands.

Duality is the illusion of fragmentation. In truth, all things work in tandem and always for a greater good, but the human *Mind/mind* cannot fathom the larger picture. Continuing down this historical path of dualistic thinking will only result in outer annihilation. Instead, *conscious inner annihilation* can create a powerful path of aliveness where your authentic nature is realized. Inner annihilation is the dissolution of all pieces, parts, and aspects that keep *You/you/YOU* seemingly separate. That includes story, identity, race, class, religion, thoughts, beliefs, etc.

Open to, embrace, absorb, transmute, and transfigure the places within that hold *You/you/YOU* back from the realization of oneness. No thing exists outside *You/you/YOU* that does not exist within *You*. Denial of such keeps the illusion operating, and duality in place. Your delusions of grandeur are *Self/self*-serving and egotistical. Ego delights in drama, contrast, and duality; that is its playground. Contrast will cease when criticism, condemnation, and judgment do.

See duality as it truly is . . . Oneness.
Life is merely the creative play of the divine absolute.
All of life is one entirety,
with no end and no beginning,
and, more specifically, no separation.

The reason the world has not seen the miracle of peace is because *you/i/we/they* continue to assert *our* individual pieces. *You/I/we/they* are the ONE sacred presence. When *You* can be in complete unconditional acceptance of life's bipolar expression, all duality and separation will dissolve. Blessed *Being/being/BEING* . . . Breathe deeply as *You/you/YOU* absorb all that is dual in the name of oneness.

May your nights be blessed,
and your days be blessings.
May the vast space of magical ether
reveal your infinite presence.
May your eyelashes fan Divine Light into the world,
opening brilliant portals of expressive creation
and closing with prayers of petition.
May Light reflect into the body
and out to others
with the power of presence . . .
freedom from fear . . .
and the grace of detachment.
Sweetly dream . . .
so to create the sweetest of dreams.

0
0 0
0
1
1 1
1 1 1 1
1 1 1
1
0
0 0
0

. . .

SECRET OBSESSIONS

What is the addiction?

**Mother Nature is like any other mother . . .
she loves, disciplines, and will get stern
when her children act up.
Unless we come together,
nature will create a way for us to do so.**

Secrets and lies are bred into familial history and become part of *your/my/our/their* genetic code. Hushed voices, whispers, and silent glances hide skeletons that are brushed under the bed, hidden behind curtains, and tucked into closets. Their bones keep creaking, as they become the ghosts that live on. The great burden today is the weight of secrets *being* held and lies *being* told. Living in this manner creates *Self/self* betrayal and dishonoring repercussions. A secret or lie can never stand alone. More secrets are needed to safeguard and protect the initial one. A lie needs many others to back it up.

Secrets sit within the uncomfortable silence between small talk, where the air holds the weight of shame and emotions that are withheld. There is a blanket of unease when not knowing what to say, how to say it, what not to say, and how to inconspicuously avoid saying anything. Lying, cheating, stealing, and corruption are embedded in the fabric of humanity from long ago. It began in your original family structure. Secrets, shame, adultery, and a lack of trust seed every new creation. Since the human *Mind/mind* naturally leans toward the negative, the energetics for secrecy and deception unfold when consistently coming in contact with the aura of a person, place, or thing that vibrates at that frequency. Like attracts like.

Dishonesty is a slow-building bacteria that weakens bodies, destroys connection, tears families apart, and obliterates societies. This is how *you/i/we/they* become serious and obsessed with the smallness of ourselves. Secrets and lies are the birthplace of patterns of shame, blame, and judgment. This is not only about how *You* withhold and lie to others. The secrets *You/you* keep and the lies *You/you* tell your *Self/self/SELF* are the most destructive to your life experience, particularly to your physical body. Once *You* face your own deception, the final frontier of healing will be forgiving the betrayal, lies, and secrets of your biological family.

**Experience has nothing to do with "out there."
It is for "re-cognition" of what's "in here";
the inner workings of your mind, body, heart, and spirit.**

History, movies, and media illustrate that power does not exists unless force, manipulation, or deception are used. *You* are fed stories of suffering, success, heroes, and villains. These are subtle imprinting within the mind. Through images and sound, *you/i/we/they* become conditioned, gaslighted, and homogenized into a world that is not real but is portrayed as real. *You* exist at a time where *Truth/truth/TRUTH* must be advocated for. All secrets, lies, falsities, withholding, and manipulations will knock *You* off your feet, have *You* running for safety, and have *You* in search of security. Perceiving yourself as a small speck in this great big universe, *You* will initially believe the lies and liars; we all do . . . until we don't.

The most insidious affect of gaslighting is the denial of your reality. Convinced that what *you* feel, know, and intuit is false, your sense of *Self/SELF* becomes lost. This is psychological abuse, and it runs rampant. *You* are told what to believe, how to think, and the way in which to feel. Even those who appear to have celebrity status, political positions, and religious leadership become puppets and pawns for a few who sit behind the scenes and make the moves.

This began in your past with accepted forms of brainwashing. Religion and school are two forms of brainwashing that condition *you* into separateness. Your outlook, expression, and identity are based on what is taught to *you*. If born into a family of white supremacists, you will be brainwashed into their version of truth. If *You* are born to earth-loving, interracial hippies whose religion is love, *You* will believe that as truth. Your truth becomes the secret obsession *You/you/YOU* live and die for, until *You/you/YOU* shed layers upon layers of identity.

Stay in the inquiry.
This is not for learning more; it is for letting go of all *you* learned.

People in positions of power want more power. Church and state are built on this premise. Religious institutions manipulate ideas of good and evil—God and Devil—for profit and penance. Love and fear are used to manipulate and harness human resources. Governments, structures, and systems perpetuate haves and have-nots—allies and enemies . . . threat and security—through propaganda. It may be real news or fake news, but it is news. *You* are given freedoms within a context of boundaries. Regardless of what appears, all things are catalysts for justice and patriotism. In this way, institutions maintain control of actions, ideas, and movements. *Mind/minds* that steward propaganda—whether news, leaked information, or conspiracy theory—facilitate the matrix that keeps individuals conditioned.

History has spun stories to satisfy the agendas of a few, so that mass consciousness follows. Each time society moves toward realigning, secrets and lies are utilized to initiate fear. It is likened to a psychological taser to get people back in line, have them play it safe, and remain small. Objectives are met each time *You/you/YOU* conform to social, moral, political, and economic *norms*. This is the art of war . . . and the game of life.

Those that step out of this man-made comfort zone are either celebrated or vilified based on the homogenized need at the time. We need those we love and celebrate. They provide the masses an escape, which maintains the illusion. These people provide entertainment, hope, and inspiration. We also need those whom we love to hate. They justify our addictions, behaviors, and states of hopelessness. They also allow us to be indifferent to pain, suffering, and corruption. And all of this plays into balancing the energies of time, compounded from the past through present day. Time takes as long as it takes.

Awaken a greater unknown.
Begin the process of unknowing.

The golden thread within the darkness of your human condition is the *greatest secret of all*. It goes unspoken, unacknowledged, and therefore never integrated, but it eternally beats within each and every cell of *Being/being/BEING*. In going back to the beginning of *Self/self/SELF*, *You* will meet your true maker. The ultimate secret to be embodied is beyond what the ego wants *You/you/YOU* to realize. This powerful *Truth/TRUTH* will trigger your ego and humanity. The great secret within all duality—and timeless reality—is that *You/you/YOU* are *God/god/GOD*. *You* are the *God* of your understanding. Not your identity or personality—and beyond personhood—*You/you/YOU* are *God*. Knowing this, what changes? . . . What will *You* change? Blessed *Being/being/BEING* . . . Breathe deeply as *You/you/YOU* release your obsession toward withholding, lying, and keeping secrets.

May *You/you/YOU* find good company in your aloneness . . .
and through that,
bring rich connection and communion into our togetherness . . .
May deepened humanity be the open doorway
in which to meet and greet.
May the *God/god/GOD* within you recognize
the *God/god/GOD* within all . . .
May your divine smile
inspire recognition and delightful reunion . . .
Sweetly dream . . .
so to create the sweetest of dreams.

OUR GLOBAL REFLECTION OF CLIMATE CHANGE

What is the mirror?

**Off-grid away from everything . . .
on-grid in connection . . .
in gridlock.
One is apathy. One is love. One is fear.
Be aware.
In the enemy is your mirror;
in the stranger is your family.
In the uncommon is a common bond.
And . . . pain holds healing.
Within the Dark
is the Light.**

Floods. Hurricanes. Forest fires. Tsunamis. Droughts. Earth is expressing everything that *you/i/we/they* will not. It has held an incredible amount of *your/my/our/their* energy, along with all that has compounded throughout history. Nature is speaking back to *You* with the same intensity *being* held inside *You/you/YOU*. She mirrors emotions that are collectively repressed. Gaia also expresses the trauma she has been forced to endure. Nature and the elements work synergistically to release pressure and restore balance.

**The universe always provides
the appropriate weather and conditions
to achieve its end.**

Your degree of emotional intelligence affects personal and collective consciousness. Life is the full expression of your emotive pattens. Your internal weather creates ripples in our world. Through what is mentally, verbally, and emotionally transmitted—consciously and unconsciously—earthen manifestations arise. This often expresses as climate change and weather patterns. *You/you/YOU* are the waters of emotion: grief, sadness, despair, clearing, purification, and cleansing. *You/you/YOU* are the fires of emotion: anger, rage, agony, destruction, passion, heat, and creation. *You/you/YOU* are the winds of change: confusion, chaos, trauma, obliteration, freshness, lightness, and ease.

Although science illustrates theories and reasons for climate change, all things stem from spiritual cause. *You/i/we/they* are the source of the cause. Unknowingly, *you/i/we/they* produce all manner of effects. Global warming is inflammation, due to the continued energetic impact of stress, trauma, and rage. Freezing and cold conditions are indicative of feeling unloved, posttraumatic stress, depression, and shock. This lack of circulation, warmth, and intimacy is reflective of what rests within the undercurrents of society. Flooding relates to the well of emotion that has backed up within the peoples of earth, and not being expressed. Fires are the buildup of rage, anger, and hostility that exists within us and the earth. We are the body of Gaia. What she expresses is related to what we hold as energetic cells within her body. Our disease is her disease, and vice versa. If she dies, it is because *you/i/we/they* are the cancer that kills her.

Emotions from those that are ravaged, killed, beaten, and tortured are discordant energies. We place life's lost sons and daughters—soldiers, children, battered women, refugees, death-row inmates—inside Gaia after waging domination and war upon her belly. Chemicals, bombs, and pollutants are poured into her waters and onto her lands. Spiritual practices—for releasing anger, sadness, hate, and vengeance performed by writing, burying, and burning—use our Earth Mother as a dumping ground for the darkness we do not want. For centuries, we have cut, torn, raped, and used her lands. Earths animals have been abused, tortured, slaughtered, and depleted, many of which have become extinct. Other animals are bred, caged, cooked, and eaten. Her birds are shot down. Her sea life is strangled and encapsulated by plastics, oil, and waste. All of this toxic energy has to go somewhere; it must transform . . . express . . . and release.

Heaven and Hell exist here on earth.
Which manifests is wholly dependent on
***your/my/our/their* capacity to feel,**
personal responsibility,
and conscious action.
In every moment you have a choice . . .
Heaven over Hell.

We are earth's latecomers. Plant and animal life have existed in balance and harmony before *you/i/we/they* began destroying it. More animal than animals, we are worse than pests, vermin, and the superbugs of the world. Voraciously destroying and consuming everything, *you/i/we/they* are uncertain and unaware of how abusive and entitled we have become. The oppression inflicted upon people of color, men, women, children, and animals is just another way we desecrate the earthen form we are a part of. Why are we shocked at our vile, animal nature that expresses violence toward each other, when we willingly clear-cut, burn, pollute, and destroy our sacred living planet?

We must endure earth's release of pent-up energy and also take ownership of her wrath. The loss many have experienced through flooding, winds, and fire is *being* given opportunity to release strong currents of grief, rage, and despair. Doing so alleviates some withheld energy. The decay, death, and disappearance of human life—due to viruses and natural disasters—are simply a response to the disease that we are. Earth is mirroring our fight-or-flight pattern. We can alleviate the planet's suffering through feeling our pain, while also bearing sacred witness to those who suffer. In this way, we not only support earth's healing but also facilitate our own sustainability. Blessed *Being/being/BEING* . . . Breathe deeply as *You/you/YOU* calm the climate within.

May the company you keep
illustrate the beauty of your personal communion.
May the moments outside

the illusion of duality.

return you inside
to the sacred treasure of your aloneness.
May each of us celebrate
life's many creations
as we dance with the whole and holiness
of all of life's manifestations.
Sweetly dream . . .
so to create the sweetest of dreams.

. . .

THE HOLE OF LUST

What is the disease?

You are an exploration in experience . . .
of the unknown becoming known,
like no other before.
Revel in each day.
Rebel in each moment.
Remember . . .
Now.

Lust, craving, and aversion have their roots in the displaced *anima* and *animus*—male and female unconscious archetypes—of each person. These animal instincts are at the core of the shadowed, reptilian brain. The base of lust stems from the survival mode of *kill or be killed*. This animalistic hunger consumes individuals, where senses override conscious action. Often associated as a sexual vice, lust can exhibit as hunger for fame, celebrity, power, money, etc. The chase is a ritualistic part of the high. To drool, want, desire, and devour temporarily feeds the inner animal. Once the object of lust is captured, the quality of *being* insatiable emerges. This builds the foundations for shame and guilt, which manifests vast imbalances and dysfunction on the inner and outer realms.

You/i/we/they are *being* sucked into a black hole, one born of hunger, cravings, and desire. Your animal impulses are alert with lust, while voraciously gorging, hoarding, and ravaging. These behaviors lead to addictions that control *you/i/us/them* and the senses, mind, and actions. Human *being*s are naturally addictive creatures, and we all have addictions. Addiction is mental illness. This insanity pervades every life. Cravings, when uncontrollable, lead to other vices and violence. In the same way, an aversion is still addiction. However, this is the addiction of *being* hunted and haunted by what we cannot accept.

Lust can appear in many different ways. It is not only addictions of sex, alcohol, or drugs. It can appear in all manner of expressions. Competition feeds the desire to be the best, to kill the competition, or to have excess. In your world of excess, amassing material things—more money, more shoes, more . . . more . . . more—is grounded in voracious desire. The hunger and desire in social media to amass followers is another expression of lust. Wanderlust . . . drooling . . . jealousy . . . stalking are all shadow animal cravings. Insatiability, dissatisfaction, and a lack of fulfillment are signs that craving, aversion, and lust are present.

> **The human race has nothing to do with running,**
> **yet so many are.**
> **The animal craves.**
> **It hunts to win . . . to conquer . . . and to kill.**
> **It is averse to what intimidates . . . threatens . . .**
> **or fights back.**
> **Are you searching for humanity?**
> **It's right where you are.**

Life's mission is to humanize the animal nature and spiritualize human nature. The animal inside hungers and hunts. Seeking to conquer and be king of the jungle, it sees only itself and its needs. To calm the animal nature does not mean to domesticate it. That only suppresses hunger. The animal will become feral. Humanizing the animal nature occurs by lovingly accepting its naturalness, and consciously transmuting the hunger moment by moment, thought by thought, action by action, and breath by breath.

Desire, craving, and aversion are seeds where illusion and disillusionment sprout and grow. Craving and aversion create suffering, where gross energies build within the body. These energetic impulses may take *you* into one life experience or many, adding layer upon layer of gross sensations to the mix. Compounding these energies initiates multiple births, many deaths, and rebirths along the way. Develop a relationship with all of who *You/you/YOU* are, especially in *being* animal. Clearly understand what *You/you/YOU* lust after . . . crave . . . and have aversion to. Upon clear recognition, *You* have an opportunity to transmute and transcend these energies, impulses, and experiences.

> **Every relationship *You/you/YOU* have is for the recognition**
> **of who *You* are in each moment . . .**
> **and equally who *you* are not.**

You are an organism that is in the greater body of humanity. Interdependence supports the health of the greater collective. Anything less is a cell gone rogue. Your stories are not the issue, but *how you carry them* deeply affects not only your life, but also the collective experience of your world. Attachment to your stories is also an expression of lust. Preoccupation with your story creates wheels within wheels that keep *you* spinning, and wounds within wounds that keep *you* wanting. *You/you* have been spiraling, but not necessarily in evolution. *You/you* might discover that *you* have never gotten beyond *being* animal in nature.

As *You/YOU* become the spiritualized human, *You/YOU* will be drawn away from worldly pursuits. Ultimately becoming a silent watcher in the world, *You/YOU* will not have the need to be seen. As a conduit for transmuting energy into higher frequencies, *You* will experience the union of aspects where you discover presence. From this space, all doing is experienced as distraction, talk becomes energetic leakage, and the *Mind/mind*'s agenda equates to force, not power. Blessed *Being/being/BEING* . . . Breathe deeply as *You/you/YOU* neutralize your cravings, aversions, and lust.

May the mind be
flexible in hard times . . .
the heart be warmed
in cold moments . . .
May the body feel safe
when in the grip of fear . . .
May your steps be calm,
when traveling pathways of strife . . .
May the Higher SELF lead . . .
and be guided
by the Light . . .
May trust always be close . . .
and wisdom walk
with clear sight . . .
May your inner authority reign . . .
and providence coincide.
Sweetly dream . . .
so to have the sweetest of dreams.

...

THE KEY WHOLE OF TENDERNESS
How is personal power activated?

The heart is vast . . .
It can hold all of the heartbreak
and all of the love that exists.
The heart is not a physical space,
but a landscape of experience . . .
Knowing that,
fathom who *You/you/YOU* really are . . .

If open to your heart, *You/you/YOU* will slip deeply in and be engulfed by the raw emotion that rests within its cracks and crevices . . . pulsations and rhythms . . . deep gullies and chasms . . . fullness and overflow. Deep inside lie a humanity that is broken open. There, *You/you/YOU* forget that *You* are *you*, and I am me. *You/you/YOU* no longer perceive that *we* are separate *being*s. Awareness of this comes when *you* go beyond the facade your heart is surrounded by. Much of what is written in this book is intended to break down the wall surrounding your heart. It is so that *You* finally face the places of heart-shattering hopelessness that are buried inside. Move toward something deeper than the illusion *You/you/YOU* desperately cling to. Your aliveness rests on the other side of walls and barriers *You* have built. Otherwise, *you* are a paper doll living a false existence. That is why *You/you* never feel full . . . satisfied . . . satiated . . . complete . . . whole.

In *being* pierced by the jagged edges of pain that cut from the outside, tenderness and compassion bleed through. These energies are within the pathways that life experiences have carved out. With tenderness, *You* begin to see a face in the brokenness of each moment. That familiar countenance holds the innocence *you* once knew. It shines with the *Light/LIGHT you* desperately long to return to. While seemingly out of reach, your tender *Being/BEING* is on the other side of the waterfall that *You/you* must shed. *You* will taste the salt of your earthen *being* through tears that stream down. These are shed for how *you* became lost . . . what was lost . . . and the loss of humanity. *BEING* rests beyond the hardened facade and various walls that have been built.

Walk with me into the Light . . .
Walk with me into the Dark . . .
Walk with me into the Higher Realms . . .
Walk with me into the Underworld . . .
***I* have been beside *You/you* all along.**

What lies between *you* and innocence is a bruised, black-and-blue, ill-shapen, shadowy *being* that is extremely tender. The sensations, ache, soreness, and pain need your gentle hand. The longing to be held exists, but the timidness of being touched reveals fear of further pain. Although the worst injuries appear on the surface, layers beneath the bruising are affected far more. There are scars upon scars . . . broken places . . . and shattered dreams. Tenderness is required. The softness of *being* must come from *You* before it ever comes from another. Safety, empathy, and trust will rebuild your sense of wholeness and capability. Tenderness will gently rock the frightened animal, so that it realizes there is no need to hunger, fear, or be on the prowl. Care, compassion, and love are necessary. *You* are giving *Self/self* the gift of receivership.

Look at life from your heart instead of the eyes, ears, or mind. *All* people are the same as *you*. Their brokenness, trauma, tragedy, and heartbreak match your own. Do not turn from them. *You* mistakenly view them as strangers, or people belonging to another clan. They are yours: your brothers . . . your sisters . . . your children . . . your grandmothers and grandfathers. Tenderness dissolves lines of separation. It creates union. *You/i/we/they* are on a crowded island, each desperately attempting to get *Home/HOME*.

Your worth is not based on who *you/i/we/they* will/might become, nor is it based on what *you/i/we/they* possess. *You/i/we/they* are enough, regardless of status, circumstances, or state. Choose the most unconditionally loving response in every moment. Have appreciation for what rests within the space. Love quenches those who are parched. This *Love* does not ask, seek, need, control, or manipulate. It is pure. This Love does not turn away, run, hide, or ignore. It is present, fully seeing and holding humanity. Communion fills those who are starved.

Walk with me . . .
In each step . . .
Together, we will create Heaven on Earth.

The distortion that makes *love* appear distant, painful, or manipulative arises from the filters, misaligned fantasy, and projectionist expectation of individuals who hide from their own heartbreak. When *you/i/we/they* are conscious of the shackles, chains, limitations, and control that *we* place on *Love/LOVE*—a renewed tenderness toward humanity can unfold. Before *Love/LOVE* can exist, *You* must *tend* to your wounds, then the ability to be tender toward others will be true. Change must also coincide in *Mind/mind/MIND*.

Give to *Self/self/SELF* and others what *you* most desire. In doing so, *You/you* will find the place where secret longings become realized. In that space, there is no longer *you* or *me* . . . not even an *us* or *we* . . . but an *IS*-ness that is true intimacy. It is unnamable, unexplainable, and untouchable; vulnerable and beautiful. As *You/you* embrace your humanity, *You* wrap your arms and head around a world *You/you* have been unable to see. My home is inside *You/you/YOU* and your home is inside *Me/me/ME*. In this sacred space, there are three. Only through safety, sacredness, and transparency can *you/i/we/they* begin to know the *One/one/ONE*. See the sick as healed, and the broken as whole. See what appears bad as good. See chaos as order. Return your eyes, heart, and mind to an original state of innocence and purity. Blessed *Being/being/BEING* . . . Breathe deeply as *You/you/YOU* turn the key of tenderness.

May *You/you/YOU* taste the world
but return to what nourishes from the inside . . .
May *You/you/YOU* see what is beautiful externally,

BEING

but discover the exquisiteness of your inner sanctuary . . .
May *You/you/YOU* explore vast lands
and know your holy land . . .
May *You/you/YOU* meet with all,
as a way to receive thyself . . .
May the maya of the world engage inner *Truth/truth/TRUTH* . . .
May *You/you/YOU* know this world was created
to discover the great universe inside *You/you/YOU*.
Sweetly Dream . . .
so to create the sweetest of dreams.

. . .

EGOIST TO HUMANITARIAN

How does purpose unfold?

Find me in your breath . . .
I sit in the marrow of your bones . . .
I roam through the canals of your body . . .
I beat the drum of your heart space . . .
I tickle you from the inside . . .
I play your organs . . .
I am on the tips of your fingers . . .
and in between your toes . . .
I am in the blink of your eye . . .
in each tear that flows . . .
I am within laughter that bellows . . .
and your moments of silence . . .
There is no place I am not . . .
I am with you always . . .
I have always been . . .
in all ways.

The ego is not bad; it is not a villain. It initially developed as your protector, a savior that shielded the child from hurts *being* experienced. Ego serves a purpose. There will be large egos and extremely quiet ones, but there will be an ego nonetheless. Superegos can also develop; these venture toward extreme narcissism where empathy and humanity are compromised or nonexistent. The egoist is driven by the outside, following the trappings of excess, importance, and significance. Through measuring, strategizing, and individualizing, the ego seeks to be loved, adored, applauded, needed, and celebrated. Regardless of heightened educational, material, or social success, people are enslaved by their egoic thoughts, patterns, emotions, and identity. Through ego, these can remain deeply unconscious.

Ego tends to look outside itself for approval, and desires to be seen, heard, and acknowledged. It becomes a teacher, businessman, preacher, politician, visionary, and revolutionary; wearing whatever hat is called for at the time. Like-minded is the ego's way of creating cliques. Ego wants to build and leave a tangible legacy. Your ego will create an attachment to who *You* think *You* are. If *you* think *You* are nobody, your ego attaches to that. In this way, you are controlled by your ego, and in service to it.

The ego projects everything outside itself, including humanity. It views humanity as the collective population. However, if not engaging your humanity, there can be no real compassion or empathy for external humanity. The shift from egoist to humanitarian is a turn inward. When willing to get beyond the ego's need to fluff its feathers, be on display, or prove its significance, an individual can begin to know the vulnerable reality of themselves and what expands inner knowing and higher soul expression. Each time *You* do nothing— taking the time to merely witness and deeply breathe—healing is activated. The false *Self/ self* or ego loses a little of its hold as *YOU* become more empowered. In this way, ego can align in service to the soul and higher *SELF*.

> **When someone's heart breaks,**
> **they don't need your words or wisdom;**
> **they need your heart, compassion, and presence.**

A humanitarian integrates and embodies their internal landscape, feelings, and emotion. Focusing inward for discovery, the humanitarian is high-minded, not simply like-minded. *Being* cultivates deep love, acceptance, connection, and compassion for *Self/self/SELF*— in the broad spectrum—encompassing light to dark. This tender embrace is how *You/i/ we/they* deepen into greater humanity. Compassion comes through individuals that have been with their own pain. Otherwise, the individual reflects pity or sympathy, which stems from ego. *You/i/we/they* must grow from the inside out.

You cannot be a humanitarian in the outer world, unless willing to engage your inner humanity. The deep understanding that *all action is reaction* will dawn amid the meditations and meanderings of inner work. A foundation of calm grounds outer experiences of pain and suffering—whether one's own or another's—within the silent spaces of the heart and body. Once there, these are seen, heard, acknowledged until felt, absorbed, and transmuted. The feelings that rise can usher out old belief systems and unresolved issues that block *You/you* from moving forward. This active devotion embodies energy much like the Ho'oponopono prayer of healing, which states, "I love you, I'm sorry, Please forgive me, Thank you." This prayer acknowledges individual responsibility for creating a world that is seen as suffering and separate. Presence to your consciousness is the epitome of a humanitarian heart and sacred service.

Dive into your caverns of withheld pain. Transmute your suffering. Not doing so shifts the legacy of pain onto future generations. Through numbing, avoidance, and distraction . . . suffering is amplified. The world requires people willing to be present and truly feel. Do not spiritualize or philosophize. Do not positivize, intellectualize, or attempt to make meaning. Do not be distracted with busyness, or a cause. Just feel, and *be with* those who can and cannot feel. In order to change the world, *You* must be willing to accept and hold the world as it appears. Cherish life as an unconditionally loving mother holds a child: close to the bosom. Regardless of what occurs, the humanitarian heart must be at the forefront. When *You* walk in another's shoes, *You/you/YOU* discover the steps of humility. If *You* have not walked those steps, tenderly hold the heart of the one that did. Blessed *Being/being/ BEING*... Breathe deeply as *You/you/YOU* vibrationally shift from egoist to humanitarian.

May there be space between us . . .
space for consciousness . . .
space for creativity . . .
space for loving . . .
space for sacredness . . .
May there be space for *You* to be *you* . . .
space for acceptance . . .
space for me to be me . . .
and for something greater than the both of us . . .
even greater than the *we*.
May there be space for listening . . .
communing . . . and cocreating . . .
space for unity . . . and freedom . . .
and *Being/being/BEING*;
space for nothing . . .
for everyone . . .
for no one . . .
and for everything.
Space as Oneness . . .
and the presence of emptiness.
Meet me there . . .
Sweetly Dream . . .
so to create the sweetest of dreams.

. . .

CULTIVATING APPRECIATION

How can peace arise?

Embrace all that walk past . . .
They too are yours. They long to belong . . .
They have only forgotten . . .
They are lost.
Hold them. Hear them. See them.
They scream to be heard.
Do not match fear with fear . . . hate with hate . . . anger with anger.
Then all is lost . . . and all become lost.
Love them. Forgive them. Accept them.
Appreciate them.
They are your love in action.
They are your creative power for good.
They are your salvation . . .
because they are *You/you/YOU*.
Do not lose sight of the message they bring.

Give thanks for all the good in your life. Appreciate everything, even the conflicts. Have gratitude for the health issues and the chaos. Money issues and dysfunction also serve. In humility, bow to the other and say, "*Your adversity gave me mine, and that brought us both closer to the Divine. When I asked life for what I wanted, I had no idea you were the way to get there. Thank you for being in my life, playing the role I needed you for strengthening my spiritual connection and empowering me.*"

What have *You/you/YOU* not had? Have *You/you/YOU* experienced love? Have *You/you/YOU* experienced limitation? Have *You/you/YOU* seen something, anything, come to fruition? Have *You/you/YOU* coped with death? *You/i/we/they* get to experience it all . . . but rather than focusing on the vastness of experience, *you* judge the situations that arise. Deepen into appreciation because *You/you/YOU* have gained experience.

Silence is sweetest when there is too much noise.

When all is lost and the darkness of the valley enters your life, find gratitude and appreciation. They will lead back to the light. These two expressions are distinctly different. Gratitude comes before appreciation. Initiated by the outside, gratitude brings *You/you* to the heart via the mind. Gratitude reintegrates fragmented pieces of the soul, supporting more of *You/you/YOU* in inhabiting the physical form. Gratitude lifts veils of illusion, heals the sick, and brings disorder toward harmony. It helps you say, *Thank you*, even for the things *you* do not want to be grateful for. It begins as a mental construct. Then it connects the mind to form.

Gratitude is easy to speak, be convinced of, and espouse . . . even if *you* really do not mean it yet. It is a pathway that softens *You/you* toward cultivating the ability to receive. The easiest area to begin expressing gratitude is for material things, people, and experiences that enter your life. Practicing gratitude brings more that *You/you/YOU* can be grateful for. In order to deepen gratitude, release your grievances, secrets, fantasies, and illusions. Release these secret obsessions and begin receiving thyself. In doing so, *You/you* transition from the external act of gratitude to an internal embodiment of appreciation.

Honor all people. Respect each life.
Adore every heart. Cherish the moments.
Forgive the unforgivable. Celebrate the failures.

Appreciation emerges from the inside. It is the full feeling of joy arising from within for a person, place, experience, etc. As a doorway to the Divine, appreciation grounds *You* more deeply into the body while also increasing your energy and vibration. Appreciation is felt within the entire body, culminating as a swell inside the heart space. It is embodied awareness and presence. This is how fulfillment is experienced. Whereas *gratitude* and *thanks* flow outwardly, appreciation is experienced inwardly. Appreciation fills *You*, activating the energy of receptivity that creates more flow within your experience.

Cultivating appreciation for those whom *You* believe harmed *you* releases the energy around the experience. Every experience brings with it the opportunity to grow, expand, and awaken gifts. Each life challenge opens *You/you* to a new aspect of *Self/self/SELF*. Each constriction leads to an expansion. Every downturn leads to aspiration. Anything that was removed from *You* creates an opportunity for insight of what *You/you/YOU* really hold.

A leap in consciousness occurs when *You* look at your life experiences and have appreciation for everything that occurred. Mastery is the ability to regard each person on your journey—and the experiences they engaged—as divine collaboration for your greatest experience and expression of *Self/SELF*. Appreciation increases worth, vibration, and joyful presence. The ultimate appreciation rests in the complete embrace of who *You/you/YOU* are, appreciating each aspect as a part of your wholeness. Blessed *Being/being/BEING* . . . Breathe deeply as *You/you/YOU* cultivate appreciation.

May there be comfort for those feeling cold . . .
and nourishment for those who hunger . . .
May a light . . . a beacon . . . a bridge . . .
rise for those wading across dark swamps.
May we outstretch and connect
as cosmonauts on a ride into space . . .
floating within the emptiness . . .
become pioneers of peace
within the discomfort . . .
and the soothing voices of spirit
who drown out the noise . . .
Appreciate all of it.
Sweetly dream . . .
so to create the sweetest of dreams.

. . .

RECEIVE THYSELF

What is the asking?

Come into your life . . .
your moments of quiet . . . times of tension . . .
and the spaces between.
Come into your heart . . .
the soft spots . . . the fractures of heartbreak . . .
and the vulnerable, guarded edges.
Come into your longing . . .
the dreams . . . the aspirations . . . the wishes . . .
and the dawnings.
I have been there all along . . .
waiting for your mind to surrender . . . your hands to open . . . and you to rest . . .
I have been waiting for *You/you/YOU*
to come to every place I Am.
The invitation is yours . . .
will you RSVP—Receive Spirit's Venerable Presence?

AFFIRMATION—CONTEMPLATION—INSPIRATION

I am capable of awakening to where I hold
fear, lies, and illusion.
I now transcend all places of *Self/self/SELF*-division.

Contemplate and journal these inquiries until inspired to take action.

Be still; see what rises as *courage* versus *conformity*.
You/you/YOU possess the answer for achieving aliveness . . . go within.

The degree to which you are *Being/being/BEING*
is the extent to which *You/you/YOU*
shall cultivate inner and outer *Appreciation*.

What is "your" self-obsessed story around duality, good, and evil?

duality.
What is your relationship with . . .
- duality?
- light?

- darkness?
- good?
- bad?
- right?
- wrong?

Who are *You/you/YOU* amid darkness?

Who are *You/you/YOU* amid light?

secret reflections.

What secrets do *You/you/YOU* keep?

What lies do *You/you/YOU* tell . . .
- yourself?
- others?

Where, and to whom, do *You/you/YOU* withhold?

How can *You/you/YOU* address internal climate changes to eliminate the effects of triggers?

How can *You/you/YOU* adjust your inner thermostat in relation to your outer climate?

How can *You/you/YOU* *Self/self/SELF*-regulate?

lust.

What role does lust play in your life?

What do *you* lust after?

Where and how do *You/you* project lust onto others?

Who are *You/you/YOU* jealous of?

What are *You/you/YOU* envious of?

tenderness.

Does *tenderness* appear in your life? How?

How can *You/you/YOU* more deeply embody and integrate tenderness . . .
- as an internal experience?
- in relation to *Self/self/SELF*?
- in relation to others?
- in relation to the world?

egoist to humanitarian.

How do *You/you/YOU* express from the . . .
- quiet ego/identity?
- loud ego/identity?
- personal will?
- deceptive intelligence?

Do *You/you/YOU* allow the full experience of your humanity?

What aspects of humanity (your emotions) do *You/you/YOU* suppress?

How do *You/you/YOU* serve outer humanity (others' emotions)?

appreciation.

How can *You/you/YOU* cultivate greater appreciation for your . . .
- body?
- life?
- shadow?
- *Self/self/SELF*?
- relationships?

receive thyself.

Do *You/you/YOU* focus on inner child / lower *self*?

What does the inner child / lower *self* focus on?

How does your lower *self* perceive . . .
- *You/you/YOU*?
- each moment?
- every experience?
- creating capacity?

Do *You/you/YOU* focus on ego/identity *Self*?

What does the ego/identity *Self* focus on?

How does your ego/identity *Self* perceive . . .
- *You/you/YOU*?
- each moment?
- every experience?
- creative capacity?

Do *You/you/YOU* focus on your higher *SELF*?
What does the higher *SELF* focus on?

How does higher *SELF* perceive . . .
- *You/you/YOU*?
- each moment?
- every experience?
- creative capacity?

May hope be replaced with trust . . .
May insecurities transform into confidence . . .
Let attachments dissolve,
as the deep intimacy of detachment surrounds . . .
May authenticity prevail in the face of all that has been fabricated . . .
Let innocence break your hardened heart . . .
Let love rule the mind,
and commitment guide your hand . . .
Let devotion steer your movement,
and gentleness take a stand . . .
May your palms be open . . .
May they be empty . . .
for the world to fall into.
Sweetly dream . . .
so to create the sweetest of dreams.

. . .

PETITION FOR UNITY

What is the shift in consciousness?

It takes two hands to clap . . .
two eyes to see . . .
two feet to walk . . .
and two opposing forces to create the experience of unity.

IN COLLECTIVE PRAYER
FOR RECEIVING . . .
EMPOWERED LASTING CHANGE
WITHIN THE GLOBAL CLIMATE

Dear Infinite Oneness . . .
Awaken our trueness . . .
disengage illusion . . .
the perception of pain . . . chaos and confusion.

the illusion of duality. 83

This is not a world of your Divine making . . .
it is minds gone mad;
some who are giving, but more who are taking.
with all that is good, we seemingly create bad.
Bring us home . . .
Remind us of our true nature . . .
Mend the separation inside . . .
Release these wounds . . . Heal our divide.
Imprint our thoughts with holiness . . .
Anchor silence within seeing . . .
Place purity in the dark nights . . . Shine innocence through being . . .
Alight thoughts of transparency . . .
into the makings of Love eternally.
Inspire our precious souls . . . these earthen bodies . . . our sacred humanity . . .
We no longer need pain as a teacher . . .
Awaken us to freedom and folly.
May we surrender to the greater will of Divinity . . .
and bow to divine destiny.
Fill our minds with miracles.
Move the mountains from our way.
Create a garden of eden.
Make us aware of your eternal embrace . . .
Strum our heart strings with harmony . . .
Meet us in castles and cathedrals . . .
cemeteries and ceremony . . . mourning and night . . .
Dissolve within us our fight, flight, and plight . . .
May we find you within all of duality . . .
Let us meet you here and there . . .
Guide us . . . so that truth and everlasting clarity
resides everywhere.

Temper our tones . . . Gentle our ways . . . Soften our smiles . . . Tender our touch . . .
Sweeten our sounds . . . Purify our words . . . Let us be natural . . . Open us up . . .
Dissolve our distortions . . . Enter our embrace . . . Bring us your bliss . . .
Sweeten our dreams . . .
So be it . . .
And so it IS!

0
0 0
0 0 0
1 1 1 1
1 1 1
1 1
1
1
1 1
1 1 1
1 1 1 1
0 0 0
0 0
0

the illusion of money.

What is the awareness?

**If you knew what *You* would find,
you might not seek to know anything.
If *You* truly understood what was being revealed,
You/you/YOU might be blinded . . .
destined, fated, and enlightened
by the obsession you are seeing,
while also shocked at how you are *being*!**

The Illusion of Money	The Awareness	Being/being/BEING
Material Obsessions	What is the addiction?	Ego/Mind
Our Global Reflection of Fashion	Where is the mirror?	The Collective
The Hole of Greed	What is the dis-ease?	The Shadow
The Key of Trust	How is personal power activated?	Essence
Businessman to Philanthropist	How is purpose fulfilled?	Humanity
Cultivating Connection	How can peace arise?	The Bridge
Heal Thyself	What is the asking?	The Embodiment

A low-grade fever keeps *you* sweating, tossing, and turning. *You* worry over paying the bills. Wondering if what is needed will appear, *You* feel tight and constricted. The heart paces. The constant anxiety of not having enough—even if there is plenty—plagues *You/you/YOU*. Wanting many things, but truthfully needing nothing. The impulse to buy the next phone . . . car . . . clothing trend . . . or great vacation pulls at *You/you/YOU*. There is an unconscious impulse toward wanting more . . . more . . . more . . . Through every action and conversation, a subtle undercurrent regarding how *You* can get, have, take, or earn—exists. There is an unconscious pull to market, buy, sell, and consume.

People no longer appear as people; they have become pathways to your needs, wants, and desires. They are the currency . . . dollar sign . . . exchange . . . expenditure . . . and disposable income. When money is involved, connection has a conditional and codependent agenda. Networking sits at the forefront of mind, as a civilized form of hunting and gathering. New methods, manipulations, and strategies keep you busy running, driving, forcing, and *killing it*. The animal inside is hungry. It pants, drools, and smells meat. Trading time for money, and people for productivity, traps *you* like a caged animal. Your feral *being* claws at the world out of protection and survival. It is hungry, needy, and wanting, scrounging and scrapping while stealthily taking what it can.

What is the fear of—and need for—money?
Why has money become a *god* in your life?
Can *You* let go, and trust?

The parasitic part of a human *being* continuously gorges, increasing the size of its appetite as time passes. People become prey. Marketing becomes manipulation. Ultimately, products, services, and ideas do not really matter; the bottom line does. Marketing and business make accumulation aesthetic, but this only feeds the hunt. The idea of being king of the jungle rests within the heated breath of wanton desire. Money is the meaty measurement of rulership. Ironically, there will never be enough to feel satiated and satisfied. This drug is captivating. What began as an inspiration, dream, or desire to create and serve will fall victim to herd mentality and quickly turn into the push to produce. In moving too slowly, *You* will be trampled on or left behind.

There is as fine a line between giving and receiving as there is with giving and taking. Ultimately, receiving is the consciousness of the prince, whereas taking is the consciousness of the pauper. Ironically, many with means embody the energy and consciousness of the pauper. It is because they live in spiritual deficit. Likewise, there are those who have little monetarily but become vessels for continual receiving. These individuals are spiritually wealthy.

Money is an illusion that feeds the addiction of material obsessions.
Fashion reveals the global reflection of the collective's
viral shadow of greed.
In turning the key of trust,
you are initiated from businessman to philanthropist.
Healing thyself cultivates connection as a bridge for embodied humanity.

There is nothing wrong with money; it is not evil or vile. It is simply energy. As with everything, money requires a balanced approach. However, currency has moved beyond its purpose of equal give and take. We have made money a measure of establishing hierarchy, class, and status. As individuals are ranked within categories—from the haves to the have-nots—money builds walls and barriers of separation. It brings people in, but it also keeps people out. Issues arise when money becomes more important than people.

Unfortunately, money has become the *almighty*. Those honest with themselves might discover a deep fear of being poor or homeless. This underlying influence creates actions, drives, and impulses that fuel the worry for money. The undercurrent of *not having enough* courses through bloodlines as generational issues around worth and value seep into the unconscious. This triggers the animal instinct for survival.

Is money your master?
Are you the master of your money?

Rather than attaining value and wealth from rich internal resources, our world illustrates that significance and value come through the size of a diamond on a hand, the type of car that one drives, or the neighborhood someone lives in. Money has been purported as a measure of success, when it is often the source of misery, conflict, and inner bankruptcy. Too much of anything brings imbalance. The quest for external worth often results in an experience of spiritual poverty. Money actually has no specific value; what we give meaning to does. Unfortunately, we have given too much meaning to the material world. Should *You* not be able to sustain happiness, satisfaction, or purpose without having money, then your inner vault is devoid of resources. Money is simply where *you* project this lack. Money represents the game *you/i/we/they* play with one another, and ourselves. It is the lie that distracts us from true connection.

Money is the drug through which *you* get high.
It makes you fatter but not fuller.

A time will come when money is obsolete. Either this structure will break down out of excessive indebtedness, or there will be so much being printed that it loses all value. People will realize the farce of minting money at will, a trillion-dollar debt that can never be repaid, and how money is corruptly used for control and dominance. *You* will see the futility of exorbitantly priced goods, and the levels of waste being dumped daily. The disparity between incomes and occupations will cease. In time, money will simply be paper. Rather than burning a hole in your pocket, it will literally be burned for warmth. People will cease *being* machines of productivity and become cocreative philanthropists of energy. As *you/i/we/they* release the fear of not having enough, money will be neutralized in its power.

The shift toward simplicity will produce a surge in creativity. As people attain higher levels of naturalness, nonconformity, and consciousness, greater trust will unfold. This manner of *Being/BEING* will more readily attract required needs and opportunities. Collaborations will increase. Attention will be aimed toward conservation. Communal living and minimalism will bring like-hearted individuals and groups together. The side effect will be the slowing of time. There will be fewer actions of unconscious busyness and a decrease in the contrast between one another.

If money is the only focus, connection will be worked out of your life and leave *You* barren, lifeless, and dull. External wealth is meaningless. It keeps you hungry, if you're not building inner riches. The metaphysical equivalent to money is relationship. Until able to realize this link, money will be a false and elusive substitute for connection. Explore what provides a rich life of experience and expression as opposed to superficial satisfaction, excess, and image. Let the riches of inner and outer connection guide *You/you/YOU*, your actions, and relationships. Develop a trusting partnership with life and experience the delight of *Being/BEING* provided for. Blessed *Being/being/BEING* ... Breathe deeply as *You/you/YOU* relate to your deep inner expanse of resources.

**May you amplify heart resonance
through harmony with the heart-mind . . .
experiencing life's miracles amid all mankind.
May those that choose to stay asleep,
or ones who believe they are awakened,
realize they have been both / and . . .
as truth and communion carry them forth . . .
As we learn to lend helping hands.
Allow the everlasting energies of Love and Oneness
to bathe your consciousness.
There is only one of us.
May all beings find unity and freedom
from within their illusions . . .
and recognize the makings of their delusion.
Sweetly dream . . .
so to create the sweetest of dreams.**

0
0 0
0
1
1 1
1 1 1 1
1 1 1
1
0
0 0
0

MATERIAL OBSESSIONS

What is the addiction?

I Am to know *You* . . . not turn from you.
I Am to embrace *You*, not push you away.
I Am to see *You*, not be blind to your need.
I Am to hear *You*, not suppress your voice.
Do not shrink back . . .
Do not place *things* between us.
Embrace the gateways of the unknown
For they are the blessings . . .
originating in illusion
that become the openings for grace . . .

With ever-growing technologies, internet conveniences, and never-ending creations of material creature comfort, the ideology of success has been gravely misconstrued. The *do* society lends credence to what can be accomplished or attained, rather than *who* a person is by mere virtue of their presence. Value is based on creating greater productivity in the shortest amount of time, for the highest monetary result. Time equals money but produces machines out of human beings. High quality becomes forsaken for quantity. People are replaced by the ease of automation. Waste is blindly disregarded for what is new. Necessities take a back seat to extravagances. For many individuals around the world, particularly in developed nations, success equals achievement, money, the ability to acquire things, and notoriety.

What hole are you trying to fill?
Is it ever enough?
Can material things ever fill the real longing resting within?

Marketing is designed to sell people the *dreams* they hunger for. Ideas of perfection become a measure of worth . . . requiring more material escapes . . . adventurous experiences . . . and fashion excellence. The *need to fit in* triggers impulse purchases, trends, and followers. Fear and conditioning teach people to be cosmetically enhanced . . . and branded or marketed as an image. Everyone is selling their story, delivering an elevator pitch, and running after the next social media app sensation. We have turned into a world that values people on the basis of material measurements.

Lifestyle, luxury, and social circles create cliques. Significance becomes the drug of choice as voices clamor to be heard and recognized. The debt of drive depletes endless hours of valuable time. Everyone is running; just running. As the ego strengthens, the addiction to *working hard* and *playing hard* somehow justifies *being* a hamster on a wheel. The endless pursuit of success is a silent and subtle cry for what is missing—the approval of and connection to others ... the relationship with *Source/SELF* ... and the experience of natural *BEING*. Should image be manipulative or grounded in greed, a trap will have been unknowingly set. This subtle form of *Self/self*-betrayal creates a veil of shame, while also chasing an image one has to keep up with. This will also create mirror experiences of betrayal from others.

True success is the ability to be present,
this moment, every moment,
giving the highest quality of *Self/SELF*
to the relationships and experiences *You/you/YOU* encounter.

Material obsession—whether physical in nature or as social following—results in climbing ladders. Running after those who can build *You/you* and your business up—while ignoring those who *You* perceive as small, insignificant, and not worthy of your time—mirrors the internal friction between the acknowledged and disavowed selves. This is illustrative of listening to mind versus heart, ranking sales over true service. The balanced perspective is hijacked by images of perfection, wealth, status, and significance. Conditioning drives your ego into buying and selling illusory dreams. The range of manipulations and sales-marketing tactics in our world includes ...

- *Romance* portrayed as a fantasy, erotica, drama, and fairy tales.
- *Living the dream* portrayed as the perfect, happy family with 2.5 kids, a dog, and a white picket fence, who travel and live a life of complete ease while experiencing carefree living through perfect home-cooked meals, memories, and lives devoid of conflict.
- *Success* portrayed as the perfect body, car, home, or lifestyle.
- *Connection and intimacy* portrayed through sex, alcohol, and the nightlife.
- *Happiness* as the result of shopping, food, vacations, cars, sexual fantasy, or alcoholic consumption.
- *Wealth* portrayed as hierarchy, fancy cars, big homes, bling, fashion, and brand.
- *Fulfillment* portrayed as fame, achievement, excess, or celebrity.
- *Salvation* achievable through charity, hero's journey, suffering, and religion.
- *Safety* projected onto weaponry, alarm systems, and identity theft defense.
- *Health and well-being* achieved through medications, despite advertised side effects that could result in other disease or even death.

Constantly bombarded by messages that everything *You/you/YOU* need is outside *You*, an inner conflict pervades. Television, magazines, and social media have become purveyors of dualistic thinking. Instead of being platforms of information, they have become another means for manipulating sales from behind a mask of connection. The underlying energy is *self*-serving, with an end goal of acquiring more money, followers, clients, and sales. Lies and illusions feed material obsessions of the ego and shadow animal.

- The portrayal of seven-figure incomes being marketed by a person in debt ...
- The illustration of a perfect and balanced lifestyle by an individual that is run ragged ...

- The concept of lifestyle and community from someone who is isolated and struggling...
- The ease of fitness through a pill, while the model actually spent hours working out...
- The depiction of peace and calm, while chaos and busyness reign

Each lie creates more shades of gray, amid a world dancing between light and darkness. These manipulations empower the separation of *Self/self*. Consumers shell out endless amounts of cash to look thinner, become younger, become more valuable, and appear smarter . . . while feeling invisible, barren, and disconnected. Distractions born of these pursuits ask the heavy price of soul *Truth/TRUTH*. Shadow consciousness seeks to fill needs through material possessions and escape: more toys, bigger things, exotic adventures, and the latest gadgets. Lives of excess are an attempt to fill the deep sense of boredom that has doused the spirit. Material goods can never fill inner emptiness. Those serve only to temporarily veneer the black hole. At some point, the realization that *nothing outside will fill the void* comes into awareness. Connection is no longer about the individual, but whether or not they can do something for *You/you*.

What appears rich externally may be empty internally.
What appears as gold may be only a veneer.
What appears huge may feel small within.

As *You* continue your earthen schooling, the soul will gently guide *you* toward higher consciousness through physical and material experiences. Instead of feeding the insecurities of the small *self*, the life that no longer serves will begin to break down. That leveling creates a blank slate where *You* can build a more enriching life. Awakening to your dharma deepens purpose and fulfillment in a way that the material world never can. Dharma cannot be figured out, sought, or manipulated by the ego. It is an experience that expresses when *You/you* are not there. Dharma finds *You/you/YOU*; it is not chosen by your identity or ego. What *You/you* have deemed your soul purpose—that which *You* place all of your time, energy, and effort into—is likely another material possession. If *You* are in any of it—with any part consisting of the *I*, *me*, *my purpose*, *my vision*, *my mission*—the ego has turned *You/you* into its material possession. *You* are possessed by your deceptive intelligence. The ego has tricked *You/you*, yet again.

Focus on real success; not greed . . . gluttony . . . or vanity.
Success is not an outcome of something *You/you* work toward.
It is not material.

Your power does not rest in what *You/you/YOU* can do or achieve. It is not reflected in how much can be accomplished, or the status *You* attain. The power *You/you/YOU* possess is not in intellect or muscle. It rests in your ability to express your *Self/SELF* authentically with intimacy, vulnerability, and clarity. That level of soul relaxation leads to the fulfillment of natural rhythm, flow, ease, and play. Go to the time when *You/you* lived simply. Release the weight of your material burdens. Begin to look at what *you* hold on to that is not necessary. These trappings are just that . . . traps.

Essence weaves through all pieces of creation with a single intent . . . to know itself and its connectivity. Become the fullness and richness you seek, by realizing the material good within. That will open doors in ways that dharma and destiny require. *You/you/YOU* do not need to leave your world; simply be the change within it. Your life experience is showing *you* exactly where to step. When there is flow . . . create, move, and do. When there are obstacles . . . stop, sit, and be. *You/you/YOU* are the material good that *you* keep seeking externally. Blessed *Being/being/BEING* . . . Breathe deeply as *You/you/YOU* build your connection with *Self/self/SELF*.

May *you* recognize who is behind the eyes . . .
seeing Light as it has shined for eons.
May *you* know eternity's radiance . . .
which fills the space before *You/you/YOU* enter.
May *you* know silence . . .
as the interconnectivity of *you/i/we/they* in undulating oneness.
May you know the *Love/LOVE*
that eternally wraps around *You/you/YOU* . . .
in your slumber . . . in your waking . . .
dawn . . . day . . . dusk . . . and night.
May *you* remember . . .
the sacred rests within every part of *You/you/YOU* . . .
May *you* realize . . .
I am *you* . . . *you* are me . . . and *we* are *I Am*.
Sweetly Dream . . .
so to create the sweetest of dreams.

OUR GLOBAL REFLECTION OF FASHION
What is the mirror?

Presence is within *you*; let it be all around *You*.
There is an *i* behind the two eyes . . . and a singular *Eye* behind the *I*.
That which witnesses also watches and holds vigil for all,
as the sacred and silent keeper of each rise and fall.
Identity is the play of *being* . . . somebody.
They are likened to coats that are worn.
With each, *You/you* speak, act, think, and behave differently.
With each, *You/you* express, interact, and communicate a certain way.
There will be a closet full from which to choose.
But to know yourself . . .
requires that *You/you* undress fully
and bare the naked *TRUTH* of who *YOU* are.

Looking good does not always mean that an individual feels good. An epidemic of exhaustion currently exists. Weariness hangs in the air—making bodies appear frenzied, round shouldered, slumped over, and dark eyed. Tiredness is expressed through well-rehearsed smiles, contagious yawns, and shortened breaths. Even the weight of wanting to care—when there are no reserves from which to care—is evident in the lack of presence to *self*-care. Even the desire to serve has become mangled and manipulated, by way of commerce and *save-the-world* complexes.

We are encountering big signs: poverty, pollution, waste, abuse, etc. . . . These outer manifestations do not gain our attention. We are becoming a bankrupt species: spiritually, ethically, morally, and relationally. Unattended social issues manifest as individual heart palpitations, digestive problems, ulcers, fevers, boils, infections, and more. The body cries out with a loud, unequivocal *Slow down! STOP! Be present!*

Where *You/you* are was created from the consciousness of yesterdays.
The consciousness *You/you* hold today creates your tomorrows.

Just as illness begins with a bacterial infection that spreads, the contagion of world issues does the same. Societal and global issues are symptoms arising out of deeper foundational issues. These stem from a lack of love and *Self/self/SELF*-care. They are illustrative of disconnection and presence having gone rogue. There is more concern with following the trends than listening to your cycles and rhythms. *You/i/we/they* are the bacteria. Each one of us is a virus. Although wearing masks of all kinds—literally and figuratively—*you/i/we/they* remain isolated, distant, and separate. There is a tendency to compete with or attack one another, rather than working together. However, as with any virus, a solution can be found within the bacteria.

The world of fashion is built on trends. However, the trends today—whether apparel, television, movies, books, electronics, social media, or travel—feed identities, fears, greed, and lust. Trends in media, television, and movies illustrate our reflections of narcissism, control, corruption, and war. Even the clothing industry is preoccupied with perceptions of itself. However, this perception is a made-up version of who you want to be, on the basis of images others show you; images that may not even be real. Fashion is akin to the nature or culture of a group, society, or time and will change. It is the rhythm of the external world and creates a wave in the collective. This may or may not be opposite your internal nature. Fashion can be seen as a temporary belief system, conditioning, and homogenization. It is subtle control and herding of minds, expressions, and people. Distinguishing among fashion, fad, culture, and individual nature is important. It is necessary to find the balance that does not compromise your unique expression, energy, cycles, or rhythms.

Fads will come and go.
Fashion is an impulse that rises and falls away.
Nature is inherent and everlasting.

At one time, *brands* held power, controlling image and the direction of the masses. As a form of hierarchy, they created the paths that people followed. Now, influencers control waves of consumerism. Certain voices rise above the fray as fashion icons for clothing, nutrition, self-help, spirituality, business, beauty, and more. These influencers portray the images and lifestyles that others desire, thus setting trends and fashion in new ways. The fluctuation in markets mirrors the fluctuation of awareness, connection, and bonding. In truth, influence is not really about the person, but more so the image they portray. In this arena, image is everything, regardless of if it is true or false. Oftentimes, what is behind the scenes is different from what is seen.

Amid current trends of following people, further mediocrity is created. Rather than uniqueness and creativity leading the way, it is often the catalyst for carbon copies being created. Current fashion urges individuals to become influencers, experts, or celebrities without realizing that the same tactics, strategies, and methods are being used by everyone. This actually depicts sameness. It also illustrates the increasing need for people to be seen, heard, and acknowledged. A mass of voices are clamoring to be heard. It appears as if everyone is listening, but in truth . . . no one is. As individuals assert more and more of who they want others to think they are, who they really are becomes lost in the mix.

Image is a mask; a glass house that can fracture and break at any time.
Authenticity and unique expression can neither be copied nor stolen.

Being a person of influence has become the height of fashion. The quest for recognition, fans, followers, and customers has *You* chasing every new trend, and trumpeting them as your own. *You/you/YOU* sell your soul for *a like, the need to be needed,* and *the high of recognition.* Unaware of how many masks are piling upon one another, the endless selfies are simply portrayals of mass hypnosis. Keeping up with the image *being* presented is exhausting over time. The body soon grows weary and the mind still clamors for meaning.

As time passes and aging accelerates, a subtle sense of melancholy and depression intensifies. When the fashion trend or fad declines, loss of purpose and confusion will set in. The farther from center *You* travel, the more distant *Truth/TRUTH* feels. Like a dog chasing its own tail, *You* run to be like everyone else, without ever truly grasping who *You* are. The ladders that have been climbed actually lead nowhere. They only feed your ego.

It is time to move beyond herd mentality. You are meant to be the shepherd or the sheep. This will occur when you're willing to hear your true nature. It expands as *You* nurture your soul's voice. This is a feeling inside you, not a strategy or destination outside. Your soul's voice will organically create externally. It has been preparing your steps all along. Your unique beauty will express fully when *You/you/YOU* show up authentic, real, truthful, and intimate. Until then, it is masks and mirrors, which can have only a superficial 3-D influence or impact. Your greatest gift to the world at this time will come in going against the trends. Be willing to be the fringe. Fashion—in whatever form it appears—is a subtle form of social conditioning, homogenization, and brainwashing. Convinced *You* are different, *You* actually are more of the same because everyone else follows the same trends. Blessed *Being/being/BEING* . . . Breathe deeply as *You/you/YOU* discover your unique expression.

May *You* realize this world is ego . . .
and remember *You/you* are here for the soul.
May *you* understand that attainment feeds ambition . . .
and breath releases that control . . .
May *you* discover that accolades poke your animal nature . . .
when nothing is required to be worthy of Love.
Business is made for the mind . . .
busy-ness for the mindless.
Bliss-ness rests in the mindful.
Have illusion in any way *you* desire . . .
but be present to the reality
You inspire . . .
Sweetly dream . . .
so to create the sweetest of dreams.

. . .

THE HOLE OF GREED

What is the disease?

The physical experience is the bridge
between your animal and Divine natures.
When greed rises . . .
and cravings swallow you whole . . .
***you* have merely forgotten that**
your value . . . your worth . . . your inheritance
is more than gold.
***You* cannot carry anything with *you* . . .**
so embrace what feels true.
It is the only way to receive what is meant for you.

Greed is within the one who is *self*-centered, as opposed to those centered in *Self/self/SELF*. Deep down, *you* want . . . and *you* want . . . and *you* want more. This hungry feeling does not leave. There is no peace in what has been given; there is still desire for more. You pray, asking for this, that, and the other to be fulfilled. Then, after receiving your want, its focus is quickly discarded. *You/you/YOU* ask for something else. Although *you* may be grateful for what was received, your eyes are hungry; your hands are open and empty. *You* want to be happier, richer, skinnier, and more loved. *You* want more adventure, purpose, and applause. There is a wanton desire for things, and more things, and then there is a desire for something else. Even in your consciousness of lack or limitation, *You* claim how much more your lack and limitation are in comparison to others. In health, dis-ease, and story, *You* speak of how much more you need, lacked, hurt, and were broken down.

Individuals choose livelihood on the basis of monetary compensation instead of soul direction. But it is not just about salaries. This is a conversation about the insanity and hypocrisy of $50,000 toilets, $8,000 screws, $50,000 sweet-sixteen parties, $100,000 weddings, etc. . . . It has to do with enormous homes and cars that cost more than the majority's lifetime savings. It is the discrepancy between pay, perks, and lifestyles. Consumption, waste, and greed have been woven into our social fabric, as individuals climb and clamor for influence. Moral values become compromised in our capitalistic society. A legion of money-grabbers exist in every industry. Enough is never enough. Simplicity is outdated in the materialistic world. Happiness is based on the latest, greatest, most popular, exclusive, and branded option, until the next one comes along.

Life placed *You* where it requires your service.
Just be *You* . . . live your life . . . field your circumstances . . . and experience fully on all levels.
Any other move glorifies the mind's whims and wants,
distracting you from the subtle service of balancing the world's energies.

Greed is all about attachment. It is an excessive love for money or possession. The greedy individual cares too much and is too attached in an excessive way. Greed affects the emotional life, creating anxiety and restlessness. When believing that accumulation will create the ease and satisfaction desired, a vicious cycle of addiction ensues. All greed is an attempt to avoid feelings, particularly the sense of emptiness inside. Somehow consumption serves as a point of distraction, at least for a while.

Greed can also infiltrate self-help and spirituality. Hoarding books and religious tokens can be overconsumption. Taking every workshop and needing to have a list of qualifications and certifications is excess. The necessity to keep seeking and collecting is a dis-ease. It can also appear in healthcare and wellness. Endless medications, protocols, surgeries, and techniques are more about gathering experiences than actually focusing on healing.

Becoming present to your interiority requires feeling the emptiness that lingers. It is necessary to succumb to the feelings of aloneness, abandonment, and lack of intimacy that are present. In delving into this space without filling it, *You* discover your true tastes, likes, and inspirations. Although spiritual tools, techniques, protocols, and teachings support this inner exploration, be cognizant about using methodology as distraction. It is not your willpower, but your why power that makes all the difference.

The mind needs, wants, craves, competes, and is never full.
The mind attempts to repair broken pieces of the past;
it is rarely satisfied.

The outside world will keep *you* chasing the next big thing. But no amount of material substance will fill your inner void. You are programmed to believe that more is better. This perpetuates a belief that the one who has more is somehow more valuable. It is the belief that the one who is materially successful is favored by on high. It is an idea that the one who is humble is not as impactful or significant. Competition and accumulation are components of greed consciousness. An insatiable drive or appetite to conquer is not about capacity; it is related to dominance and greed. It stems from a need to measure up, have worth, and overcome deep feelings of insignificance and worth. Greed can appear as pulling things continually toward *Self/self/SELF*. It can equally be about pushing away those things that *You* do not want to identify with. The dilemmas of life come about when becoming ensnared in the pursuit of the transient: beauty, youth, money, power, or the illusion of independence.

The deep need for anything opens the door for self-deception and ignorance. What is important becomes neglected. There is an inability to see the cost, or what will be lost. To take more than one needs obstructs the balance of nature and energy. Taking too much will create the counterbalance of being required to give up a lot in some other way. Release from the clutches of greed arises through letting go of the world and stepping into the humble abode of the heart. Create deposits of presence, awareness, love, compassion, and kindness. Deepen your connection to *Self/self/SELF*. Nothing outside *You* compares to the treasure within *You/you/YOU*. When rich internally, it does not matter what life brings to your door, because balance, joy, and peace prevail. *You/you/YOU* are your greatest asset.

The heart has no agendas.
The heart does not seek status or labels, nor does it care if money is earned.
The heart encompasses the path to peace.

Life is not about trying or striving, pushing and working, toiling and making. Your agendas, goals, and illusions for affecting others is how *you* avoid being with *You/you/YOU*. One day, *You* will sit back and laugh at yourself. *You/YOU* will have spent decades of intense effort, when presence, play, and allowing were the only things required. When *You/you* stand in who *You/YOU* are, it does not matter who others are *being*. Every life is with purpose, even the ones that do not look like yours. Blessed *Being/being/BEING*... Breathe deeply as *You/you/YOU* selfishly leave your outer distractions for inner revelations.

May human beings express the highest level of respect by ...
increasing diplomacy and communication with all sisters and brothers ...
and deepen conversations that awaken understanding.
May every person understand what it means to walk in another's shoes ...
see through another's eyes ...
witness the wisdom of another's experiences ...
and lift up each other's dreams.
May we see, hear, and acknowledge each other fully ...
By being in communion,
knowing we sit with a sacred steward father Divine.
Sweetly Dream ...
so to create the sweetest of dreams.

. . .

THE KEY WHOLE OF TRUST
How is personal power activated?

**Do not worry about what people say;
their opinions mean nothing.
The only thing that matters is your opinion of *Self/self/SELF*,
respect for *Self/self/SELF* . . .
and, acceptance of *Self/self/SELF*.
Nobody can destroy your dignity . . . or take your life from *You/you/YOU*.
This is not dependent on anybody else . . . their perspective . . . or their power.
Come out into the open, even if it goes against the whole world.**

There is truth in the body. It knows of things. The body possesses wisdom and creates from that place. This unconscious creator of experience feels your nervousness, constriction, and anxiety. It also feels your expansiveness and boundless possibility. The *Mind/mind* is the gateway and guardian of both. Doubts, insecurities, and challenges create lives layered in control, reaction, and inaction. Due to a history of deception and self-denial, it is not always easy to trust what is outside *You*. This requires practice, trial, error, and the experience of truth.

Lies cause dissension, drama, and struggle. More lies are needed to explain, justify, and defend what you attempt to convince yourself and others of. The deceptive intelligence will travel down many rabbit holes due to the experiences of deception. These keep *You* separate and in fear of real connection. *You/you* do not trust the world. *You/you* do not trust others. Ultimately, the lacking of trust exists because *You/you* do not trust yourself. In each moment, evaluate if *You* think, speak, and act from the deceptive ego or the intelligent heart. The first is restless and fast-talking. The latter is still and listens. Are *You/you* talking or listening?

**You either know you are safe,
or believe you have never been.**

The reason for distrust relates to your interference with life. Subconsciously *You/you/YOU* are aware of how *You* deceive others and yourself. *Your* body feels each betrayal and manipulation. It tightens with how deeply *You* control everything. Life is constricted by the actions *you/i/we/they* take. Even your breath illustrates this control and constriction. Little do *You* realize that *You/you/YOU* have been following the anxiety, fear, and conditioning of your rearing. *You* have been entrained to follow impulse, reactivity, and control mechanisms. These behaviors have become second nature; however, second nature is an artificial expression.

You/i/we/they came as open, relaxed, and trusting infants. However, the world taught us to close off, tighten up, and be on guard. *You/you/YOU* lost the innate knowing of your organic, natural connection to the world, the support available, and your interconnectivity. *You* also distanced yourself from Spirit, and the eternal cosmic assistance that union provides. *You/you/YOU* separated. *You* isolated. *You/i/we/they* were conditioned to be takers when we were born to be receivers.

Learn from your brethren species. They show *You* how to commune with the rhythms and cycles of earth. They illustrate the expression of naturalness, receivership, and trust. All other life is grounded in unconditional trust. Animals, plants, and elementals live in harmony with the ebbs and flows of life. This rests within the essence and ease with which they live, cycle, and die. Plants illustrate a powerful example of this. They grow without need, want, or worry. There is no resistance to wilting, dying, or falling away. They gently unfold in full blossoming and flowering, allowing the space and time required for full radiance, Every movement is in collaboration with all that surrounds it. Plants receive each day, month, season, and year what they need in order to thrive. Cycles of life rise out of the absolute.

All of life hums within this ecstatic rhapsody and relationship. The vibration and resonance of each natural expression plays a critical part in the ecological balance of matter. As such, life simply is. There is no will, agenda, or resistance to ebbing and flowing. Even struggle and death are not pushed against. The rhythm of birth, life, growth, decay, death, and rebirth is as natural as the sun rising and the moon waning. In this way, life experiences permutations and continually encounters new versions of itself. Throughout this endless, unfolding unknown is an underlying trust in creation.

You either believe in a divine plan,
or you do not.
You either trust in a higher power,
or you do not.

There is a distinct difference between how nature pushes upward and human beings push forward or against. The first is surrender; the latter exerts control. Life pushes upward—a seed bursting into a plant, a lily rising through murky waters, a chick cracking through a shell—as essence revealing in right time. There is no attachment, agenda, or need; neither is there an assertion of direction, timing, or expression. Despite the energy and effort nature expresses, life moves with fluidity and ease. The components interdependently cocreate within a dance of infinite expression.

Human beings respond differently to obstacles. *You/you* push against life. More often, the energy of struggle and *fighting what is* creates experience, which results in a longer path of unfolding. While transformation does occur, it is replete with control. Armed with material obsessions, *You/you* push your way forward, issuing rights, desires, demands, goals, intentions, missions, and visions. Through personal will, every step is controlled until what *You* have in *Mind/mind* is achieved. Rather than utilizing the barriers as guidance mechanisms designed to pivot or shift your course, *You/you* bulldoze through them. Either they will break or *You* will break down. All the while, *You/you/YOU* disregard life's callings and messages, no matter how blatantly they appear. This illustrates a lack of trust.

When *you* shove God into the back seat of the car with energy that says,
I've got the wheel. I have this.
Source will not get in your way;
only *You/you/YOU* will.

The irony is that *You* have no idea what *you* are doing. *You* believe *You/you/YOU* are listening, following, serving, and fulfilling your purpose. Actually, *you* are being led by the scent, taste, and vision of greed, hunger, and cravings. Amid your greed, life adjusts. Life takes a back seat to your agenda. Once your aggressive energy subsides, life will recalibrate and work with what exists. Life utilizes everything in its path to end in balance.

Life is not testing *You/you/YOU*; nor are people. Circumstances do not either. *You/you* test yourself as a way to deflect from the anger, fight, rage, and frustration living inside. It is easier to convince yourself that the world is against *You/you/YOU*, rather than dealing with the fact that *you* are not in control. The only thing to overcome or conquer is your ego.

You cannot push against life and not expect a pushback.
You cannot turn away from *what is*
and not be brought face to face with consequences of such *Self/self*-betrayal.

Your speed and agility are talents for the ego, but immaturity for the soul. Follow no thing. Subscribe to no one. These are distractions, merely illusions and delusions. Trust your inner guidance. Be the *eye/i/I* in the center of every storm. Trust in the unfolding of each moment. You will discover that everything is available and provided when required.

Learning to trust the beat of your heart and the pulse of Spirit strengthens this earthen experience. Becoming life—as opposed to doing life—synchronizes *You/you/YOU* with tides and streams that flow with abundant inspiration, innovation, and abundance. With trust, *You* become the perennial plant that flowers, rising rhythmically in the full expression of your essence.

Life uses *You/you/YOU* and your circumstances
—mundane and boring . . . drama-filled or colorful—
to unveil your unique service.
You are here to be *used well* by the universe.
Merely surrender to your life, exactly as it presents itself.

Trust that something larger is always occurring. Life is infinite in its wisdom and uses *You/you/YOU* for a greater good. *You* will not be privy to what that is. Your mind can not comprehend the vastness or simplicity of the grander plan. Do not resist anything that comes your way. Embrace it wholeheartedly so that *You/you/YOU* receive the benefit of such powerful medicine. Deepen your ability to trust, through the art of doing nothing. Watch everything unfold by divine design. Let things come to *You/you/YOU*, instead of running after them.

Who *You/you/YOU* are is beyond what *Mind/mind/MIND* can comprehend.
You create what is familiar, but *You/you/YOU* encompass much beyond that.

Trust arises out of living intimately, vulnerably, and courageously. This does not mean *You/you/YOU* are fearless; it means that *You* have grown in your ability to embody confidence, endurance, and high-mindedness. Trust emerges out of mastery, which elicits change from the core of *Being/BEING*. *You* do not have to do anything to open the heart; it is already an open space. This is all it knows. The *Mind/mind* must be managed. When *Mind/mind* follows the *way of the heart*, freedom and connection build. Through deepening trust of *Self/self/SELF*, personal power, purpose, and peace awaken in increasing increments.

Trust is the embodiment of relaxation. This is the relaxed mind. It is a relaxed body. Trust is *Being/BEING* with everything, seeking nothing, and allowing everything. Your spirit can fully breathe life on your behalf when *You/you/YOU* trust. Blessed *Being/being/BEING* . . . Breathe deeply as *You/you/YOU allow life to take the lead.*

May the whisper of love wrap you tenderly . . .
May the kiss of kindness open your heart . . .
May the gentle touch of tenderness be the fragrance that lingers . . .
May your angelic nature be seen within every smile . . .
divine essence experienced in each movement . . .
and consciousness heighten with each word spoken.
May all doubt of unity dissolve . . .
all duality be seen as oneness . . .
and all fragmentation be reunited into wholeness.
May remembrance Be . . .
celebrations decree . . .
and jubilation reign free
within creation's capacity . . .
Trust in the flow of life . . .
Trust in the spirit of creation . . .
Trust *Self/self/SELF,*
as you embrace life's celebration.
Sweetly Dream . . .
so to create the sweetest of dreams.

...

BUSINESSMAN TO PHILANTHROPIST

How does Purpose unfold?

**Open your mind . . .
Your heart is big enough to handle it.
You hold an endless capacity from which
to love, give, and cherish.
Expand your perspective . . .
Look beyond where the *eye/i/I* can see.
All decisions stem from personality;
see from beyond the masks,
the past, and your drive.
Sink into your beautiful soul topography . . .
and discover a sacred landscape of philanthropy.**

We have become a world that is continually running, in the name of progress. Goals, projections, and desires tease us into busyness . . . and business. Businesses are like a human body, and employees the cells. The wellness of an organization is dependent on the health of those within it. Shadow cultures within corporate and business structures create deficits within human resources, if the only focus is profit. Not only does this produce negativity and exhaustion within the environment, the soul of the company becomes entrenched with the energy of greed and slothfulness. When a culture feels void of connection, humanity, and empathy, individuals within it become numb, worn-down machines.

The heart of an organization is personified by the CEO, board of directors, and upper management. In small-to-medium-sized businesses, the businessman/businesswoman is the heart space. The leadership illustrates whether the environment is grounded in love, fear, or indifference. Unfortunately, in many environments, there is a tendency to value profit and productivity. People and personal connection are not necessarily valued as important areas of focus. The image and success of a company will flat-line if the hearts and souls of those working within it do. The energetic and emotional rhythms within a company culture might resemble a volatile stock market graph, due to increasing demands for productivity.

The need to be good enough creates immense pressure on the business leader. This need to please—stemming from early childhood—solicits more hours, more energy, and more action to create what is necessary. This persona will also demand more . . . sell more . . . and produce more. The underbelly of this beast is fed by material obsession. The desire to influence, lead, and be followed overtakes humanity, if those within the company are disconnected from their own. Oftentimes, the business leader's drive usurps the energy, nature, and talents of company associates. The wound of *not good enough* is overshadowed by the superiority of *being better than*.

Every impulse *You/you/YOU* have is from your conditioning and programming. That is your doing. Being need do nothing.

Whether business, politics, religion, or spirituality... the shadow *eye/i/I* will justify what *you* are doing, who *you* are helping, and why the world needs what *you* are peddling. This plays into your need for position, significance, and worth. In the same manner, *You* barter your *Self/self/SELF* in exchange for what others are selling. Some things are out of necessity, and others from desire. But oftentimes, your business relationships are purely for manipulation; tit for tat. There is no real relationship. The mighty dollar sees the other as a means to an end, for another dollar; and the other views you the same way. This will be subtle, but the taste of it will linger inside.

The smell of the hunt lingers in the air, as animals become clans, and clans grow into packs. Trends and influence turn packs into herds and tribes. The need to feel worthy and significant feeds into the deception. Unknowingly, *You/you* play into the other's unconscious *Self/self*-perception of smallness, and they buy into yours. It is all in the name of *big* business. This can manifest as fat bottom lines, massive followings, successful businesses, and powerful leaders... but beneath it all are wounded *being*s trying to outlive their pasts.

Identities anchor strongly. Who they once were is buried beneath layers of masks and manipulations. The individual must keep running to escape their past. Because they do not desire to embrace all of who they are, they often experience disconnection from partners, children, spouses, friends, or family. Time and space are not something these people have, because they do not give that to themselves. The avid businessman/woman's business becomes their lover, escape, and infidelity. Although there can be much good that comes through business ventures, this is just another scenic route that will eventually hit a dead end... a blowout... a burnout... or a crash.

The harder *You* work outside is a reflection of how much work is still required within. But, the ego will convince you otherwise.

Projecting inner work onto the need to empower, heal, fix, change, save, and satisfy others is how businesses are born. Businesses are created to provide solutions. However, if digging into the psychology of the founder, it is easy to see that the solution relates to a childhood issue that sits in the recesses of *Mind/mind*. The businessman is attempting to solve problems; namely, his own. *He/she* creates a product or service, perhaps out of enthusiasm, but soon after the focus turns to money. Very quickly the free energy of creation shifts toward the costly energetic of need. The right demographic becomes the focus, as opposed to initial creative expression. As hunger increases, business shifts to ways of *luring* people and *capturing* clientele. As the hunt expands into dark shadowy woods, subtle manipulations and marketing methods are designed to bait, catch, and lead.

When *You* understand how animal hunger drives impulses and desires, your conscious creations will hold the energy of fulfillment and celebration as opposed to selling this to get that.

In businesses where individuals experience person-to-person connection, there is greater satisfaction. When a product or service is purchased from a business where connection exists, the overall experience is more deeply fulfilling. This product or service is not only valued, but also the emotional connection creates genuine heartfelt relationship, celebration, and worthwhile exchange. Along the same lines, individuals who promote connection within business interactions are those who are likely to connect inwardly.

Increased activity does not always equal increased productivity. In a world caught up in busyness and business, the most important but least valued action is stillness. A few moments of presence has as much power as a week's worth of activity. Stillness creates space for something new to occur. True wealth does not build through your ability to toil, produce, or build. It is not in how hard you work, networking, or your ability to sell. Your wealth is affected when *You* invest in *Self/self/SELF*—your dreams, your spiritual practice, your genius, your essence. When *You* embody the experience of *feeling* rich internally, and *knowing* the wealth that *You/you/YOU* are, external abundance is attracted into your life. *You/YOU* are the bank! Build interest with your investment in personal and spiritual growth.

The joyride of success does not have to be a rollercoaster of ups and downs. It can be a continuous high. Your desire to ride the wave is how *You* succumb to peer pressure. Success is not the outcome of something *You* are working toward. It is not material. True success encompasses your ability to be in the moment—every moment—giving the highest quality of yourself to the relationships and the experiences encountered. Success is the expansive feeling of fulfillment from the inside out. It is grounded in a sense of *Self/self/SELF*-worth and satisfaction.

Hierarchical structures create shadow gods and goddesses;
they are the makings and manipulations of man and money.
Philanthropy removes the ladder of hierarchy,
so that humanity is rung free to flow in prosperity.

You/you/YOU are not here to serve ego. Do not let ego take over your life. It is here to serve your soul. The ego will always have you do more, need more, want more, push more, work more, etc. . . . The ego follows the constraints of society; the soul's calling does not. The ego conforms to conditioning, policy, and procedure. The soul knows those are trappings of illusion.

The philanthropist's product is *Love/LOVE*. This is not sold; it is given through connection. Philanthropists do not negate business or money. They approach it differently. True philanthropists build on the foundation of connection. They seek to achieve social change that is both scalable and sustainable. *Philanthro-preneurship* goes beyond providing temporary quick fixes or Band-Aid solutions. They seek to eradicate problems. These are people, companies, and organizations who bring a creative approach combining philanthropy and entrepreneurship. They utilize collaborations that effect positive change in the world. Their aim is often to alleviate suffering, and they do so through inspired action. The primary expression of philanthro-preneurs is creative capacity.

These individuals are grounded in emotional intelligence, empathic sensitivity, and compassionate presence. They realize people are their first resource, with an understanding that those connections compound all other resources. Through heart-centered relationships, these individuals create communities. Those communities create *change*. This begins through individuals giving from their high-minded, whole-hearted *SELF*.

To clear the mind of greed
—impulse, drive, need, and agenda—
is to clear the world of ego and animal behavior.
Begin by seeing what drives *you*, instead of being driven.
Move past the program, see the programmer, and the see the true operator.

Tempering the reactivity and projection of *self* is the stand *You/you* make, as your charitable contribution to the world. Adopt this effort as your cause. This sacred activism is the umbrella for all others. Issues will find resolution as each individual finds their resolve. Expressing from your highest *Self/SELF* is philanthropy. Encompass the deep inner work that cultivates the high-minded, open-hearted, empathetic expression of *YOU*. Be compassion in action; devotion in motion. Let doing serve *Being/BEING*. Leave every person, place, thing, and experience better than when *You* encountered it. Imagine and embody that version of *YOU*.

Philanthropy unlocks the free energy of service and expansion. Heart intelligence exacts the still mountain of peaceful presence to exude from your *Being/BEING*. In that vast flow of *Love/LOVE* . . . seeing from the higher perspective magnifies solutions that would not otherwise be seen. What results is a catalyzing movement of people as resources, which builds into a wave of abundant generosity and collective prosperity.

Let the *i* serve the *I* . . . and the *I* serve the *WE* . . . and the *WE* serve the *ALL* . . . and the *ALL* serve *I AM*. Herein is infinity, and the supplication of illusion to reality. In truth, it is all *I AM*. Be led by the courageous heart, not by the fearful mind. This asks of your patience, discipline, and devotion. It calls to your mastery, perseverance, and commitment. This is philanthropy. The heart know things beyond what the *Mind/mind* fathoms. There is no other; all is Divine. All exists as Source expression. Here, all things arise out of pure *Knowing/KNOWING*. Blessed *Being/being/BEING* . . . Breathe deeply as *You/you/YOU* transition from the force of business to the power of philanthropy.

May hope be replaced with trust . . .
May insecurities transform into confidence . . .
Let attachments dissolve as the deep intimacy of detachment surrounds . . .
May authenticity prevail in the face of all that is fabricated . . .
Let innocence break through hardened hearts . . .
Let love rule the mind and commitment guide each soul . . .
Let devotion steer your movements and gentleness resound within each footstep . . .
May hearts be open . . .
May hands be empty . . .
May minds be inviting and accepting . . .
for a world to trustingly fall into.
Sweetly Dream . . .
so to create the sweetest of dreams.

. . .

CULTIVATING CONNECTION

How can peace arise?

**Human nature is like the beauty of Mother Nature.
We need only be natural . . . and organic . . .
Growing with trust . . . and ease.
This is intimacy . . . connection . . . aliveness.
Stop all your hidden ways of disconnection.
Your world keeps asking this of *You/you/YOU*.
Be still.
Feel the impulses. Let them pass.
See what runs *You/you*. Watch your programming.
You/you/YOU were not created to just keep moving . . .
It goes against nature.**

Life's essence and vitality wanes when there is a lack of fulfillment, connection, and compassion. When people are cast aside, the true resources of the world are being wasted. People are not to be farmed . . . bred . . . or herded; nor are they to be disregarded, put in cages, locked up, or eliminated. By slowing time, we return to what is fulfilling. We return to balance. Ways of connecting more deeply with one another arise from expanded expressions of communal empathy and compassion. As *you/i/we/they* balance the energetic spectrum, our collective experience will reflect the same interplay of energy within structures, institutions, and society. Our world holds an unending supply, when not blocked by our individual actions, emotions, and energetics. Humans are powerful conducters of energy.

The ultimate purpose of any incarnation is for the reconnection to *Self/self/SELF*. No other can heal *You/you/YOU*; ultimately it is yours to do. Until this begins, a person remains bound by the programming, patterns, and addictions that were taken on. Healing requires acceptance of where *You/you/YOU* are, and the willingness to do the inner work to shift. It involves connecting deeply to every aspect of *Self/self/SELF*. It is a whole-bodied experience that enlists your life, mind, emotions, energy, body, and soul. It is not always easy, but it is profoundly enriching. *You* must be willing to connect . . . deeply . . . honestly . . . objectively . . . and devotedly. Because the ego creates all manner of distraction and excuses, life has designed all manner of connections—people, places, things, and experiences—to support *Self/self/SELF* realization. Duality, dis-ease, discordance, and separation are life's most powerful tools for supporting the human in remembering.

**Every person is Essence; pure and holy.
See them as innocent, for we all are.**

Relationship is the single most profound experience given to human beings. It occurs in a multitude of ways with the seen and unseen, animate and inanimate. The construct of relationship is the precursor for yoking with spirit. The prerequisite for Divine connection is relationship to *Self/self/SELF*. The greatest container for personal growth exists within relationship. Engaging with another individual provides a mirror from which to see yourself—in both light and shadow aspects. Relationship will also reveal your wounds through any triggers that come about. Your relationships are powerful ways in which *You/you/YOU* heal, grow, and empower yourself. These containers will expand your ability to listen, cooperate, cocreate, and respond, should *You/you/YOU* choose. Connection exercises trust, voice, boundaries, and love.

When ego is not tempered, connection can become distorted, guarded, or distant. The human condition is a play of separation, utilizing many human puppets upon life's stage. The drama of your sanskaras plays out in combination with that of others. This built-up residue of many lifetimes is here to be reconciled and resolved. It is *you/me/us/them*—as God—immersed within the full spectrum, experience, and expression of connection, disconnection, and interconnectedness. What began as *ONE* endlessly separated into entities and identities. The illusion is that *You* are working toward unity and connection with many. In truth, there is only *One/one/ONE* of us here. Ironically, *you/i/we/they* must connect to our belief in disconnection in order to transcend it. When doing so, all separation will dissolve, revealing *ONEness*. The joke is on *you . . . me . . . us . . .* and *them*.

This is the Garden of Eden.
It is not outside You; it exists inside *You/you/YOU*.

Just as a rosebush stems from a single seed, it births branches that supply many buds. Each eventually flowers. The seed is individual. The branches host communities. Stems host multiple buds, extending from branches like families. Every bud is a congregation of petals, unique in its flowering expression. If you stand back, the entire unfolding is a collective experience, a world of its own. Although each bud may have a short life, the rosebush lives on until its story is complete. Everything has a beginning, a middle, and an end.

We are the same; a flowering collective, ripe with the thorns and beauty. Each human being is intricate and textured. There is softness, color, and opening. Wilting, fading, and dying will also happen. Within each birth and death, the original blueprint is present. Even in the harshest conditions, *you/i/we/they* thrive if the divine plan warrants. At some point, *you/i/we/they* return to cosmic dust. This is a universal story of cosmic architecture. *I Am . . . You Are . . . We Are . . .* the flower of life . . . in endless fractals . . . through frequency and form.

The extraordinary is hidden in the ordinary. Every creation—from a grain of sand to the complex human being—is embedded with the simplicity of Essence, and the intricacy of many universes. The experience *You* came from is connection. Your elements, emotions, thoughts, and senses offer a multidimensional experience in which to experience the same. Your journey from *Me* to *We* parallels your path of *fear* to *Love*. The original sin of fear is separation. The miracle is Love as connection.

Dance with me in the shadows.
Meet me in the Light.
Be kissed by my tender moments.
Behold my precious plight.
This is Me.
My name is Nobody.
And . . .
in that I am Everybody.

To cultivate a relationship with the Divine, deepen your connection with *Self/self/SELF* by integrating what *You/you/YOU* feel, think, and emote. *You/i/we/they* are designed to connect, care, and cooperate. We are hardwired for compassion toward others. The space between us is Love. Ultimately, that is the connection being sought. The soul longs to experience its fullness in resonance with the rest of itself, which is the whole. Hold every moment and every thing with reverence because it is all in divine relationship. It is all connected. Blessed *Being/being/BEING* . . . Breathe deeply as *You/you/YOU* realize the connection between earth and heaven.

May each heartbreak make *You*
Love larger . . .
every challenge make *you*
stand stronger . . .
each obstacle build a bridge
of greater compassion . . .
Through it all, may you celebrate
the whispers,
the wonders,
and the wounding
for all their hidden treasure.
Sweetly dream . . .
so to create the sweetest of dreams.

. . .

HEAL THYSELF

What is the asking?

We are the same.
You have your version of where *I* have been.
There is no shame to be held by either of us.
No judgment either.
Let us celebrate our humanity . . .
Beautiful.
Brilliant.
Bold.
Crazy.
Fucked up.
Dysfunctional.
Chaotic.
Divine.
Embrace all of it . . .
in *You/you/YOU*.

AFFIRMATION—CONTEMPLATION—INSPIRATION

I AM capable of awakening to my distraction and dis-ease.
I now transcend all places of *Self/self/SELF*-absorption.

Contemplate and journal these inquiries until inspired to take action.
Be still; see what rises as *wealth* versus *poverty*.
You have the answer for achieving aliveness . . . go within.

The degree to which you are *Being/being/BEING*
is the degree to which *You/you/YOU*
shall cultivate inner and outer *Connection*.

What is your self-obsessed story of the material world, your needs, and desires?

money.
What is your relationship with . . .
- money?
- value?
- worth?

How is money your master?

How are *You/you/YOU* the Master of your money?

How do *You/you/YOU* value yourself daily?

In what ways do *You/you/YOU* connect to inner wealth?

What can create an empowered relationship with money?

material reflection.
How obsessed are *You/you/YOU* with the material world?
What does material obsession look like in your life?

Do the things *You/you/YOU* acquire bring happiness?
- What do *You/you/YOU* seek more of?
- What do *You/you/YOU* desire to simplify?

What feeling are *You/you/YOU* seeking through the material objects?

What story from childhood do material obsessions represent?

greed.
What role has greed played in your life?

Where has it shown up . . .
- in *You/you/YOU*?
- in word?
- thought?
- deed?

How have *You/you/YOU* been slave to your material cravings?

trust.
Where is *Trust/TRUST* required within your experience?

What would *Trust/TRUST* look like?

How can *You/you/YOU* embody greater *Trust/TRUST* with . . .
- your emotions?
- *Self/self/SELF*?
- others?
- the world?

businessman/woman to philanthropist.
How have *You/you/YOU* been treating your life; as a business, barter, or exchange?

How do *You/you/YOU* treat your relationships; as business, barter, or exchange?

What does it mean to give and receive?

What would exchange look and feel like?

Where are *You/you/YOU* philanthropic?
How can *You/you/YOU* embody greater philanthropy with . . .
- *Self/self/SELF*?
- life?
- relationships?
- world?

connection.
How wealthy is your connection to . . .
- *Self*
- *self*
- *SELF*?
- others?

Are you in debt to *Self, self,* or *SELF*?

Are you invested in *Self, self,* or *SELF*?

heal thyself.
What vision does Higher *SELF* hold?

Where do *You/you/YOU* require healing in . . .
- mind?
- body?
- heart?
- spirit?
- relationship?
- life?

**May all hearts open
a little more each day . . .
all minds expand in broader ways . . .
May all souls remember
their essential nature . . .
and all ego surrender
their burdens and false stature.
May all beings see
the one great family that exists . . .
where all men behold their brothers . . .
and women lift up each sis . . .
Sweetly dream . . .
so to create the sweetest of dreams.**

PETITION FOR RESPECT

What is the shift in consciousness?

Awaken the healer within . . .
Let that one serve *You/you/YOU*.
***You* are not sick, weak, or small;**
***YOU* are the infinite expression of wellness, strength, and power.**
***You/you* simply fell into dis-ease and delusion.**
Stand taller;
***You/you/YOU* are *One/one/ONE* . . .**
***You/you/YOU* are all.**

IN COLLECTIVE PRAYER
FOR HEALING . . .
OUR GLOBAL RELATIONSHIP
TOWARD THE PRESERVATION OF WHAT MATTERS

Dearest Infinite Oneness . . .
Within the fluid memory of our reflections,
inside the elements of our nature,
lay a seed of material obsession.
What has been so incredibly daunting
is our ever-present wanting.
Wild and weary, the seed has grown
into poisonous streams of thoughts that flow.
Out into the world, polluting our connection with other souls.
We have begun seeing with lack instead of what grows.
With no regard to the equality of our sisters and brothers,
or the personal power, purpose, and peace for ourselves or others.
Our mental manipulations have resulted in vice-filled actions.
While forgetting about what is created through the law of attraction.
We have become takers instead of givers, and haters instead of lovers.
We look to what may be gained, not from what can create satisfaction.
Humans push agenda, goals, and bottom lines, rather than connection and inspired action . . .
This has become the sign of our times. No longer can money be our master.
Fabricated resources only cost us, leading to all-out disaster.
We needlessly waste and horde . . . while ignoring the least among us.
In accepting these human flaws, we open more-abundant ways of being, seeing, and trust.
May care and compassion for one another be our cause.

Let no man be hungry,
or any go without shelter,
Let no child be without comfort,
and no animal live unprotected . . .
Let no environment be destroyed,
or any natural resource be wasted or disrespected.
Let our business be philanthropy . . .
our goals in collaboration . . .
Let the only agenda be of cocreation
with the golden key of devotion.
Let the soul nature lead and guide . . .
as shadows dissolve,
and highest selves be the ones we greet
as we discover our resolve.
Let our currency become relationship.
May we be the product of accumulated self-worth.
May we tend to each other's needs
and remove one another's hurt.

Let us see equality as a new economy is birthed.
Let us heal . . . and know when enough is enough . . .
to reveal simplicity in the name of trust.
May we watch philanthropy expand as greed wanes . . .
To live as equals where freedom reigns.
So Be it . . .
And so it IS!

0
0 0
0 0 0
1 1 1 1
1 1 1
1 1
1
1
1 1
1 1 1
1 1 1 1
0 0 0
0 0
0

the illusion of hierarchy.

What is the awareness?

You are all faces,
every body, and every thing,
within all time, amid all space.
You/you/YOU have no face,
You/you/YOU are no body,
You/you/YOU are no thing,
in no time,
beyond space . . .
Do *you* look from top to know the bottom?
Do *you* look from bottom to know the top?
Why don't we just meet in the middle
and see no difference?

The Illusion of Hierarchy	The Awareness	Being/being/BEING
Personal Obsessions	What is the addiction?	Ego/Mind
Our Global Reflection of Human Rights	Where is the mirror?	The Collective
The Hole of Envy	What is the dis-ease?	The Shadow
The Key of Balance	How is personal power activated?	Essence
Politician to Servant Leader	How is purpose fulfilled?	Humanity
Cultivating Conversation	How can peace arise?	The Bridge
Know Thyself	What is the asking?	The Embodiment

Every human being has a desire to be the best . . . the fastest . . . at the forefront . . . number one . . . the winner! Even within the animal kingdom, it is survival of the fittest. This begins innately; it is what we are made of. From the point of conception, a race ensues, with a single sperm making it to the finish; winning the prize of *a lifetime*. Anywhere from 40 million to 150 million sperm swim upstream toward the fallopian tubes on a mission to fertilize *one* egg. Only a few hundred even come close. Once a sperm penetrates, the surface of the egg changes. At that point, no other sperm can enter. That egg becomes *You/you/YOU*!

This is the *human race* . . . the fight and flight to the finish. *You/i/we/they* are born with innate stamina, perseverance, and a predisposition to compete. Within *You/you/YOU* is the spirit to keep going, despite all odds. *You* are a born winner! You already have proof of being a winner built into your DNA. But also, there is an inherent biological understanding to compete. Separation existed before *you/me/us/them*. And yet, this is—and has always been—a unified experience of life unfolding.

Hierarchy is the illusion that feeds the addiction of personal obsessions.
Human rights reveals the global reflection of the collective's
viral shadow of envy.
In turning the key of balance,
you are initiated from politician to servant leader.
Knowing thyself cultivates conversation as a bridge for embodied humanity.

We are at a turning point that not only creates social currents of change but also challenges the shadows of subconscious culture. In some cases, social issues drive us further into the currents of diversity—equal pay, Black Lives Matter, gender equality—while at the same time illustrating the great divide. Hierarchy and division pull *you/me/us/them* away from truly seeing each other as souls. Instead, it further engenders separation, greed, and envy. Climbing higher materialistically does not always hold the promise of illumined, conscious *Self/self/SELF*-realization. It most often deters this because story, ambition, and identity become firmly anchored.

Fight and competition in and of themselves are illusions, because struggle is internal, typically existing in mind or body. Each *personal* obsession stems from deeply embedded shadows of codependency, neediness, and dishonesty. These expand into our structures of government, law, and economics, which have long held hierarchical roots. These civilized forms of ancient caste systems are meant to serve but are corrupted when driven by personal agenda. Hierarchy always serves those at the top first.

As *you/i/we/they* climb over one another, hierarchy is the tower built to escape where we are. Within your cellular structure are eons of climbing toward higher expressions of life. *You/you* are bred to believe life is about achieving and significance. Even now, this is embedded in every aspect of *your/my/our/their* lives, from caste systems and heads of households to organizations and states. Governmental, religious, and business structures are built on ladders of rank and importance. Although status is temporal, money solidifies this illusion.

Our world is locked within the vices of greed, envy, and gluttony in small and large ways. In a world clamoring to be seen, the ladder of success is proselytized as the measure of those who have made it. On the way up, perspectives change. New views do not allow a balanced and equal approach to all people because the vision becomes skewed. When continually reaching for the skies, it is difficult to remain with both feet rooted in the ground. Hierarchy is a mechanism of distraction, keeping people from realizing layers of untruth. It is hypnotizing.

Varying levels of society and structure create a foundation for judgment, gossip, and competition to thrive. These behaviors are the shadow nature. When projected upon others, these morph into corruption and manipulation. Ultimately hierarchy creates only further separation, widening the divide between peoples, cultures, and nations.

Your stuff is my stuff . . . My stuff is yours.
That is what oneness means.
Oneness is not just the soft, fluffy, feathery stuff;
it embraces everyone and everything as its own.

The ego unknowingly categorizes and separates. It creates hierarchy all of the time in order to feel important. A friend returned from San Francisco and shared about seeing large numbers of homeless people living on the streets. She hierarchically spoke of sending healing energy to release them from their plight, as she flew out of the area, believing that as why the universe really took her there. She explained that she performed certain energy techniques to clear them of past karma and living condition. The dialogue became increasingly about how her vibration, consciousness, and knowledge—being higher—had the power to shift their circumstances. She truly believed that she was their blessing and healing.

A few months later, I flew to San Francisco. The numbers of homeless individuals were startling. More apparent to me was the rest of the population. Everyone moved very quickly. The energy of the city was rushed. Noses were in phones, even as people crossed busy streets. No person looked at another. Every place was busy. Within the area were many homeless people; most of them were just sitting in the park area. The city's energy is frenetic. The homeless population helped ground the energy. Their stillness was a counterbalance to the constant movement. As a sign, they also depicted how spiritually homeless—or disconnected—people around them were.

I thought of the conversation that occurred weeks prior. That friend is also frenetically busy. She believes her constant doing is presence and power. In my view, the homeless were doing more to serve her than she could do to serve them. Due to unconscious hierarchical thinking, she couldn't appreciate the service in front of her.

You cannot truly see the homeless for who they are, if not having given a home to the painful and lost parts of *You/you/YOU*. There can be no compassion for the poor unless *You/you* define your poverty. *You* cannot aid the sick, if not addressing personal ills. Ironically, *you/i/we/they* see all of these issues, and we do not see our own. Attempts to serve them are wasted energy. They serve *You/you/YOU* in looking at yourself. Honor them by healing yourself. Their souls chose to live that specific experience in order to reflect yours. Take note of the people *You/you/YOU* look down upon or arrogantly attempt to fix. You are caught within an illusion.

Inequality will create only dissidence and friction.
Equality brings forth the fluidity of cooperation and true cocreation.
Do not be a leader or a follower.
Be an equal.

The world is at a loss for real connection, because people have become commodities, and money the master. We trade stock in families for a gain in status. The race to the top has consumed the mind to such a degree that morality becomes trampled on. When hierarchy no longer exists, real connection will root. Communication will be rooted in soul recognition. This requires listening. Really listening. As long as superficiality prevails, the aura of distrust will be present. This is not someone else's work to do; it is your work. To create a world of equality, *You* must regard others in an equal way; all people. In addition, *You* must see yourself as an equal to all people.

With younger generations caring more about the earth, inclusion, equality, and love . . . old paradigms of selfishness, greed, and manipulation will crumble. Times are upon us where the *haves* will share with the *have-nots*. The poorest nations and peoples have always been the happiest and most peaceful, despite their conditions. They are not conflicted by attachments that have to be protected. When a person loses everything, the material world can be seen for what it is; a shiny bauble that was plastic all along.

Richness is derived through intimacy, vulnerability, and presence. True wealth is experienced within a relationship to *Self/self/SELF*, others, and inner fulfillment. When *you/i/we/they* see one another as equals—allowing interdependent exchanges—opposing experiences among earth's creatures, peoples, and nations will decrease. When pure service strikes, it will exhilarate *You/you/YOU* beyond your senses. It will terrify *You/you/YOU* at the same time—obliterating the ego— because the task will no longer matter, nor whom is doing it. Recognition will not be required. Camaraderie and communion will be of greater importance. Connection creates wealth beyond measure. Blessed *being/Being/BEING* . . . Breathe deeply as *You/you/YOU* experience equality.

May *You/you/YOU* realize the illusions that trap *you* . . .
and awaken to the Source that has *You*.
May life know the beauty of your uniqueness . . .
in celebration for your *Self/self/SELF* and others . . .
May *You/you/YOU* stand in your radiant feminine energy . . .
and revel in the strength of your masculine sensitivity . . .
Sweetly dream . . .
so to create the sweetest of dreams.

0
0 0
0
1
1 1
1 1 1 1
1 1 1
1
0
0 0
0

. . .

PERSONAL OBSESSIONS

What is the addiction?

At times *You/you/YOU* are in the moment,
in other times prophetic.
Always both,
because there is no time . . .
This is as true now as it was then,
and as it shall be tomorrow.

You/you/YOU want to be seen as a good human being. *You* want people to like *You/you/YOU* and desire to like yourself. This is how people-pleasing and do-gooding begin. It is why *You* are a *nice* person. It is why people say *You* are kind. Deep down inside, *you* question this. *Am I a good person? Is my life meaningful? Have I made a difference? Am I leaving a legacy? Do people like me?* Have I done enough? The shadow craving to hear words that affirm you are always present. *You/you/YOU* want to feel worthy, good enough, and significant. Deep down, *You/you/YOU* equate *Being/being/BEING* with your level of doing.

You/you/YOU reach into other people's lives, whether they ask or not. Taught to place the world upon your shoulders, *You/you/YOU* carry the weight of friends, family, and those appearing downtrodden. This burden is taken on in hopes of being seen as a *good* person. *You* equate worth with *doing*. But goodness is merely an extraneous effort for counterbalancing the *badness* that you unconsciously hold. The chains of societal bondage enslave *You /you/ YOU* into codependent relationships early on. *You* learn to take care of others needs, despite your own. The most unconscious addiction human beings have is *the need to be needed*.

The *need to be loved* will have you act as a people pleaser, oftentimes partaking in tasks you believe you "should" do. The *need to feel worthy* will have you give your time often to places and things to help you feel good enough. The *need to be significant* will dupe you into believing that a certain status or attainment is your purpose in the world that no other can fulfill. The *need for meaning* will keep you in an endless search for purpose. This is the foundation of all personal obsessions. Yet, each step—on any of these staircases—removes *You* further from yourself, and into the outer sphere of projection. This is why tiredness, depletion, and lack of fulfillment appear.

Your power is in your pain.
Embrace the pain, unleash the power.
The illusion of what looks good has value only if it feels good.
Discern reality from illusion.
Discern the difference between heart and mind.

Many healers, teachers, coaches, mothers, fathers, and servers become exhausted and depleted because energy is extended in excessive and codependent ways. They take on weight, illness, and other people's energies. *You/you/YOU* have your version of this in areas *You/you/YOU* feel consistently tired. Your attachment to *helping others*—change, heal, learn, or do better—controls your life. That attachment engages codependency and *self*-betrayal. It creates a cord that pulls energy from the other—keeping them in their state—and keeping *You* in yours. This is how oppression is created for *Self/self/SELF* and others. *You/you/YOU* need people to be where they are in order to feel needed, worthy, and purposeful. Because of this neediness, they remain locked and bound in their conditions. They give *You* something to fight for. You give them something to fight against. They also become your excuse for not living a bolder, more vibrant life of aliveness and freedom.

Doctors *need* sick people. Therapists *need* individuals who are mentally and emotionally conflicted. Lawyers *need* for people to be at odds with one another. Healers *need* people with issues. Coaches *need* individuals who are disempowered. Motivational speakers *need* an audience to motivate. All of these professions—and many others—require people to be in deficiency in order to be significant. These professions would not exist if individuals were healthy, vibrant, and empowered. The consciousness of codependence keeps these need-based relationships in place. Focus and vision are anchored in deficiency, dis-ease, and lack rather than wholeness, ease, and abundance.

Can you imagine a world where individuals are grounded in creativity—music, art, travel, dance, photography, design—as opposed to fixing problems? Is it altruistic? Yes. Is it possible? Yes. To achieve this end, a shift in *Mind/mind/MIND* must occur. What if the necessary shift in consciousness is not within the broken, ill, or dysfunctional, but, instead, within the minds of those who treat them?

Empowerment is not only required by the other; it is necessary within the *Self/self/SELF*. The other's state exists due to your projections, wounds, and inhibitions. Because *You/you/YOU* unconsciously need an individual to be in a state of dysfunction, they are. Is this your child? Your parent? Your spouse? With their issue, *You/you/YOU* keep yourself caged as well. The endless grind exists because *so many people need help*, or so you *think*. The whole world operates in this way. Your personal obsessions keep *You/you/YOU* from freedom, joy, and the lightness of *Being/BEING*.

> **If you were to release past wounds, conditioning, and imprinting,**
> ***You/you/YOU* would not be attached to your current purpose.**
> **The capacity to see with clear vision would open you to something new.**
> **When you let go of all identification . . .**
> **you find the true *SELF*.**

Regardless of who *You* are, what modality is practiced, or how smart, the only one who can change, fix, or heal the other . . . is *the other*. However, your consciousness and personal obsessions obstruct their ability to clear themselves. If *You/you/YOU* require an individual to behave or experience life in a certain way—for *You* to find fulfillment, satisfaction, and purpose—*You* are operating out of deficiency. When *You* get out of your way, they will get out of theirs. Don't dupe them or yourself into believing that *You* have the power to heal them . . . only they can do that. Your need to believe that *You* are their savior is your need to feel important and significant. Give them the space to empower themselves through a belief in their capability. Allow them your presence, listening, and witnessing. See others as capable. The truth is that *your presence is enough*. You need do nothing. Your *Being/BEING* present is required.

> **To paint this, and sculpt that . . . to carve then, and create now . . .**
> **to melt . . . to smolder . . . to burn . . . to solder . . .**
> **from formless to form; no thing and every thing.**
> **To reconcile a division that was not real.**

The ego craves significance. Each action, pursuit, and agenda may stem from the desire to prove your existence matters. The human ego will justify anything as a subtle way to escape the simplicity and purity of the soul. It will be convinced to keep doing what it is doing. Everything *You/you/YOU* fight for—including the ladders *You/you/YOU* climb in the name of ambition and agenda—is out of *a need* to feel significant. And yet, in the expansiveness of space and time, *you/i/we/they* are insignificant minuscule particles of cosmic dust. Slow down; inquire why *You* do what *You* do. Listen intently for agenda and impulse. Find your clear notes and let them be heard. Be your true *Self/self/SELF*; otherwise *You/you/YOU* remain lost within the lie. Such an act betrays the unique beauty and brilliance *You/you/YOU* bring.

> **It is never about what is achieved outside,**
> **who you can be in the world, or what you want to fix;**
> **the only true everlasting transformation will be internal.**

Awareness leads to soul's illumination, purpose, and true service. Your soul expression will be silent, consisting of small gestures. *You/YOU* will be more present and filled with vision. There is a fine line between expressing yourself out of need, fear, and want . . . to that of celebration, love, and communion. Do not be too quick in listening to the loudest voices—inside or out. The softest voices often speak the greatest truths. Meet your *Self/self* in the dark . . . and *You/you/YOU* will see others in the wholeness of their light and dark. Meet yourself in the light, and *You/you/YOU* will see others with celebration.

> **True advocacy sees another's greatness, even if they can't.**
> **To be of service, you must get out of your story and empower theirs.**
> **They must get out of their story and empower another.**

Allow the organic nature of life to awaken infinite possibility. The heart will always move *You/you/YOU* in a different direction than *Mind/mind*. It has an intelligence that *Mind/mind* could never comprehend. The heart will find the simplest route to create the soul's goals. Within it is no attachment to fame, fortune, status, or attainment. It only desires to love, create, and serve. The heart knows what will bring fulfillment. Life will always create levels of support and expansion organically. Your expression and creations are clean when *You/you/YOU* are in the full celebration of your own voice, unattached to what anyone else says or does. Creative capacity has the highest frequency when not weighted down by agenda. Your work must engage the experience of joy and celebration, then the energy is clear for the other to stand in their power. Your only purpose is to remain in a state of inspiration and creativity. Blessed *being/Being/BEING* . . . Breathe deeply as *You/you/YOU* experience communion within and without.

> May you realize that hierarchy is an illusion;
> there is none better, or greater, than another.
> May you see that money is simply energy;
> merely a means of relating to our needs and desires.
> May you acknowledge that status only separates;
> it is a modern-day caste system,
> creating the ladders that you climb.
> May you level the playing field,
> where the only difference between us
> is the genius that expresses through us.
> Sweetly dream . . .
> so to create the sweetest of dreams.

. . .

OUR GLOBAL REFLECTION OF HUMAN RIGHTS

What is the mirror?

> Let sacredness be within your sounds.
> Let Essence reveal boldly through your expression.
> Let holiness be the crown you adorn.
> Let Divinity fill your doing,
> and humanity ooze from your being.
> Life is the grace for endless human rites of passage.
> Experience is your divine and human right.

Your world is threatened by many factors: terrorism, climate change, security, human rights, and more. What is written here has the potential to threaten all of those issues into extinction. It does not necessarily mean they will disappear. However, *you* may choose to release the fight and angst around them. The relationship between individual and collective consciousness is an interwoven experience of illusion and reality. It is reflective of the *Self/self*-obsession that rages through identity. Your perception of who *You* are subsequently creates a belief in hierarchy that is used to hoodwink yourself. By placing others above you, the experience of duality is more deeply entrenched.

Social activism and *Self/self/SELF*-help must be viewed differently, if *You/you/YOU* desire to transcend the experiences of your world. A new paradigm of embodiment not only eliminates the illusion of hierarchical structures but can also bring *You/you/YOU* into present time. *Self/self/SELF*-help and social activism are based on past and future thought. The issues of our world are marched, picketed, and stormed against because of issues that built over time, and a fear of the future not changing. Although *You* actively crusade for something happening in front of your eyes, this is distraction depicting a wounding reflected from your psyche.

Human rights encompass an umbrella of issues relating to gender, race, wellness, lifestyle, healthcare, voting, and equality, among others. The ongoing fight for human rights continually affirms and anchors structures of hierarchy, thus making them stronger. What *You/you/YOU* push against will push back. That which *You/you/YOU* hate, *You* unconsciously envy. Issues can feel like wake-up calls to fight the establishment, but they are not. These are siren calls to deepen into the reactions of the body and mind as *You* rise into your highest *Self*. This is derived from becoming aware—not seeking or evolved— but completely present to how disengaged you are. Your upset is not about overcoming the institution, nor is it about processing through all that *You/you/YOU* encounter. Both of these are tied to your need for significance. Upset and angst will subside as *You* immerse within the waves of feeling and emotion to find your balance.

Forgive the institution . . . and the process.

The self-created insanity of needing to build an identity to protect, survive, and fight comes from separation and suffering. This disease of thought creates the realm of fight or flight that compounds over time, creating reaction, defense, and opposing forces. It is the foundation upon which to claim right or wrong, good or bad, just or unjust, and significant versus insignificant. Even the most conscious individuals succumb to this mind-control mechanism with the right trigger, circumstance, or dangling carrot. Such insanity is subjective to internal and external influences that justify reasons for actions and reactions.

As a thought process produces swings of positive and negative, the pain and pleasure cycle is introduced. This cyclic rhythm becomes the drug that keeps *You/you/YOU* getting high and swinging low. It begins to control *You*, creating inner climate change that produces filters and lenses that maintain echoing inner affects and external effects. Once *You* are on your drug of choice—albeit greed, wrath, gluttony, lust, pride, envy, or slothfulness— withdrawal will be challenging and painful.

The dark asks/seeks nothing of you.
The Light asks/seeks nothing of you.

Want to change the world? Any focus on an issue creates more of the issue. Your upset or your denial, even your activism, empowers the state of hierarchy, not equality. Your focus can no longer be about human "rights"; the focus must shift to human "rites" of passage. The time has come for individuals to no longer conform to a false world; those who are ready to let go of the control paradigms that are in place. This means creating internal freedom despite conditions. This level of *Self/self/SELF*-awareness is not for the faint of heart. This degree of courage is grounded deeply into the feeling heart.

Rather than fighting for human rights, view each experience—even those that the world illustrates—as a sacred rite of passage. Each one is for mastering yourself mentally, emotionally, physically, and spiritually. Your willingness to let go of the fight is course correction and prerequisite training for Mastery. Life is designed to challenge every aspect of *You*: mind, body, emotion, personality, identity. This experience of physicality is a Master's curriculum, especially for those desiring to remove all obstacles to godhood. Viewing personal and global issues in this manner will bring about increasing degrees of present-moment living. Embrace each creation and miscreation as the *Self/self*, and the *SELF*. Your life is asking for the bold truth . . . the cold truth . . . the hard truth . . . the whole truth . . . the blasphemous, brazen. and unbridled collective truth . . . and finally, the nonexistence of truth. These are likely to have *You/you/YOU* spinning, until finally surrendering.

Be still. Be witness.
Behold the dance of duality.

Living an aligned life means standing in divine equality with everything that exists. *You* fall victim to hierarchy by holding those outside *You* better, greater, and more powerful than *You/you/YOU*. *You* must not grovel or shrink back. *You* are equal to those perceived as the highest among *You*. It is not necessary to qualify yourself. *You* either live it or do not. Regardless, this exists in truth. There is no in between. Get neutral and live in the vibrational resonance with which *You* were made. Hold steady focus and vision, aligning to the highest state of consciousness for yourself and others. View the sick as whole, the malevolent as good, the evil as Divine, the broken as whole. Everything that occurs facilitates various rites of passage for *You/you/YOU* to uncover expansive levels of mastery on this physical plane.

To neutralize the extremes, *You/you/YOU* must move beyond your ideas of struggle and fight, approaching human rights from a different angle. This shift cannot be surface philosophy. It must be an embodied integration and lifestyle change. In the past, *You* attempted to do what was "right," politically correct, and aligned with perceived social norms. Protest is as much a social norm as conformity. The movement from citizen, politician/lobbyist to heart-centered, servant leadership will engender a new focus and vision, removing energy from the problem.

Your energy must pivot toward growth, expansion, and the curiosity of *Self/self/SELF* within existing conditions, issues, and problems. This realignment will open the way for deeper communication internally and establish a new baseline of government that exists within rather than externally. This is a move from oppression to optimism, which reveals the distinction between real conversation instead of performance-based, outer-focused dialogue. This shift leads to a stronger *Self/SELF*-concept for *Knowing/knowing/KNOWING*. Authentic conversation must first occur with *Self/self/SELF*. With that, inner authority will strengthen, so that the divide created by hierarchy decreases. When anchored in a higher *Self/SELF*-concept, equality becomes more prevalent. It is an outgrowth of your residence within confidence, creativity, and curiosity.

Hierarchy is a subtle belief in victimhood and unworthiness.

There are a lot of happenings . . . natural happenings . . . human happenings . . . inhuman happenings. *You/you/YOU* view a world of your own making. In truth, *You* are fighting with yourself. Your oppression is *self*-inflicted. Hierarchy even exists internally; *You* rank your animal above your shadow, while the shadow dominates your humanity. With the weight of all three, *You/you/YOU* oppress your godhood. Through this illustration of inner domination and limited government, it is easy to see how collective consciousness holds energy externally. It is withheld inside . . . outside . . . and hidden away by amplified expressions of the very same.

This moment is for remembering only one truth . . . inner truth, whatever that is for *You/you/YOU*. It is time to decide who *You* are, and where *You/you/YOU* came from. No more illusions. The disciplines of empathy, compassion, and love have been calling to *You/you/YOU* through the violation of your human *rites*. Do not clamor for things to change. *You* must change. The imbalance in the world mirrors the imbalance in your inner world. Hierarchy existing in society, systems, and structures is equal to the hierarchy held in your mind. A new world experience of aliveness must be based on present-moment experiencing. A global playground of inspired peace—instead of a world in reactive conflict—is possible only when we stand in the world with a firm footing of equality.

Petition only yourself. Protest against your mind's need to react. Fight the inner constructs that keep *You/you/YOU* looping in pain, hierarchy, and illusion. Your *Self/self/SELF*-love should be tender, but in fierce advocacy. This means your devotion to internal government. The ultimate hierarchy to challenge exists between *You/you/YOU* and God. *You/you/YOU* have placed this infinite Source high above. *You/you/YOU* have created *his* wrath, karma, and ideas of punishment. *You/you/YOU* have placed *her* high in the heavens. Put yourself on equal footing, not by bringing God to your level, but by raising yourself to Divine capacity. God has never been above and beyond *You/you/YOU*, but wrapped around and within. Once knowing this, *You* will see the outside world for what it truly is. Blessed *being/Being/BEING* . . . Breathe deeply as *You/you/YOU* recognize the truth of equality.

May you see know . . .
you are more than a spark of Light . . .
your voice as a beautiful harmony . . .
and that you give breath to beauty and bounteousness.
May you truly know how the Divine
see through your eyes . . .
hears through your ears . . .
touches through your skin . . .
and weeps through your tears.
May you know the power of your thoughts . . .
the ways of your words . . .
and the effects of your actions.
May you know there is nowhere you will go
that the Divine will not be.
Sweetly dream . . .
so to create the sweetest of dreams.

...

THE HOLE OF ENVY

What is the disease?

Don't be fooled by the illusion . . .
sometimes what appears winning may be enslaved,
and what appears bound may be free.
Look at your lens
to know how you see . . .
and where you hold
the green eye of envy.

Jealousy and envy are similar negative emotions that will make *You* miserable and spoil your relationships. Although both are detrimental to experiencing balance and peace, jealousy is a more natural state existing in humans and other species. Because others possess something *You/you/YOU* think belongs to *You/you/YOU*, resentment builds. Jealousy is often accompanied by possessiveness, insecurity, and a sense of betrayal. When out of control, jealousy is destructive. Envy is relegated to humans who have embodied a darker, animal nature. Both have roots in anger.

Jealousy has to do with *who* others are, whereas envy is derived from *what* others have. Envy begins early—in the younger years. Media and marketing create initial comparisons, cravings, wants, and desires. This only grows as we age. As adults, envy can often be the foundation that creates a need to have the most toys. Abuse of rank feeds envy. The illusion of hierarchy is a proponent for competition and greed because those that are powerful, rich, or of high stature do not always follow the same rules as others. Additionally, these individuals can use status as a weapon against others.

Envy is ill will toward the blessings and achievements of others.

Envy is also resentment toward others, but because of their possessions or success. The one who envies craves things that others have, which they do not. The envious individual does not necessarily believe they deserve what the other has; they simply do not want the other to have the experience. In alternate cases, the envious person wishes the individual harm, a negative experience, or a detrimental outcome. Those who are envious lack confidence and tend to have a sense of inferiority. The envious person can be very rich, very poor, or average. Envy is a deep-seated sense of resistance to what is, because the individual is more grounded in the lives of others as opposed to themselves. Their distorted perceptions are laced with greed and desire.

Spiritual envy tends to be the worst kind—we resent the spiritual gifts of another.

The hole of envy is rooted within ingratitude. Comparison fuels envy, feeding the hungry and ravaging nature of one that is dissatisfied with themselves. Often carrying the characteristics of criticism and condemnation, envy will display as rudeness and boorishness. Envy is a form of hate for what another has or does not have. When caught up in envy, *You/you/YOU* become someone else's prisoner. *You/you/YOU* let what they do—and what they have—determine how *You/you/YOU* feel about your life. It also carries a subtle desire for harm to another, in order to feel better about oneself. Envy is passion gone awry, eating an individual down to the core. Envy erodes joy and destroys true intimate connection with others. It is a deadly sin that destroys the soul. When innocent, alive, creative capacity mutates into the green-eyed monster of envy—where morality and integrity are discarded—this dis-ease of mind will create sickness in one's spirit. This merely creates more imbalances in an already cracked foundation.

Ignorance and delusion are the primary causes of evil and misery;
envy is a weed within both.

There are several antidotes to envy: gratitude, humility, and pure sight. Gratitude supports creating inner fullness, which also increases frequency. Humility anchors *You* into the presence of the Divine. Pure sight sees no separation and knows all things that exist are with *You*. Grounding into these states gives access to broader perspectives. Each person fulfills an aspect of experience on the planet. As an interconnected *Being* of the *ONE*, you have the ability to see, feel, and imagine the experience of any other individual's life. *You* can experience it as your own. Simply move your focus from behind your eyes and place your vision behind the eyes and life of the other, from the sense of celebration and gratitude that they must feel. Hold the gaze steady and anchor into the intimacy of their experience. In this way, you will begin to understand it really does not matter who is having the experience, because we are each here to fulfill a different piece of the divine puzzle. In union, *You* are able to have it all. *You/i/we/they* must teach ourselves to avoid looking upon the fortune or misfortune of others with envious eyes, and to hold on to the essential communion shared with one another. Blessed *being/Being/BEING* . . . Breathe deeply as *You/you/YOU* experience celebration.

May you give your life . . .
to the death of all things that no longer serve.
May you be the dreamer . . .
and fully live your greatest Dream.
May you rest in that . . .
so that no other's life takes the focus from your own.
Sweetly dream . . .
so to create the sweetest of dreams.

. . .

THE KEY WHOLE OF BALANCE

How is personal power activated?

True leadership understands there is not one leader;
it knows there are no followers.
The pure leader receives guidance,
rather than giving direction.

Imagine being on a swing. If *You* move your legs out or pull them back, the intensity increases. Your body will go higher and faster, as you move forward and back. If you stop generating the movement, the swing will slow down, eventually bringing *You* back to center. Still. Calm. Life is like this. The further forward one goes, the further back they must venture. If *You* were to see the energy amid all of the movement, it would appear as infinity.

Balancing opposites creates waves within the resistance of highs and the lows. *You/ you/YOU* are to surf these waves, externally and internally. At first they may pummel your body and life, pulling *You/you/YOU* under. There is something beneath the surf that *You* must discover. Do not fight it. Interference, struggle, and fight only delay balance.

Do more nothing.

If you desire happiness, **you** will also encounter sadness. Darkness always encounters Light. Success and failure are bedfellows. Through finding balance, *You/you/YOU* discover the ability to ride every wave, even the extremes. Tidal waves are especially generous in all they can bring, but *You/you/YOU* must endure and survive them. Patience will be your greatest ally in these moments. Noninterference will allow space for the highest good. Justice and truth organically unfold according to the laws of nature. Give in to your experience **of** timelessness and receive transformation. Equilibrium and equanimity are the ultimate threshold of a life well lived.

A design . . . a destiny . . . a deity
lives inside you.
It knows what it's doing.
You do not have to.

Life does not always appear fair, but it does achieve balance. This applies both to man's law and universal law. This does not mean in the time you desire; balance follows divine time. Every step *You/you/YOU* take is the unwinding of something that became tightly wound. In this way, life exhales what was once inhaled. Be silent and witness the beauty of your entire saga . . . and the intricacy of each note, stroke, and character. Behold the big picture. Let life lead; it will take *You* to places never imagined. It will grow and expand *You* through experiences that feel like challenge, upset, or unfairness. These are simply the landscape of life, just like mountains, valleys, and deserts. The scales will balance as *You* master each level of *Self/self/SELF*. This reveals the beauty and strength of your human spirit.

Whatever *You* walk into or bump up against is life's way of steering *You* closer to freedom, authentic living, and greater receiving. Pay attention to your spirit's soft guidance, so that life does not present a hard sign. Things that call for attention are fine-tuning and honing *You*. Balance is an important element toward manifestation, sustainability, creation, and flow.

Karma is not inflicted by anything outside *You/you/YOU*; it's all *You/you/YOU*. Your body keeps a record of injustices and inequality inflicted or received. The body knows what to do with this. It is nature. It knows balance. Life lessons continually bring *You* back to *self/Self/SELF*. Going to extremes and allowing all lessons provides the *re-vision* necessary for clarity. Once *You* master your outer persona, every action and response eventually brings about the perspective of higher self. Soul lessons balance creations of time and space. Your soul is unwinding old memory ... and, at times, ancestral ... ancient ... and collective memory.

Don't underestimate the power of your spirit; it is eternal.
Your ego doesn't, which is why it tries so hard.

When *You* feel the freedom of wise choices, immature desires will no longer rule your experience. Temperance honors the rhythms of your nature. It allows *You* to be open to what passes by, while also having the ability to let it pass unscathed. A temperate person honors desires and passions as gifts but holds a steady line of higher expression. It is not wise to follow every whim, impulse, or fantasy that enters the mind. That leads to imbalances. Seek to experience simplicity, sweetness, and sacred presence. Only that which is real remains. All else will be a whirlwind that has you teetering to find your footing. Remember that *Love/LOVE* holds *You/you/YOU* . . . *Light/LIGHT* guides *You/you/YOU* . . . *Essence* moves in, as, and through *You/you/YOU*. Therein is true human, spiritual, and social balance. Blessed *being/Being/BEING* . . . Breathe deeply as *You/you/YOU* experience balance.

May there be moments when there is nothing to say . . .
no one to talk about . . .
no noise in the mind, on the airwaves, or static in space.
May there be vast spaces of stillness . . .
where the richness of space is valued . . .
the timelessness of love abounds . . .
the quietness of being quenches every thirst
and feeds each hunger.
May there be days when there is no division . . .
no side to take . . .
and no separation
because all are clear enough
to see the beauty of being One.
Sweetly dream . . .
so to create the sweetest of dreams.

. . .

POLITICIAN TO SERVANT LEADER

How does purpose unfold?

Let every single choice be heart centered,
understanding within each moment
my words, thoughts, and deeds arise out of . . .
my past or my Presence . . .
my story or my Clear Vision . . .
my wounds or my Wholeness . . .
my ego or my Heart-Centered Divinity . . .
my addiction or my Innocence . . .
my lack or my Fullness . . .
my unworthiness or my Worth . . .
my craving or my Creativity . . .
my aversion or my Acceptance . . .
my indifference or my Love . . .
my pain or my Power.

What is currently identified as power in the world is actually force. This type of forced power draws from the external world. It is a "taking" energy rather than a "giving" one. Forced power amplifies and reflects the energies it takes in from the world. Anytime words and actions are bullying, dominating, or threatening . . . the "grave shadow" of power is present. This is the mask of one who is deadened to their senses and sense ability. Such dark use of power is concerned only with its own image, status, and agenda. It is grounded in fear—at times, unconsciously—and can express with charisma or a hard edge. Its most identifying characteristic is "*my way or else*." Power of this type is "slave" to the ego. This is the "God complex" of the head and ego. This person behaves as a politician, by telling others what they want to hear while every move is for personal agenda.

To move from this "shadow mask" of power and into authentic power requires humility. Real humility knows itself as an extension of Source. Grounded in the "God-spark" of the heart, one wills not to inflict pain but instead aims to transmute it. This individual lives in full trust and acknowledgment of life's innate wisdom, cycles, and rhythms, even within the difficult, challenging, and hard moments. This person is engaging servant leadership.

One cannot love another greater than they love themselves.

Shadows are the smoke screen, the veil that we hide behind to dupe ourselves into believing we are in control. Criticism, condemnation, judgment, and gossip keep people distracted from the truth . . . their truth . . . THE TRUTH. When around those who engage in these shadow activities, it is easy to get caught up in the spin. But doing so will send you off-course.

There is a natural tendency to remain in patterns and habits that are not beneficial; there is a payoff. That payoff can be material, status, fame, or a false sense of power. The politician archetype is one who mimics what others want to hear. They begin in good faith and service but soon turn toward the shadow side of greed and false power, becoming parrots for those can boost them up. The politician uses a mask of service to feed a deep insecurity of wanting to be loved, liked, and accepted. With this deficiency, it is difficult to stay true to one side for too long. The politician will flip back and forth like a wave, taking what is needed in order to advance, win, and achieve the agenda at hand. There may be a rise, but there will typically be a fall that follows. To be a politician is to be a people-pleaser, which is entrenched in codependency, manipulation, and bartering. It is feeling the soul for a quick fix. As *You/you* release yourself from the *self*-created prisons, chains, and bonds of trying to morph into what everyone else wants and needs, *You/you/ YOU* will be cut loose. When choosing to serve something bigger than yourself, everyone wins. This is a natural side effect of personal power and authenticity. The innocent service heart will begin to bloom. The very nature of this balancing allows inner wildness to rise, and outer responsibility to take root. This is the great legacy that selfless service, sacrifice, and surrender embody.

SHADOW EXPRESSION	SOCIAL AFFECT	SOCIAL EFFECT
Criticism	Conditioning/ Homogenized	Branding/Labeling
Condemnation	Rejection/Guilt	Politician/Networking
Judgment	Shaming/Following	Celebrity/Influencer
Gossip	Enslaved/Complicit	Marketing/Salesman

Regardless of others' circumstances, hold them as capable. You cannot fall victim to the codependent need to save, fix, or heal others. If *You* have engaged in inner work in the areas they face, *You* will be able to appreciate where they are. Compassion will rise for the visceral steps they are to encounter, because you have been there and done that. This is the empowerment and service today's world requires. A resurgence of true humanity and real humility can awaken a new world.

The task at hand is to radically love *Self/self/SELF*. The world cannot and will not change unless *Love/love* is brought into its purest and most unconditional essence. *Love/love/LOVE* has morphed into a method. Extending oneself in exchange for something else is not *Love*. It is bartering, trading, and commerce. Needing another to feel whole and complete is not *Love/LOVE*; it is a version of addiction. *Love* does not use, abuse, or manipulate. It seeks nothing. It requires nothing. It yearns for nothing, because it is full and fulfilled within itself. Seeking love is an attempt to fill oneself, but there is no one that will be able to fulfill that need. The emptiness *being* felt is the vacancy of having given yourself away.

To truly love means not giving yourself away but instead grounding deeply in your truth of completeness. It is the innate truth of *Being/BEING* whole. Real love sees the other as the *Self/SELF*, also whole and complete. Many are in a relationship, but it is convenience instead of *Love*. It's a trade. "You do this for me; I'll do that for you." It is politics. That creates division, opposition, and resentment.

Authentic power is rooted in Love that shines bright like a diamond.

Authentic power is grounded in love and compassion because it draws from its gentle experience of intuition and a deep connection of the heart. True power knows "to give is to receive back in greater measure." The soft whisper of internal guidance always considers the whole, and its interconnection with the greater body as a catalyst for good; for unity instead of separation. Authentic power is never swayed by money, status, hierarchy, or fame. It knows these things as temporary, understanding that real wealth is in connection, equality, balance, and equanimity. Authentic power can be expressed softly or firmly, but with grounded simplicity and brevity. Power of this manner exhibits being "Master" of one's environment and world, where every experience is embraced fully.

When uniting with others, do so from heart and Essence, not mind and ego. The latter is driven by fear, lack, and programming. The first is pure heart, soul, and essence. Personal agenda and *self*-absorption focus on the *self* and what it can take. We are in the pendulum swing back to center from the far-reaching, grabbing hand of forced power. Individuals who ground authenticity—holding, purifying, and keeping their personal energy in check—create greater quickening. A return to inner authority and servant leadership slows the world down so that people are truly seen and heard. Servant leadership has no personal agenda. It is right action, based on seeing the other as the Divine. Servant leadership builds unity and community. There are no sides. There is no partisanship. There is no yours and mine; it is all ours.

True collaboration and cocreation focus on the whole, not individual parts. True leadership resides in knowing there is not one leader, and there are no followers. The pure leader receives guidance, rather than giving direction. Those sacred activators who act as pure witness sit and ground transformation. Sometimes those who stop and appear to be doing nothing are the ones that are truly doing everything. There is only one question to ask your friends, your frenemies, your framily and family . . . *How can I serve?* The only agenda to be present with is . . . *Have I served the soul, and its allegiance to the whole.* Blessed *being/Being/BEING* . . . Breathe deeply as *You/you/YOU* experience servant leadership.

May you aspire to illuminate insight . . .
May you lead yourself into laughter . . .
May you generate goodness throughout your Being . . .
May you make Love to your longings . . .
May you ground into the beauty of your humanity . . .
so that your service is wholeheartedly
experienced and expressed.
Sweetly dream . . .
so to create the sweetest of dreams.

. . .

CULTIVATING CONVERSATION

How can peace arise?

I bow down. Not in submission, but in devotion.
I have come before humanity, humble and naked,
not broken, but broken open.
Nothing that occurred made me weak;
everything made me stronger.
I see from beyond my eyes. I know beyond any sense.
I am still within my core, while the body moves with ease.
I can walk this earth with humility;
I have nothing to lose.
Living . . . being . . . and knowing . . .
are my incredible steps of divine unfolding.

Ripples and reflections are the projections of individual *Mind/mind/MIND* . . . and collective thinking. Your relationship to others—or nonrelationship—is the magnified version of your relationship to *Self/self/SELF*. When something has been done, taken, or put forth against what the relationship stood for, *You/you/YOU* are encountering an angel in disguise. Their soul purpose is to catalyze your growth and awareness.

Your best relationship will arise beyond your need for one.

The nemesis, codependent, and villain of your experience will provide intensity that deepens *You* into *you* and *YOU*. These people are translators and facilitators of shadow emergence. They will assist *You/you/YOU* in meeting the deepest, darkest parts of yourself. However, until aware that they are showing *You* . . . *you*, there will be an inclination to project onto them. Although they may be deceptive, devious, mean individuals, they will be your greatest teachers, guides, and gurus. Their job is to break *You/you/YOU* of your ego. At some point *You* must leave everyone and endeavor upon a bold dialogue with *Self/self/SELF*. Having a direct relationship—instead of this middle man or interpreter—is an enriching part of the journey. *You* will discover your light and dark sides.

Speak and act with nonviolence;
compassionate living is the only cure for our world.

The most-insidious and subtlest forms of violence are gossip, secrets, and the little white lies we tell ourselves and others. Every distortion of truth dilutes your integrity and inner authority. Each secret held is a sickness that festers within. White lies are parasites that keep growing, becoming bigger and bigger. All of these create illusions where truth once stood, which results in *self*-hate and internal anger.

If *you/i/we/they* desire to clean up relationships, societies, and this world … it begins with our thoughts and words. It is necessary to become impeccable in word, truth, and integrity. How *you/i/we/they* give is how we each shall receive. Gossip, lies, secrets, and withholding are grave and deadly shadows that work against *self*-care, *self*-love, and *self*-respect. Speak the truth. Live in absolute integrity. Most importantly, have compassionate presence for every person. They are doing the best they can with what they have been taught. Support them by *Being/BEING* the example. Model something different.

> **Your awareness is the remembering …**
> **Your remembering is the discovering …**
> **Your discovering is the acknowledging …**
> **Your acknowledging is seeing …**
> **Seeing is believing!**

Your belief, mindset, approach, and energy have everything to do with the conversation taking place between *You/you/YOU* and *Mind/mind/MIND*. The other person can say only what *You/you* silently believe about yourself. They reflect *You*. Use clear, conscious conversation. Follow what your gut requires of you, and no less. In doing so, *You/you/YOU* begin the return to your authentic voice. All of life is an exploration in Mastery. This mandates connection to *Self/self/SELF*. Have an ongoing conversation with every aspect of *Self/self/SELF*. On a moment-by-moment, day-to-day basis,

> **master your mind, thoughts, beliefs, opinions, judgments, and ideas.**
> **master your emotions.**
> **master your physical body and physical environment.**
> **master the frequency of your energy, and where you place your energy.**
> **master the Essence of your Spirit.**

This is your soul/sole life purpose. The only life purpose for every human being is *SELF*-realization, integrating your divine confidence and creativity capacity. *You* must cultivate the ability to know *self*, before becoming aware of *SELF*. In achieving this, conversation is vital. Inner dialogue and outer dialogue are equally necessary. Cultivating authentic inner conversation is the pathway to maintaining clear, bold, authentic, and loving conversation with others.

> **Let conversations today be Soul to Soul instead of role to role.**
> **The role personality, just a small piece of who you are.**
> **Lead with what soul knows.**

Connect with the voices inside. Connect to the strong voice: the bold, courageous, aggressive risk taker. Also, speak with the more timid voice: the fearful, weak, shy one. Bring them together, asking them to teach each other. Both have great gifts to share. There is something deep inside, so much bigger than who *You* currently express as. Go beyond the small mind's need, craving, and desire. Let the stillness inside . . . out. This happens when you connect, commune, and have conversation.

There are many paths to the Source, but none that use fear. Just be present and in the now. Be in each moment, devoted to what is *Being/BEING* asked of you. Sometimes that is emotion. Sometimes work. Sometimes rest. Sometimes play. Be in conversation. Opening a deep dialogue with *Self/self/SELF* produces intimacy and transparency. *You* will find yourself immersed in safety and trust beyond anything *You/you* have known. In time, deep communion opens the way for *Knowing/knowing/KNOWING You/you/YOU* and the Divine as *One/one/ONE*. Blessed *being/Being/BEING* . . . Breathe deeply as *You/you/YOU* experience the many languages that exist inside.

May government stand for the purity of leadership,
rather than personal or party agenda . . .
May justice stand for truth, not the manipulated story that might win . . .
May money be a means of true exchange for connection,
not a way of buying and selling out each other . . .
May social activism be the internal transformation rather than an external fight . . .
May healthcare focus on health rather than purport the vision of treating illness . . .
May business be less busy and relax into the art of philanthropy . . .
May we value each other more than the things we create . . .
May our bread be beholding of brethren . . .
And wine, the intoxication of wisdom . . .
May this life be nourishing . . .
And each death rise in fulfillment.
Sweetly dream . . .
so to create the sweetest of dreams.

KNOW THYSELF

What is the asking?

Nothing can change on the outside,
until you create change on the inside.
Beyond mind is no mind.
Beyond thought is no thought.
Knowing arises through unknowing.
Unbecoming is the path to becoming.
To understand me,
You/you/YOU must know thyself.

AFFIRMATION—CONTEMPLATION—INSPIRATION

I AM capable of awakening to where I hold judgment and arrogance.
I now transcend all places of *Self/self/SELF*-righteousness.

Contemplate and journal these inquiries until inspired to take action.

Be still; see what rises as *intelligence* versus *ignorance*.
You have the answer for achieving aliveness . . . go within.

The degree to which you are *Being/being/BEING*
is the degree to which *You/you/YOU*
shall cultivate inner and outer *Conversation*.

What is your *Self/self/SELF*-obsessed story of hierarchy—gods and servants, princes and paupers, celebrities and fans, politicians and people, priests and sinners, CEOs and janitors, police and criminals, judges and judged, heaven and hell—and anarchy?

hierarchy.
How are *You/you/YOU* obsessed with hierarchy—being a star, being a leader, making a difference?

How does that keep your world in the state of *have* and *have not*?

How does that keep *You/you/YOU* distracted from true intimacy and vulnerability?

personal reflections.
Who do *You/you/YOU* place on a pedestal?

How are they your mirror?

How are they used as a weapon against yourself? (e.g., negative self-talk, nonaction)

By placing them higher, how do *You/you/YOU* sabotage your personal power or purpose?

Who do *You/you/YOU* look down on or have pity or sympathy for?

How are they your mirror?

How do *You/you/YOU* use them as a way to feel better about yourself?

envy.
Whom do *You/you/YOU* envy?

Who do *You/you/YOU* think is jealous of *You*?

How does envy drive . . .
- *You/you/YOU*?
- your choices?
- your addictions?
- your shadow nature?

balance.
Where does your life continually ask for balance?

What needs to be embraced for balance to become embodied?

When is enough enough in your . . .
- life?
- career?
- status?
- attainment?

What do *You/you/YOU* have to lose/release to achieve balance in . . .
- mind?
- heart?
- soul?
- life?

politician to servant leader.
How do *You/you/YOU* play the politician?
How do *You/you/YOU* manipulate . . .
- others?

- through conversation?
- your *Self/self/SELF*?

What brings servant leadership out in *You/you/YOU*?

What aspect of Essence do *You/you/YOU* feel and express when in servant leadership?

conversation.
Which *Self/self/SELF* predominantly speaks when engaged in conversation?

Who is the *Self/self/SELF* that predominately perceives?

Who is the *Self/self/SELF* that listens?

Are *You/you/YOU* in intimate, vulnerable, and truthful conversation daily with
- your *Self/self/SELF*?
- others?
- Spirit?

How do you embody servant leadership when in conversation with . . .
- *Self/self/SELF*?
- others?
- Spirit?

> May presence abound for all of life . . .
> where silence rings in truth . . .
> flowing in the spaces between the quietest stillness.
> May presence fill bodies and beings . . .
> where each communes with powerful forces
> that stand quietly among us . . .
> May you meet all people where they are,
> by disrobing your identities and personalities . . .
> removing your masks and masquerades . . .
> and discarding conformity . . .
> to embrace that which has no name,
> no sound,
> no thought,
> no form . . .
> This is . . . *Is*ness.
> Sweetly Dream . . .
> so to create the sweetest of dreams.

...

PETITION FOR DIVINE EQUALITY

What is the shift in consciousness?

**This is my allegiance to Godhood...
my devotion to the Divine Feminine...
my mission for the Divine Masculine...
my presence to Powerful Providence...
This is my fierce love
wrapping itself around everyone and everything,
every moment of every day...
because this is what You deserve
and who Eye/i/I deserve too.**

IN COLLECTIVE PRAYER
FOR KNOWING...
THE TRANSFORMATIONAL STEPS OF RE-CREATING
FOUNDATIONS AND STRUCTURES FOR THE GOOD OF ALL BEINGS

*Dear Infinite Oneness...
Let the strings of longing play within us,
and the gifts we forgot be given back to us.
Bring the awareness of SELF into full view.
Let Eye/i/I sight see only YOU.
Help us cross every ocean of existence
in order to know our true place of listening.
Guide us upon every path,
sustaining us amid every desert
until we see your holy face.
No ocean can hold the joyful tears
we have yet to shed
through knowing complete Oneness of you
embodied in heart, action, and head.
Squeeze from within us
anything that is not truth.
Wring out all that is illusion,
that we receive our divine due.
Pull away any deception we have come to see, know, and believe.
We call unto the Light to bring us home with each deepening breath.
Opening our hearts to all that is divinely conceived.
Carry us through any valleys of death.*

Remove all the masks that still exist.
Take away all coverings of identity and personality that bind.
And dance with us, through all that is.
Hold our hands; guide our steps.
Bring us full spiral,
to Love, Light, and Illumination . . .
Letting that go viral.

It was a free-will choice to incarnate . . .
for learning and lessons
experience, expression, and blessings.
We now know duality,
and polarity;
a full spectrum of emotions too.
May we claim our right to be Divine . . .
in everything we say, think, and do.
Be the sacred presence
that moves within us . . . exudes through us . . . and all around us.
Let us be in service to thy name.
So be it . . .
And so it IS!

0
0 0
0 0 0
1 1 1 1
1 1 1
1 1
1
1
1 1
1 1 1
1 1 1 1
0 0 0
0 0
0

the illusion of identity.

What is the awareness?

Are you someone that knows nothing?
Are you no one that knows something?
Amid the questions is an experience . . .
forgetting and remembering . . .
imagining and manifesting . . .
dreaming and waking . . .
desiring and fantasy . . .
craving and aversion . . .
Life becomes the illusion
of what *You/you/YOU* want to know.
Set me free . . . Set us free . . . Set the world free . . .

The Illusion of Identity	The Awareness	Being/being/BEING
Masked Obsessions	What is the addiction?	Ego/Mind
Our Global Reflection of Wellness	Where is the mirror?	The Collective
The Hole of Pride	What is the dis-ease?	The Shadow
The Key of Innocence	How is personal power activated?	Essence
Homogenized to Genius	How is purpose fulfilled?	Humanity
Cultivating Naturalness	How can peace arise?	The Bridge
Free Thyself	What is the call . . . to action?	The Embodiment

You never had a chance because *you* were born into a body and environments that created a culture of memories, perspectives, and prejudices. It might look like *You* are growing, but *You* are merely follow patterns. With each experience, identity solidifies. Through different age stages, new costumes are worn. You will take on identities from the beginning: daughter, son, sister, brother . . . a tennis player, pianist, gymnast . . . popular girl, the jock, nerd, delinquent . . . college grad, employee, employer . . . wife, husband, mother, father . . . the list goes on. Each identity has its own patterns, behaviors, and stories. All of these garments are put on, and few are discarded. Alongside the image portrayed is viewpoint, language, and agenda. This is learning. In time, *You* will realize that everything *you* learned requires unlearning, if *You* want to be free. Then, all garments must be shed. Until *you* are bare naked, *You* will not know who *YOU* really are.

Identity is a construct. It is who *you* are, the way *you* think about yourself, the way *you* are viewed by the world, and the characteristics that define *you*. Consisting of self-image, self-esteem, and the mental constructs ascribed to these, your identity is a composite of your qualities, beliefs, image, experiences, and expressions. Your identity will build from childhood. This will be the basis for many other roles and personas taken on. Each age stage forms new ways of identification.

Don't get locked in your identity; *You/you/YOU* are so much more than that.

Identity is your image to the world. This is the part of *You/you* that shields the real *YOU* from everyone else. It is the picture everyone else has painted of *You/you* as fixed, but it can morph in an instant if your soul dictates. There also exists a shimmering veil of personality, *dressing* the many light and shadowy parts of *You/you/YOU*. This celebrates, defends, loves, fights, and stands as the face *You* show the world. It knows all of your secrets and insecurities. It gives *You* the ability to be strong and weak, vulnerable and rock solid. The personality is a beautiful stained-glass image of who *You* are; splintered colors of the many facets that *you* posses and can express. Identity is not who *You/you/YOU* are. It is the attachment to what *You/you* have come to believe. It is an *entity* as opposed to true *SELF*. This false *Self/self* is a fabrication of *Mind/mind/MIND*. To see and embrace all of life, *You* must become empty and become free of all attachment.

Identity is the illusion that feeds the addiction of masked obsessions.
Wellness reveals the global reflection of the collective's
viral shadow of pride.
In turning the key of innocence,
you are initiated from homogenized to genius.
Freeing thyself cultivates naturalness as a bridge for embodied humanity.

For a moment, set aside what the ego wants . . . what society would say *You* must be . . . what lives up to your parents' expectations . . . your children's needs . . . and what impresses your friends, coworkers, or boss. The seed of identity requires your attention; this shall yield a more powerful awakening than anything else. *You* were sold an *idea* consisting of the good life and the need to be relevant. *You* created an identity to match that concept.

What began as an exploration and game of life was actually a leap into the field of all possibility. Human beings are division to the *nth* degree. Each separate part held within it what came before, encompassing *what had been created* and *the ability to create*. From the most sacred of places, *You/you/YOU* came. At birth, *YOU* were complete; a trinity of one, the *third I*. As *YOU* grew, the eyes opened, and then *You* were gifted a dual perspective. The *eye/I* took in the surroundings, and then there were three. Division narrowed the focus, moving *YOU* from *You* to *you*—the multidimensional, multifaceted *eye/i/I*.

This is the *i*.

The little *i*'s focus narrowed to an "*i*"dentity and made the most of it. This little *i* could not see it was connected. Every action, reaction, and creation was based on the needs, wants, perspectives, and inner dialogue of the little *i*. But as it got smaller and smaller, the mirrors with which to see itself loomed larger and larger. This *i* became the center of its own world.

In love with its own reflection, it creates unconscious reflections in the global mirror in order to see itself. Every person *You/you/YOU* meet . . . everything *You/you/YOU* experience . . . every place *You/you/YOU* go is speaking back to *You* about *you*. Through the *i*, see your childish wounded *self*.

This is the *eye/I*.

There is a second *I*, an expanded *Self*, but it is not one above *you*. Instead, it is *One/one* that walks with *you*. The *eye/I* projects and looks outward. When the eyes are opened, the brain is connected. It is processing, thinking, judging, and projecting. The *eye/I* has the capacity to see from the ego, persona, and identity *Self*, while also having the ability to access objectivity and wisdom from the higher *SELF*. *You/YOU* are also this *third eye/I*—the higher *SELF* when the two eyes can see as *One/ONE*.

**This is the play . . .
your play . . . my play . . . their play . . . our play.
Tumbling upon the playground of life
until *You* re-member self,
seeing many *Selfs*,
in return to original *SELF*.**

The internal *you* is always having a dialogue with the external world. This partnership— created to know *Self/self/SELF* in a better way—continually guides *You/you/YOU*. Even in chaos or challenge, the world will reflect the *i* . . . *eye/I* . . . and *I*. In meeting multiple reflections within the world, *Love/LOVE* was falling . . . falling . . . and falling in *Love* with itself. Just as Narcissus deeply loved his own reflection, *you/i/we/they* have become enamored with the mirror of the world.

In forgetfulness, the reality of our abundant, expansive, creative *BEING*ness fades into the background. The person, place, or thing becomes something to have, to hold, to court, and to lust after. It is within this dual world that *you/i/we/they* meet the little *i*. This childish one takes *you/me/us/them* by the hand, into the land of mischief, mayhem, and old haunts. The ghosts, goblins, and masks of *your/my/our/their* making create the levels and layers in which we play . . . get lost . . . and are found.

You are energy in motion . . . exploding in a myriad of colors . . . resounding as a range of frequency . . . expanding into the full spectrum of light . . . awakening to the polarities of your bandwidth . . . and coloring with emotional spectrum . . . unfolding into a plethora of play. If *you* want to know the end of something, seek to understand its beginning and all spaces in between.

This is the Third "*I*."

The *third eye/I* bears witness to reality, knowing it is all illusion. The *third eye/I* can change the channel and watch all that exists, remotely viewing from any perspective when detaching the cord of identity. Its antennae are attuned to many stations of the *One/one/ONE*, with the ability to see, hear, and know itself. This has been part and parcel to life's purpose—to incarnate, individuate, initiate, excavate, eradicate, obliterate, and annihilate—so to discover peace and uncover partnership. To recognize smallness in bigness—and the infinite in the finite—is the greatest love affair of all time and timelessness. Higher *SELF* obsession will be your path of transcendence. Become obsessed in *BEING* your Higher *SELF*.

The greater the ego . . . the bigger the identity.

Who could *You/you/YOU* expand into if not attached to who *You* are and what your life looks like? Identities are garments *You* take on and off. Choose at random what color and style *You* wish to present each day. However, to do so, *You* must be willing to loosen your hold on image. Cherish ALL that *You/you/YOU* have known, felt, and experienced, but do not be defined by it. Imagine a planet where you removed complete identification with *I* and saw yourself as every other. Dissolve your identity into the expanse of all that is, and anchor into the fullness of the life. The Source of all things smiles through *You/you/YOU*. Another's smile is the Source smiling upon *You*. Give and receive these blessings; honor the real rather than illusion and delusion. Blessed *being/Being/BEING* . . . Breathe deeply as *You/you/YOU* dissolve identity.

May the identity dissolve
so true *SELF* appears.
May the persona serve
the highest of good,
and shadows rest in peace.
May self-realization be
the common man's intelligence,
and the gift we give
by fully receiving.
Sweetly dream . . .
so to create the sweetest of dreams.

0
0 0
0
1
1 1
1 1 1 1
1 1 1
1
0
0 0
0

MASKED OBSESSIONS

What is the addiction?

There are no closed doors; only closed minds.
What you deeply want wants you.
Only ego, false belief, and doubt can keep it from you.
Pain is not a required course.
No real loss exists; never despair.
Let go of who you think yourself to be . . .
Release all past and all future . . .
An instantaneous, blissful, infinite moment is present
at any point you choose.
Turn your attention within
and see what great power plays there.

You/you/YOU give, serve, tithe, and provide charity. These expressions fit nicely into the image of a productive member of society. Although *You* may huff and puff from exhaustion by the end of the day, *You* are driven to give more, do more, and serve more. The ego's need to be seen as a *good and kind person* grows. The praise, applause, and admiration is a high. This is how masked obsessions grow. The actions appear to be for the greater good, but the underlying energy is manipulative, seething, and filled with insignificance.

You/i/we/they have been taught that charity means to go out into the world: helping, fixing, and saving. It is focused on *doing good* for the purposes of solving the world's problems. *You* use it to solve your problem of *Being* seen as good. As beautiful as the charitable focus appears, it is from a state of codependence; giving to get . . . *self*-value . . . *self*-esteem . . . *self*-worth . . . *self*-assurance.

How would you treat yourself if you knew you were sacred?
How would *You* treat the other if holding them as Divine?
What if nothing was wrong?

Hidden beneath the mask of service is the one who does not feel good enough, feels insignificant, and feels unworthy. This one silently berates, judges, criticizes, and condemns *self*. *You* are trying to feel worthy. *You* need the other person to be in their condition for *You/you/YOU* to have a purpose. Your mission helps *You* feel good about yourself. In being sick, poor, homeless, or oppressed, they serve your mission. That person serves your ego. They help *you* feel better about *You*.

The unconscious vibrational shadow of support, charity, and service emits frustration, rage, guilt, sadness, and pity. These exist within the giver and the receiver. The receiver has unconscious resentment for *being* where they are. The giver holds unconscious resentment of time spent, because in doing so they neglect themselves and their own. The shadow of service and charity keeps the other locked in cycles of pain through a codependent web. Those cords create dominance and oppression out of *your/my/their/our* pride to feel purposeful. *You/you* require them to be poor, sick, broken, enslaved, and held to their circumstance, because it gives your life meaning. Their issue gives *You* purpose. *You* are not their savior. *You* are not their guru.

What are *you/i/we/they* to do with the world
—all of the sick, poor, indigent, warring, and oppressed—
that require service, charity, and support?
Dare I say nothing.
They are actually here in service to you.
Your codependent need for significance keeps them locked and bound.

The people and situations requiring support, charity, and service illustrate where *You* must go within. The poor illustrate your poverty of consciousness, connection, and fulfillment. The abused illustrate your *self*-talk, and how *you* oppress your sacred nature. Everywhere *you* see abuse and prejudice—some blatant, others subtle—are mirrors of energies within *You/you/YOU*. Keep digging, cleaning and clearing where *You/you/YOU* have been deaf, dumb, and blind to *Self/self/SELF*. Social injustices reflect the division that *You* carry within *Mind/mind/MIND*. Throughout all actions and impulses of service, *You* are driven by your brokenness, wounding, psychosis, and past. *You/you/YOU* are in service to the ego when trying to save others. But *You/you/YOU* cannot save them. *You/you/YOU* can only take care of, save, and heal yourself. They can only care for, heal, and save themselves.

If *You* are a healer attached to healing a client or having a certain experience, then *You* have made their issue about *you*. The healer must understand that the individual is healing themselves. The healer is present to enjoy the experience of themselves and the technique they use, without attachment to its effect on another. Speakers who believe that their appearance and message will change others' lives have made those individuals' experiences about themselves. A speaker must simply be excited about their own voice and experience. Their value, worth, or mood should not be dependent on having an audience. Nor should there be an attachment to changing anything. The creative act is the gift.

Before leaping into any endeavor, especially service and charity, it is necessary to become neutral. *You/you/YOU* must discern your outer attachment, which includes the need for something to change. If there is emotional energy behind a cause or person, *You* actually strengthen that which *You* desire to change. If there is internal attachment, the same occurs. Internal attachment relates to your need to appear as a good, positive, or helping person. If support, service, and charity bring *You/you/YOU* a sense of identity or image, *You* will create more people or situations that require your service. Clear any attachments that are present.

Do not be with a person or situation with a focus of saving, fixing, or healing.
Be present to the aspect in *You/you/YOU* that they represent.
Dissolve the emotional trigger;
it is an indicator of where energy must be neutralized within *you*.

Your focus on charitable expression and service must begin closest to *You/you/YOU*; at home. The body. *You.* Come home to your physical form. How can *You* give to yourself in a manner that is profoundly intimate? How might *You* delve deeper than money or a material fix? What would serve your body on every level? What is your body aching for? Where are your aches and pains? Where is your poverty, hunger, and pollution? In what way are *You* prejudiced, abusive, and oppressive to your physical and human nature? Charity must begin with *You/you/YOU.* Knowing yourself as a divine revelation means *Being/BEING* in service to the highest expression of Source expressing in, as, and through *You.* To truly be at home, *You* must be in service to the divine nature within, not the lower nature or brokenness of the world. Service to divine nature means living from a vision of celebration, inspiration, and embodied wholeness inside yourself. It is also holding that clarity of vision for others.

The next closest area would point focus toward your family, household, friends, and community. However, this state of giving requires only presence, listening, vision, and love. Take care not to move into codependent actions of attempting to fix, heal, or save the other person. Advocate for their greatness, not their woundedness. If a stand, statement, or position is to be taken . . . it must be with a neutral stance. Your desire to act should stem from inspired action, not reaction.

Being/BEING in service to your divine aspect does not mean ignoring your brethren. *You* will be with them, but how *You* will be with them must change. Remember, they serve as reflections for taking *You/you/YOU* home to *Self/self/SELF.* People in dire circumstances are humble gods that have come to guide *you/me/us/them* up the stairway of consciousness. In achieving this height, your presence will become pure, loving, and compassionate as an equal. It is in no way *being* above, greater, or separate.

When *you/i/we/they* see a world at war as a world in peace—the broken as whole and the sick as the healed—we hold them capable through the divine power of humanity. We hold them as divine revelations, endowed with the sacred capacity to transcend anything that binds or limits them. There is an understanding in consciousness—*yours/mine/theirs/ours*—that creates what is made manifest. By doing *your/our* work to shift the consciousness held, we have the honor of walking beside the other as a soulmate, in reverence for the service they bring. *You/I/We/They* maintain a high vibrational vision of one another's truth and expression by carrying no energy of attachment. In doing so, the energy surrounding them may dissipate.

Be in the moment.
Explore what is inside.
***You/you/YOU* are a divine revelation.**

Live the life that grounds satisfaction and fulfillment where *You* do what *You/you/YOU* love and love what *YOU* do. It doesn't need to make sense or be approved of by any other. Every light is unique. Give thanks for who *You/you/YOU* are and appreciate the individuality of your example. Your presence is enough. Your Love and your Light ask nothing of you. They are not required for any other either. They exist for *You/you/YOU* to reclaim and remember the full experience of *SELF.* Blessed *being/Being/BEING* . . . Breathe deeply as *You/you/YOU* experience your pure and true face.

May you know every moment in its entirety,
holding these as precious pearls.
May each encounter be given the everlasting glance of graciousness,
and the expanding embrace of empathy.
May you become fully aware of the Now,
knowing it is the golden treasure that awaits.
May you receive it,
and in doing so be the wealthiest in the world.
You are sacred currency;
your breath . . . your life . . . your experience.
May you invest in your Eternal Being
and know the prosperity of peace.
Sweetly Dream . . .
so to create the sweetest of dreams.

. . .

OUR GLOBAL REFLECTION OF WELLNESS

What is the mirror?

From one came many.
The many revealed only One . . .
obsessed with seeing . . . hearing . . . and acknowledging *SELF*.
You are the unending obsession of *SELF*.
Even your selflessness is a quest to be defined as Divine.
Only by claiming this self-obsession
will you find your way home.
It is time to wake up . . .
to all you have done . . .
to that which you have been . . .
for discovery of the unknown.
This road leads to highest *SELF* . . .
a *DIVINE* beautiful, magnificent,
all-powerful, all-knowing, all-seeing, all-being *SELF*.

Some lives are short stories that appear normal. Others are long, dramatic escapades of insanity. Several are epic adventures. All of these have pieces and parts that feel like chapters in a great book. Sections weave together as beautiful beginnings . . . maddening middles . . . and extraordinary endings. If present to the intricacies of your script, *You* can discover an invisible thread within your history. It is hidden amid the fabric of ordinariness. It weaves together different aspects of your life and holds a common theme. Listen for the faint echo of timelessness to resound through life's shadow-scape. Your life enlightens *You* to each moment through ongoing subtle calls from spirit.

The visible and invisible are intertwined. Catch hold of this triple-braided cord of magic, mystery, and miracles that rests within your DNA. The soul has equipped your life with an enduring wellness. The entire span of time is for the care of the soul. There was never anything to evolve from or into. Your only mission is to experience tender, gentle love; that of *Self/self/SELF* love and fulfillment.

> **You have been entwined in a net of illusion . . .**
> **drifting through time and space.**
> **In a great divide, one became two.**
> **Two became many.**
> **Running to opposite ends of creation,**
> **many were separate but not apart.**
> **An explosion of energy in motion.**
> **Seeking the wild abandon of realization.**

The intention for embodying form is to forget, for the purposes of navigating the path to remembrance. This maze through time allows many opportunities to escape, hide, or be distracted from your essence. That perplexity is why the world is where it is. This is not to say that *it's anyone's fault* or that *it is bad*. Instead, it is to realize the power that has been available all along. *You/you/YOU* have held the power of creation in your minds, hearts, and hands. Sustaining that power required a discipline and focus of wellness.

What is within affects the grand scheme of life. Any part of *You/you/YOU* that has been denied, repressed, or dis-eased must have your attention now. Simply put, those areas are feeding the collective issues that hamper our world. *You* are that powerful. Life is continually guiding *You* into greater *Self/self/SELF* discovery. This is not a burdensome path. *You* are not here to be a martyr. Taking on the world's suffering means diving deeply into your own. In doing so, *You* not only model change but also become a healthy cell that affects the cells around it.

> **When *You* acknowledge the vices that became your unconscious rulers,**
> ***You* engage a reawakened sense of nobility.**
> **We each must reclaim our individual kingdoms**
> **and garner crowns of holy virtue to create a new world of sacred aliveness.**

As you heal the depths of your mind, emotions, body, and soul—*You* will realize everything is connected. *You* will see how experiences began as thoughts in consciousness, followed by feelings of the heart. History required certain events and eruptions to illustrate the consciousness being held. Now, *You* have an opportunity to create differently. Any resistance is where *You* must initiate a deep cellular and multidimensional cleanse. All notions of fear, violence, control, lack of safety, and protection require your presence. These lies are calling for care; care of the soul . . . and care of the human being. Life is advocating for your wellness.

Decide who *You/you/YOU* are. *You* are either "the illusion" of your stories, ills, beliefs, and conditioning . . . or willing to move beyond that. The soul journey asks that *You* move beyond fears, brainwashing, and conditioning. Wellness means discarding the trappings of history, culture, lineage, religion, and family. *You* can remember your connection with Source at any moment. Have a direct relationship, instead of a middle man or interpreter. In time, *You* will discover safety and trust beyond anything you have known. *You* will uncover the union with all that is God, and that *You* are the Divine One.

There is a moment beyond story, outside perception, past the past, and forgetting about the future . . . where all goes to *Light/LIGHT.* Explore the immersion that is beyond the *You/you/YOU* that *You* know . . . beyond the "I" that speaks, hears, sees, and thinks.

Beauty existing within the world depends on how you see this world,
how you hold all that occurs,
and whether you are a part of it,
or apart from it.

As a child, *you* were independent . . . adventuring, exploring, and curious. *You/you* did not want help. *You/you* knew yourself as capable, until others began saying, "*Let me help you,*" "*You can't do that,*" "*Let me teach you,*" "*Be careful,*" "*I need to protect you.*" In this way, they implanted the idea of incapability. They placed power over *you*, as the seed of care-taking. As *you* grew into adulthood, *You/you* were taught that "goodness" comes from doing; care-taking people, situations, problems, and causes. The weight of the world increasingly became heavier and heavier. Your neck and shoulders grew tighter and higher.

The "need" to be needed . . . the "need" to make a difference . . . the "need" to be seen as significant is the shadow of incapability that is taken on. There will never be enough service to fill that void. Until *You* see yourself as capable and autonomous, the world will appear heavy, daunting, and in pain. Seeing yourself as capable means *You* must see others that way as well. Then what? Will the world fall into disarray? Who will save the world?

When we release the energy of outcomes and power over others, people are freed to tap into their own power and capability. If *You/YOU* did not have a cause or someone that "needed" *You* . . . who would *You/YOU* be and what would *You/YOU* do? *You* will discover that as you free yourself, *You* free the other. Then, we will not have a world that needs saving.

The voice of Love does not condemn, judge, gossip, or abuse.
But the call for Love does.
The world is calling for Love.

Little by little, throughout life, every negative thought or lie is an act of self betrayal. This is how *You/you/YOU* get hacked. This wounds and weakens your sense of *Self/self/SELF* and inner security. When boundary violations go unrecognized, the outer world will follow suit. The greater the *Self/self/SELF*-betrayal, the more dominant the inflictions of those outside *you*. All of this occurs so that *You* turn inward, set appropriate boundaries, use you voice, and see where *You/you/YOU* went against your *Self/self/SELF*. The world does not do this to punish, shame, or berate *You/you/YOU*. It solicits every possibility for giving *you* back to *You*. The other person or group merely plays a role based on the energetic vibration *You/you/YOU* emit. Their souls *Love* you enough to be this for your awareness to rise.

Self/self/SELF-betrayal begins with small acts, such as lack of self-care or not saying how *You* feel. It is not choosing what your heart wants in order to please another. Self-betrayal is saying no to your dreams, not standing for what is rightfully yours, or walking away even though what *You* walked away from was meant for *You*. The *Mind/mind/MIND* will say *You* are being kind, humble, or better, or that *You* can create what is required. But the child inside feels betrayed . . . treated as if they don't matter . . . and do not feel seen.

No thing lies outside you that does not lie within you.
Any denial of such is how you keep illusion and duality in place.
To think otherwise are delusions of grandeur.

The most difficult task for any human is a consistent practice toward *Self/self/SELF*-care. To put oneself first in life will always be a difficult task. There will be many distractions that pull *You* from *Self/self/SELF*-care. When *You* choose to be present, *You/you/YOU* will find wealth in little things, tender moments, gentle gestures, and sweet nothings. *You* will discover the richness and beauty of solitude and reflection. *You* will consciously make each moment one that responds to the *Self* with care. The love *You* have now is not the love *you* were taught. It will no longer be conditional or codependent. In this way, *You* become an example of inner calm and grounded peace. Give yourself the gift of *You/YOU*.

SELF-CARE	Right Word	Right Thought	Right Action	Right Energy
Physical Self-Care	Affirmations, Positivity	Intention and Commitment	Exercise, Water, Breathing, Food	Grounded
Mental Self-Care	"I believe . . ."	Positive Thinking, Silence	Listen, Speak, Learn, Exercise	Clear
Emotional Self-Care	"I feel . . ."	Compassion, Love, Gentleness	Journal, Express, Feel, Drink Water, Bathe, Emote	Neutral
Energetic Self-Care	"I see . . ."	Tender, Pauses, Kindness	Energy Healing, Meditation, Baths	Clean
Spiritual Self-Care	"I am . . ."	Appreciation, Unconditional Love	Stillness, Prayer, Gratitude, Quiet Nature, Walking	Knowing

The more deeply *You* see your *SELF*, the less *you* need others to see *You/you/YOU*. The deeper *You/you/YOU* venture into unknown spaces of *Self/self/SELF* . . . the greater your experience as witness. *YOU* are all of life, yet identifiable with none of it. The human perspective sees through a small set of eyes. Your higher *SELF* sees through the all-knowing *eye/I* and stands in the gap for your growth, healing, awareness, and expansion. When identity is allowed to dissolve, there is no attachment to be, do, or have anything. This occurs when *You/you/YOU* no longer peer through a single set of eyes. Blessed *being/Being/BEING* . . . Breathe deeply as *You/you/YOU* let this moment be the moment *You* commit to your highest and greatest *SELF*.

May you be the calm in every storm . . .
the peace within chaos, and the light amid darkness.
May you recognize holiness in all things . . . respect the nature of what rises . . . and
acknowledge your power amid the forces that wield.
May you realize all the earth has been asked to carry . . .
how you have dumped waste into her . . . how you have bruised, battered, and cut her . . .
how you have buried your emotions inside her, asked her soil to take your pain,
and given what you have not wanted to ground in.
May you hold her while she rages . . .
while she burns . . . when she becomes flooded with grief . . . in the midst of her opening up.
May you love her . . . give her peace . . . pray with and for her . . . give to her,
and appreciate her with humanity.
We love and hold you Mother Nature . . . Gaia . . . Goddess Earth.
Sweetly Dream . . .
so to create the sweetest of dreams.

. . .

THE HOLE OF PRIDE

What is the disease?

Your need to be right
does not mean that you are.
When you require an audience
to confirm your stance,
the only one you really convince is yourself.
If you keep holding tightly to where you are,
you will lose what you could have had and more.

What appears to be real is an illusion. *You* drank the kool-aid long ago and passed along that sacrament. It passed through many generations and runs through bloodlines. Little do *You* realize that this house of mirrors strengthens shadows, illusions, and false identities. Do not cling so tightly to what *you* know, what *You/you* believe, or who *You* are. Do not be rigid in your rightness or perspective. Your pride is getting the better of *You/you/YOU*. What *You* perceive is distorted. Pride will get *You* high on yourself. It will take *You/you* into many worlds and across varied landscapes. *You/you/YOU* will unknowingly wear many masks, interfere in all types of things, and need to fight for your rightness.

Pride is an inflated sense of *self*, worth, and power. It engenders superiority and entitlement while continuously being focused on *self*-interest, *self*ish ambition, and vanity. This *self*-focus guides every word, thought, and action. Pride affects how *you* see. It distorts reality. *You/you/YOU* will see yourself and others through a lens that is twisted. It even colors your negativity, ugliness, and wrongdoings as beautiful and worthy of applause. When pride does not hear or see what it desires to hear . . . harshness, defensiveness, and fault finding will ensue. Superficiality, false humility, and a desperate need for attention are aspects of pride, eating away at possibilities for love, contentment, and common sense. Pride is spiritual cancer.

Your victimhood is a display of narcissism.

Self/self/SELF-obsession is destroying *you/me/us/them* from the inside out. The inability to see our *Self/self/SELF*-absorption and narcissism is the Achilles' heel of our existence. This insanity is creating the world as we know it. Stories initiated by misguided perceptions have forced misaligned actions upon the outer landscape. History passes down the burden of separation between us. Pain amplifies resentment and entitlement, resulting in increasing degrees of low *Self/self/SELF*-esteem, which is the opposite of humble divine confidence that is *your/my/our/their* inheritance.

What plagues our world most at this time is a lack of empathy, the force of apathy, and a rampant cultivation of entitlement. We must recognize our narcissistic tendencies and the pathology that this mental dysfunction is wreaking. Collective narcissism appears in how we are enamored by reflections of fame, injustice, wealth, fashion, and negativity within the global mirror. Gossip . . . haters . . . war . . . drugs . . . violence . . . sex . . . image . . . and politics are things we love to hate. The addiction to fight, save, fix, or heal ourselves and this world is keeping us from seeing and hearing what is really dying within. Continual outer pursuit and gratification keeps us from addressing the inner conflicts that wage.

How much is enough? How much money? How much power? How much success? How much fame? How much violence? How much corruption, and control?

Narcissistic individuals are deeply wounded and have been since childhood. Often possessing very charming masks, these individuals need to fabricate lies, stories, and images to suit their agendas for dominance, and the bottomless need for *Self/self/SELF*-validation. Narcissists have an inability for *Self/self/SELF*-work. They are pathological in creating fantasy. Everything and everyone are seen through the veil of ownership. These minds will stop at nothing to win or have revenge.

The lessons and gifts for those who get caught within a narcissist's web are ones of autonomy, boundaries, *Self/self/SELF*-care, and *Self/self/SELF*-worth. The narcissist appears for *You* to step into empowerment, to stay true to heart and soul, and for protecting the innocent; especially younger ones to the ability that *You/YOU* can. Narcissists utilize methods of emotional, psychological, financial, and physical abuse. Unfortunately, most people walk past these individuals, turning a blind eye to how they treat others, their acts of corruption, and their ability to gaslight young and old. Sadly, systems and structures fall victim to the narcissist's wiles, unknowingly empowering malintent. The legal system and governmental structures unconsciously reward their ability to manipulate the system. Our world is currently cultivating and harvesting narcissists through neglect, materialism, and gaslighting.

There is nothing to say,
because only the ego needs to hear itself speak.

True change occurs by those who have come before . . . The oppressed can fight for their rights, but only those who have won their own rights have the ability to take a stand for the oppressed. Slavery was not abolished purely by slaves; it was abolished by those who stood with the slaves but were themselves free. When people stand side by side as equals banded together, change is possible. In ridding ourselves of pride, greed, and anger can people begin to see and hear each other again. Living in a culture that puts such an emphasis on achievement, credentials, and results can largely affect how we see others and how we see ourselves. We may be tempted to think that our worth comes from what we do, and so we strive to do more, achieve more, and be better than those around us.

Let your conscience guide you . . .
Let truth rise above the ego's need to belong.

Pride not only appears in day-to-day life experiences; it can also reflect within spirituality and religion. A sense of superiority can appear within those who believe they are more evolved, enlightened, or devout. In this one-upmanship, others are judged for where they are, how they speak, what they think, and how their lives appear. This ultimately limits spiritual awakening. Self-righteousness can appear as dressing or eating in a certain way. Some individuals have an heir of specialness about them on the basis of their qualifications, studies, or honors. It can also appear as competition. For example, criticizing another path or holding every yoga pose the longest are expressions of this. In these cases, the individual is attracting more attention to themselves than to God. This harms the individual more than those around them. The ego is further inflated, while attention is distracted from truth. The individual will become lost inside their illusion of themselves.

Time will tell . . .
Truth always reveals . . .
Life always creates the best circumstances for humility.

When *You/you/YOU* let all ambition fall, all desire disappear, and all need be released, *You* will find yourself witnessing; being aware of all that is, in its range of form and beauty. That is a "peace-full" moment. Your attachment to what was, what is, and what could be is the distraction, angst, and distortion of the truth. Heights . . . success . . . goals . . . dreams . . . visions will never fill the well inside, unless grounded in your roots, their humility, acceptance, and love.

Your main fear is that *You* are invisible. *You/you/YOU* desire to be seen and heard. *You* want life to be meaningful and have meaning. The ego will have you flaunt, flail, yell, and scream toward these ends. Pride loves an audience. However, the illusion of what looks good will have value only if it feels good from the inside out. In time, a realization of truth will arise. *You* will learn that silence speaks louder. *You* will discover that stillness holds greater presence. *You* will find that the celebration of others is the celebration of the *Self*. Humility and compassion reduce pride. Compassion removes judgment of *Self/self/SELF* and others. The combination of humility and compassion will point toward the play of *Self/self/SELF*-realization. Blessed *being/Being/BEING* . . . Breathe deeply as *You/you/YOU* experience your shallow nature.

Open . . . Open . . . Open your mind . . .
Open your heart.
Confront your enemy—in-a-me—and release fear, doubt, and ill.
Release judgment, jealousy, ill will.
Release the fight.
Your enemies are not outside;
they live inside.
Free yourself from the ties that bind.
Sweetly Dream . . .
so to create the sweetest of dreams.

. . .

THE KEY WHOLE OF INNOCENCE

How is personal power activated?

Be open, vulnerable, and defenseless.
Do not control.
Do not react.
Experience the flow of life.
Let things unfold,
waiting for the invitation to be inspired.
Then respond.

You/i/we/they began life innocent, curious, and wide eyed. *You/i/we/they* take on the stories, soak up the energy, and absorb emotions . . . in innocence. *You* keep viewing the world through eyes of innocence. Even now, your sight beholds from a state of innocence. All others interact with *you* from innocence. They also have newfangled lenses of shady influence. Yet, they are innocent.

The person who fights believes in their fight. They innocently believe in what they are fighting for. The one that pushes against you innocently learned to push against life. The one that hates innocently took on hate. Even his hate is innocent because he believes so purely. When individuals believe in something, they do so because of what they were exposed to. Innocence does not change, nor does it leave. Every action, reaction, and impulse comes from that original state of innocence. *You* did what *you* did with what *you* knew. Your parents did what they did with what they knew. Innocence does not need to be reclaimed. This simply must be acknowledged.

You are sacred.
You are pure perfection.
Your life is a sacred text.
Your body is holy ground.
You carry your temple with you.
You are innocent.

You/i/we/they are here to become . . . unbecome, and then, simply be. There is nothing logical, material, or physical about that. Ultimately everything desired—material, emotional, intellectual, scientific, spiritual, or achievement oriented—is purely a search for what cannot be seen. What *You/you/YOU* seek can be felt, experienced, acknowledged, and embraced only through innocence, humility, and aloneness. Your aloneness will teach *You* all about your togetherness. In that aloneness, *You* will discover that *you* have never been alone.

Time spent alone is incredibly valuable. It is the only place that dissolves all your shades of gray. In your aloneness, who *You* were dissolves into who *YOU/you* are. The grand plan is to let go of what *You* know. To touch that horizon, *You* must be with what is in front of *you*. Embrace the experience of aloneness. That is the true place of wholeness. Within *You/you/YOU* lies the potential and presence of an entire universe.

Through innocence, each word commands a reality that unfolds. Each thought becomes a prayer. Innocently, your expression is the breath of God. With that power and presence, all of life is created. The deeper your inhale, the more *You* receive the Divine within. The greater the exhale, the more expansive the Divine can express through *You/you/YOU*. The inhale and exhale of life throughout all experiences is holy communion. What *You* seek outside lives inside *You/you/YOU*, the true grasp of which rests within the pure gaze of your innocence.

Your life is information.
You are always in formation; you are in form, yet formless.
You are every thing and no thing.
You are real, and the play of all illusion.
Your return to Oneness . . . is your innocence.

Defenselessness and vulnerability are reflections of strength. When living from these states of relaxation, *You/YOU* say to the world, *I open my heart to experience. I am willing to know more of you, more of me, and more of what rests between us.* This viewpoint embraces life as an adventure, regardless of whether *You* walk blindly through the dark or immerse within bright experiences of Light. Wonder, curiosity, and delight bring forward this energy of childlike resonance. There is no more powerful gift than your Divine innocence. Until *You/you/YOU* are aware of this truth . . . *You* are not really alive.

The *eye/i/I* is the most important part of *You/you/YOU*. It sees . . . visions . . . knows . . . interprets . . . receives . . . and creates. The more strongly *you* hold on to what is false, the less likely truth will filter through. The real *YOU* is amid the layers that have built up around *You*. The truth is simple. It has no words. It takes no space, nor any time. It presents

the illusion of identity. 157

no boundaries. Be willing not only to dream the new dream, but also to see, be, and embody it without past filters. Let your life epitomize your dream. Although life can be intense—and at other times monotonous—it is a wild and organic endeavor in which to discover how . . . *You/you/YOU* are everything.

Freedom can exist internally regardless of what appears externally. This requires mental strength, emotional intelligence, and a consciousness of neutrality around everything and everyone. The magic talisman is your original innocence. You are *Self/self/SELF*-equipped. In fact, *You/you/YOU* are a universe unto yourself. Allow the purity of *Being/being/BEING* to bring forth the *Knowing/knowing/KNOWING* of innocence.

> **Within the heart lies the poet,**
> **the dreamer, and the dancer.**
> **Within the mind lies the controller,**
> **the critic, and the judge.**
> **The latter bows down to time . . .**
> **The other ascends with timelessness.**

Go to the place of softness that is vulnerable and deep. Within the high heart, see the vast choices of Spirit. From that vantage point, view all perspectives. Upon the bridge where love and fear coexist, walk in the space between these partners and bedfellows. They are fellow actors and conspirators, although they appear as strangers and enemies. Innocently, see all of life's intricate perfection by lightly holding the nuances of seeming imperfection. Every step *You/you/YOU* have taken was in innocence. Each choice made was of a simple mind playfully taking in an adventure. Innocence is how *You/you/YOU* began. It is how *you* accrued beliefs, experiences, woundings, and identity. Only through innocence can *You* return to Source. See each new day through fresh eyes.

Drop your ideas, stories, beliefs, and perspectives. Let go of your resentments, grievances, and hurts. Free all people from your mind and heart, and *You/you/YOU* free yourself. There is nothing to forgive. There is no one to forgive. Every person began as innocently as *you* did. They truly believed in what they were doing and saying, on the basis of what their innocent mind was told. Each one believed and became what they believed by way of innocence. Your innocence is the salve that brings insight, sensation, and wonder.

> **Love like a child . . . Laugh like a baby . . . Play in wonder like a toddler . . .**
> **Dream like a youngster. Create through imagination . . .**
> **Embrace your innocence.**

Innocence is not lack of worldly wisdom but the presence of spiritual actuality. You are not innocent because you are a blank canvas, but because you bear a divine imprint. Innocence arouses the softest, gentlest, most-tender emotions in the heart of the onlooker. It provokes the Higher Self to force its way up through the rubble of negativity, despair, and cynicism. Innocence means being totally in the moment. It means no judgment of oneself and of others.

Your innocence is a state of power and purity, free from judgment. It engages heart intelligence. Purity is the basis of innocence. There is no manipulation, no personal agenda, no need to prove anything. There are no expectations, so there can be no disappointments. Naivete is not innocence. Innocence is purity; close to godliness. Spiritual maturity is an ally of innocence.

Be curious. Befriend as children do. Judge nothing . . . Embody the openness, willingness, and fearlessness of the child. Children live in the moment. They stay committed to their heart's desire, fully immersed in their play. They have no agendas, and no need to impress. They do not judge whom they play with—what they play with—or for how long. They *believe* in their play. The innocent do not compare. They embrace everything—openly and willingly. The key to all embarking on anything new—and everything old—is innocence. Innocence is at its peak when we know that love, security, and acceptance is unconditional. When we know we will never be rejected for committing mistakes and making errors. When we have no doubts about the abundance of everything we need. Blessed *being/Being/BEING* . . . Breathe deeply as *You/you/YOU* see life through your purity and innocence.

> **May purity be a halo**
> **around your head . . .**
> **and beauty become**
> **the way you live . . .**
> **May you wear inner authority**
> **as your crowning glory . . .**
> **and wear a cape of coeur-age**
> **on your back . . .**
> **May your shoulders stand strong**
> **in personal power . . .**
> **and your body be filled**
> **with peace.**
> **Sweetly Dream . . .**
> **so to create the sweetest of dreams.**

. . .

HOMOGENIZED TO GENIUS

How does purpose unfold?

No need to keep looking for the Light.
Honor the Essence that lies inside.
Acknowledge the Spirit that resides.
It IS . . .
Time to stop . . .
Be Still . . . and Know . . .
You are genius . . .
in a bottle.
Your wish
is your command.

Society is designed to make us all the same. Our systems and structures create socialization that matriculates children into specific routes where sameness becomes celebrated and awarded. However, it is not blatantly clear that this is occurring. The ways in which *You/you/YOU* are boxed in begins early on: preschool, school, college, marriage, clubs, cliques, religion, political affiliation, etc. . . . *You* are homogenized by way of your conditioning. We all are.

You/i/we/they live based on who we believe we are—who others told us we are—and who society makes us believe we need to be, in order to be loved and accepted. And yet, a majority of people in the world feel like they do not fit in—or will never get it right—despite the fact they are homogenized. Ironically, even with homogenization, *You* won't fit in or get it right. *You/you/YOU* are not designed to. *You* will feel that uniqueness, even if completely unaware of what it is. That feeling is a warning sign that *You/you* are living off-compass. If *You* really stopped, *You* might do things a little differently . . . well actually, a lot differently. *You* might realize that *You/YOU* do not want the life *You* currently have, because it is not fulfilling. That is a wonderful point to arrive at. Stop doing what *You* are doing. A pause is a good way to uncover what *You* really want.

The voices of trends, styles, sameness . . .
and even oneness can create layers of conformity.
In consciously attempting to be unique,
it becomes easy to replicate
the manifest thought forms of mass consciousness.

As *you* walk back through your illusions, do so with reverence. *You* were innocent when they were created; your walk back is a return to innocence . . . and more specifically a return to Essence. Embrace . . . Allow . . . Embody. There is a moment that arises where *you* know everything must change. *You* don't want what *you* have always had. *You* cannot be the person *you* have been.

You will be ready to let all that go. Sometimes it is because the pain hurts bad enough. Other times, numbness feels like a slow death. And then, *You* may just realize that *I deserve better. I know better*. That moment is the moment *You* question everything. With that, the experience of deconditioning begins. *You/you* begin the path toward freedom … authenticity … and genius. Enlightenment comes the moment *You/you* stop … really stop. This means *You/you/YOU* stop doing what *You* have been doing. Stop being who *You* have been. Stop reacting—or responding, for that matter—in ways that have become your patterns. *You/you/YOU* just stop.

**To rise beyond the need to fit in . . . to be like or liked . . . feeling the same or sameness . . .
is how the inner ember of light is fanned into a brilliant blazing fire.**

You/I/we/they can continue running, moving, and being busy. We can keep going and become tired out. We can be seekers, milling about. *You/i/we/they* are the human race, after all. Is there a finish line? How did we begin running in the first place? We live in a world that dangles the carrots of purpose, celebrity, and attainment. Your true soul work exists inside. *You* are compelled in a certain way, if you have not pushed it aside or become deafened to your inner wildfire. *You* have tamed yourself, kept dreams caged and feelings restrained, and clipped your wings. What will it take for *You/you/YOU* to be released from your shackles and chains?

**There is no one here but *You* . . .
and *You* are everyone else too.**

In choosing a path, don't judge it, or anyone else's. *You* must make your own way. Celebrate your uniqueness. *You* have a specific path of genius, unlike any other. Everything common about your life is conditioning. The rest is uniquely *You/you/YOU*. No other can fulfill that piece. Be nothing. Embrace everything. Be new with each experience and moment. In the nothingness is everything! Be so intoxicated that *You* cannot find the form any longer. In the invisible spaces of your mind, heart, energy, and body lies a vast untapped unknown. This cannot be accessed by what *you* know. Genius comes through what feels natural to *You/you/YOU*. It is so natural that *You* have been unaware of it. It feels easy and flows without effort, although it may require study, devotion, and time. It is something that makes you happy *You* move into timelessness.

As *you/i/we/they* move from homogenized beings into the celebration of individuality and genius, *we* complete the divine puzzle and awaken a new world experience of aliveness. Engage with all that swirls inside *You/you/YOU*. *You* are a multidimensional *Being/being/BEING*, so change will integrate in a multifaceted manner. Open to your higher resonance and illuminate the countenance of spirit. *Now* is the moment of return to *Knowing/KNOWING* … which is beyond time, space, and form. Touch bottom; grab hold of your fragmented parts. *You/you/YOU* are the art form born of cosmic alchemy. Blessed *being/Being/BEING* … Breathe deeply as *You/you/YOU* transform from homogeny to genie.

**May all beings know their power . . .
in clearing consciousness
for new skies to dawn . . .**

May the vision of sunlight, hot and blazing,
radiate through each one
to clear the sleep from our eyes . . .
May *You/you/YOU* imagine the grass, the trees, and the flowers . . .
May we know children excitedly learning,
joyfully inspired, and happily playing . . .
May we see couples holding hands in outdoor cafes,
lovers kissing in the park,
and families present with one another . . .
Blessed Be . . .
That every dark night hold
Sweet dreams . . .
so to create the sweetest of dreams.

. . .

CULTIVATING NATURALNESS

How can peace arise?

Life gives *You/you/YOU* the chance to play,
in any direction and in any way.
You can have what *you* want.
Choose what is good for *YOU*.

What is natural within *You/you/YOU* seeks to rise. What is false will always reveal first, so that it may be discarded. Emotional transparency is the real gift of intimate connection. Masks keep *YOU* from your *Self/self/SELF*, and the world. Remove the masks; witness the beauty that reveals so that *You* can be truly comfortable in your skin.

Naturalness of *Being/being/BEING* dampens and depletes with age when moving away from the pure state of celebration. This begins in your younger years. It is first evident through the constriction of your body. It also appears in the shortening of your breath. Suppression of emotional, physical, sexual, and creative energies creates inner climate change, which builds an expanse of energetically correlating experiences. The greatest resource—your individual storehouse of energy known as prenatal ping—depletes as *You/you/YOU* expend energy in unhealthful ways. Life force is your natural resource. It is sustained, empowered, and increased through your breath, inner fulfillment, joy, and love. It is energized through expressions of creativity and nurturing beauty in life.

**If it is not your normal behavior,
perhaps it is your natural behavior.**

As *You/you/YOU* transition from being a *self*-focused and *self*-absorbed accumulator of worldly illusion into an intimate, globally connected, *Self/self/SELF*-actualized presence who stewards natural *BEING*, life will feel uncertain. An identity—or many identities—will be disintegrating. The bridge of disintegration is more than a *self*-obsessed personal growth fling. It also goes beyond the seduction of a healing crisis. Those efforts—albeit supportive for centering and growth—relate to survival. In naturalness, things are discarded in order to experience aliveness. What is happening here—should *You/you/YOU* fully receive it—is the shedding of skins that have become too small, too tight, and too limiting. This endeavor is one of remembering that *You/you/YOU* are more than form. Your constricting veils of identity keep *You/you/YOU* from experiencing the fullness of your Essence. With each identity leaving, *You/you/YOU* will experience more of your natural essence. The new is not yet formed. But trust that it is on its way.

You/you/YOU **are chosen . . . gently held . . . and created for something.**
You/you/YOU **are life, in its magnificence;**
a divine blueprint never to be replicated or repeated.

Heaven met earth when *You/you/YOU* were born. *Being* initiated blessings for deepening truth, growth, energy, and wisdom. *You* are experiencing—and BEING witness—to an epic saga of life, love, and transformation. Through time, your *Being/being/BEING* is carved and chiseled . . . shaped and honed . . . polished and shined. In becoming differentiated, You did not lose anything. Although most of *YOU* is covered up, inherent hidden gifts are available when *You/you/YOU* desire to express them. In reclaiming wholeness, *You* reduce all of your identities down to one. The final step into naturalness requires that *You* sink into your true essential nature.

Naturalness emerges by realigning to the rhythm of . . . your soul melody . . . the global song . . . celestial harmony . . . universal symphony . . . and the sound of silence. Although these seem etheric, they can ground into the physical realm. Naturalness is found with beauty. It is the ability of holding everything as a state of wellness from the mind, heart, and eyes of innocence.

Until then, *You/you/YOU* travel the scenic route, which encompasses an adventure through many landscapes and immense topography. In this hilly wonderland, *You* will meet your pride and judgment. This walk can be long or short. It might be arduous. But do not worry—it is a virtual reality. *You/you/YOU* are eternal. No matter where *you* go, how *You* get there, or the distance *You/you* travel . . . *You/you/YOU* will eventually discover that *there is no place like home*.

Rid yourself of lists and plans. Do away with *to-dos* and agendas. Remove your timepieces and alarms. These are not conducive to present-moment living. These things do not allow the organic rising of natural genius. They do not make space for natural living, or for the relaxation required to unite with universal power. These distractions and delusions keep *You/you* living in the future and, when not fulfilled, in the regret of the past.

When thoughts cease, peace comes.
When emotions stop, feelings start.
When doing ends, being begins.
Naturalness *IS*.

You are not here to dream, *You/you/YOU* are the dream. Open to your intelligence. Share your heart and voice. Be wrapped within your own essence . . . Listen for the still, small voice that whispers of passionate celebration. Ecstatically dance in the expanse of your emanation. Let your spirit fly. Lift your feet off the ground, raise your mind to the sky, and spread the wings of your heart. In doing so, the portal that appears is that of loving and being loved. It first shall inhabit your selves/cells, injecting Love into every place of disease, and eventually enveloping the whole body with the organic expression of nature. Cultivate sweetness in your heart. Nurture it. Be devoted to it. Let the flowering of conscious awareness and sacred activism be the nectar of inspiration in your life.

Live each day in the moment, organically and naturally. Be life unfolding as a flower opening. Flowers do not push themselves to flower, reach a certain height . . . or have a particular number of leaves. Flowers are in full receiving, and in *BEING*. They bud and blossom in the perfect moment. Nature is wise and nurturing. *You/you/YOU* are that when in remembrance. When willing to go into the places where there is no path, the ultimate destinations open up.

You/you/YOU are the elements. This is your nature. Until *you* claim the truth of your precious and sacred nature, *You* cannot treasure the jewel that *You/you/YOU* are. Go beyond the illusions. The real *YOU* is amid the layers that have built up around *You/you.* Rid yourself of all that is unnatural. Relax. Relax. Relax. Be natural. Wild. Organic. Beautiful. Every creation—from a grain of sand to your next-door neighbor—is embedded with the simplicity of Essence and the complexity of many universes. All of life thrives by doing nothing—except *You/you/YOU*. Surrender to your nature and dissolve into the real *You/you/YOU*. Blessed *being/Being/BEING* . . . Breathe deeply as *You/you/YOU* experience naturalness.

May the knowing of truth birth within each breath . . .
the Being of wisdom walk the way . . .
and living as Love resound within each heartbeat . . .
May humans rise to new heights
where hearts and minds of great good prevail . . .
May the earth hear only the laughter of creation
each and every day . . .
Sweetly dream . . .
so to create the sweetest of dreams.

. . .

FREE THYSELF

What is the asking?

Remember who *You/you/YOU* are . . .
Life is a dream . . .
A wink of a Divine eye . . . a flurry of human sleep . . .
Life is a story . . .
A creation for humanity's glory . . .
Remember why *You/you/YOU* came . . .
for such an adventure . . .
A leap in time . . . a making of the human mind . . .
Remember . . .
You/you/YOU created all of it.

AFFIRMATION—CONTEMPLATION—INSPIRATION

**I AM capable of awakening to where I hold escapism and narcissism.
I now transcend all places where I am in *Self/self/SELF*-delusion.**

Contemplate and journal these inquiries until inspired to take action.

Be still; see what rises as *oneness* versus *separation*.
You have the answer for achieving aliveness . . . go within.

**The degree to which you are *Being/being/BEING*
is the degree to which *You/you/YOU*
shall cultivate inner and outer *Naturalness*.**

What self-obsessed stories, beliefs, behaviors, woundings, insecurities, judgments, ambitions, and drives keep you tied, victimized, and bound?

identity.
What are the identities *You/you/YOU* claim?

How do the stories *You/you/YOU* keep determine your perceptions and future actions?

Who would *You/you/YOU* be if *You* were not *you*?

masked obsessions.
What identity and personality masks keep *You/you/YOU* limited, locked, or confined?
What beliefs and masks affect your appearance, demeanor, and actions?

How does your attachment to identity and personas affect your wellness . . .
- physically?
- mentally?
- emotionally?
- spiritually?

pride.
Pride loves an audience; who is your audience?

What story are *You/you/YOU* desperately holding up?

Which would *You/you* choose, happiness or success?

What would that choice look and feel like to *You/you/YOU*?

innocence.
Do *You/you/YOU* believe *you* are innocent?

What are *You/you/YOU* feeling . . .
- guilty of?
- ashamed of?

Do *You* view others from the same *eyes/i/Is* as yourself?

homogenized to genius.
How has society homogenized *You/you/YOU*?
How have *You* passed this homogenization on?

What gifts have *You/you/YOU* forsaken through your homogenization?

What is your genius?

How must *You/you/YOU* engage with *Self/self/SELF* differently to speak from your genius?

How must *You/you/YOU* engage differently to experience and express your genius?

conversation.
How would *SELF/BEING* engage in conversation?

How is that different from the way identity engages?

Do *You/you/YOU* engage vulnerably and intimately with others?

free thyself.
Are *You/you/YOU* ready, willing, and able to set yourself free?

What story or belief must *You/you/YOU* release at this time?

Whom do *you* have to set free, in order to free yourself?

What identities must be dissolved in order to be free?

**May you fully taste the universe . . .
and be the embodied sanctuary of a star seed.
May you explore vast lands . . .
and know your holy land.
May you seek to know all that I AM . . .
May you deepen your engagement of inner truth.
Sweetly dream . . .
so to create the sweetest of dreams.**

. . .

PETITION FOR ONENESS

What is the shift in consciousness?

**When we become nothing
amid each other,
everything is possible.
We find union.
Therein is peace.**

IN COLLECTIVE PRAYER FOR FREEING . . .
GLOBAL POPULATIONS TO
BALANCED AND COOPERATIVE EXPRESSIONS OF
INTERDEPENDENCE

*Dearest Infinite Oneness . . .
Mother, Father . . . Essence Divine
We are your little children.
With many names and faces,
varied religions, and colorful races,
playing in the experiences and expressions
of seemingly free will and your graces.
We have known every emotion
and ventured through trails of thought.
We are within each ray of golden light
even through the havoc we have wrought.*

A form, a body, a Being/being/BEING . . .
created from your starry night.
We walk with an invitation to stillness and presence,
under the infinite protection of your overarching Eye.
Almighty Mother . . . Benevolent Father . . . Holy Essence,
We hold sacred all life,
this grand gift and birthright,
dreaming a dream,
each day and night becoming the embodied hue man,
slowly realizing, We are One soul in flight.
To feel every moment,
To know every breath,
To taste every flavor,
To partake of every step.
Gifted time in a place that is timeless . . .
and the boundless ability to experience form and space.
One song . . . one melody . . . one voice . . . one world,
swaying in ecstatic rhapsody
That comes to know true LOVE.

Let us be the reflection of Divine Wellness.
Clinging to no thing . . .
being one with every thing . . .
Awakening to naturalness,
seeing all of the world
with the eyes of innocence.
May there no longer be id,
but only what IS.
So be it . . .
And so it IS!

```
     0
    0 0
   0 0 0
  1 1 1 1
   1 1 1
    1 1
     1
     1
    1 1
   1 1 1
  1 1 1 1
   0 0 0
    0 0
     0
```

BEING

the illusion of evolution.

What is the awareness?

Are we *there* yet?
If you knew where you were going,
you might run the other direction.
Are we *there* yet?
If you truly understood where it was leading,
your arms would spread as the wings of a phoenix . . .
ready and willing to burn to ash!
Are we *there* yet?
Where are you going? Will you ever get there?
Are we *there* yet?

The Illusion of Evolution	The Awareness	Being/being/BEING
Spiritual Obsessions	What is the addiction?	Ego/Mind
Our Global Reflection of Security	Where is the mirror?	The Collective
The Hole of Gluttony	What is the dis-ease?	The Shadow
The Key of Fulfillment	How is personal power activated?	Essence
Visionary to Mystic	How is purpose fulfilled?	Humanity
Cultivating Presence	How can peace arise?	The Bridge
Accept Thyself	What is the asking?	The Embodiment

Evolution and awakening are illusions that keep *You* seeking, striving, and sleeping. This collective mask encompasses your insatiable hunger and need for endless supply. The need to escape the emptiness that quietly plagues *You* is built upon the loss of dreams, and mounting feelings of hopelessness. The endless search for advancement, technique, and technology—whether physical, biological, spiritual, scientific, or through artificial intelligence—is an illusory way of avoiding *Self/self/SELF*. Gluttony has been born out of your desire for security.

You are not here to upgrade the person, but to transcend your thoughts of personhood.

Bamboozled into the concept of evolution, *you/i/we/they* chase our tails, while mindlessly consuming the latest information, gadget, method, or belief system. In reaching for an illusory destination, *you/i/we/they* continually look back in order to move forward. However, that is not evolution; it is death. This is why life never seems to fully work, nor do *You* find completion. It is why history repeats itself. *You/i/we/they* keep doing the same things in different ways. We just call them something else. Although it appears as if advancement occurs, *you/i/we/they* are on a treadmill going nowhere. If anything, we are devolving. Becoming more animal than human, *you/i/we/they* are decreasing in our ability to empathize, connect, or create the inner security that is longed for.

Visionary thinking can provide some paths to follow, but the way of the mystic will bring presence to the foundations that reflect the breakdown. At the core of collective humanity is an inability to feel safe. There exists a fracture within your grounding that stems from religions and spiritual teachings being consumed and regurgitated, rather than digested and integrated. Such spiritual bulimia never fully absorbs; thus *you/i/we/they* are never completely satisfied or fulfilled. By rapidly moving on to the next tool, technique, process, or leap . . . nothing remains sacred. Deepened presence to what truly feeds *You/you/YOU* on every level is the only way to achieve a nourishing, satisfying feeling of safety, security, and completion.

Evolution is the illusion that feeds the addiction of spiritual obsessions.
Security reveals the global reflection of the collective's
viral shadow of gluttony.
In turning the key of fulfillment, you are initiated from visionary to mystic.
Accepting thyself cultivates appreciation as a bridge for embodied humanity.

There is nothing to evolve *from* or *into*. Every frequency and state already lives inside *You/you/YOU*. Whatever *You/you/YOU* desire to experience requires only presence to that realm within. Every expression and dimension exists within *You/you/YOU* in this very moment and always has. To know to whom and where *You/you/YOU* are anchored requires clear and active presence. Awareness of your current dimension opens the opportunity for a different expression and experience. It does not matter how shadowed or animal your current state is, immerse in that energetic expression. Allow your life to lead *you*. If your experience holds drama, the lens *being* peered through reflects *you*. When experience elicits Love and joy, the lens *Being* sees through is *You/YOU*. The holy and sacred appears when *YOU* do. Consciousness comes in many shades of *You/you/YOU*. Life knows how to utilize your colorful range.

Positive thinking runs the risk of being only skin deep for many individuals. What is buried beneath can be anything but positive. In running toward one distraction or another, a sea of unconscious thoughts and feelings rage beneath the surface. Those underlying issues never quite allow what *You* truly desire to manifest. Anyone can talk the talk; are they walking the walk? Do their actions reflect their words? If things do not line up, *You/you/YOU* are not lined up. This has nothing to do with materialism or if life looks like a train wreck. Alignment is indicted by *how* your circumstances, interactions, and relationships are navigated.

**Let go of the idea that you are here to evolve
or help anyone else do the same.**

Through the concept of evolution, *you* move further into the illusion of time—allowing history to solidify. Believing *You* need to evolve anchors the belief that *you* are not enough ... not good enough ... not smart enough ... not ... not ... not. Do not seek a visionary future; be in relationship to the mystical present. *You* are not awakening to something, and there is nothing to awaken from. Life just *IS* ... what it *IS*. You simply are ... All that *IS*. To fulfill *Being/BEING* in a true state of presence—unconditionally and purely—give up the evolutionary impulse that has controlled *You/you/YOU*. This belief shifted *You* out of *Knowing/knowing/KNOWING* and *Being/being/BEING* into doing and doing and doing. The world asks *You/you/YOU* to *accept thyself* ... through the lens of Divine creative capacity. Blessed *being/Being/BEING* ... Breathe deeply as *You/you/YOU* let go of the belief you will awaken or are here to evolve.

**Do not seek to evolve; instead, become more aware.
There is nothing outside you that remotely compares to what is within you.**

Originally, *you/i/we/they* came from that which was absorbed with knowing itself. This world and everything in it came into *Being/being/BEING* through an obsession ... a *DIVINE SELF*-obsession. Creation wanted to see the image and likeness of itself. Life is a *SPIRIT*ual obsession. Imagine that *BEING* that desired to see its own face in eight billion humans, in addition to every plant, animal, and energy that exists. In an ecstatic obsession of reflections, the expansive spectrum from *self* ... to *Self* ... to *SELF* ... is the experience and expression of the mess, messenger, and message as one holy instant. *HOLY SELF*-absorption!

Let go of waking up; there is nothing to awaken from or into. This is not an experience of ascending toward some alternate reality beyond where *You/you/YOU* are, nor will galactic alien beings lift *You* off the planet. Let go of your fantasy of a blissed-out moment on a meditation chair where *You* are filled with the knowledge of the universe through an apparition. There is no awakening to anything outside. There is only awareness of your ongoing *Self/self*-obsession—your story, fantasy, wounding, emotions, and ancestry—and the absorption or dissolving of that. By doing so, *You* will become aware of something much larger than *Self/self*, its obsessions, or its perceptions. Deep insights do not come from claiming how awake or conscious *You* are, but in the willingness to face how asleep, busy, unconscious, and *Self/self/SELF*-absorbed *You* have been. *You/i/we/they* were taught to look from a single viewpoint; a very small one. Blessed *being/Being/BEING* ... Breathe deeply as *You/you/YOU* realize that awakening is an illusion.

**May kindness seep from your pores ...
and a smile shine from your eyes.
May love be the scent of your aura ...
and compassion glisten from your skin.
May tenderness drip from your fingers ...
and gentleness dangle from your ankles.**

Sweetly dream . . .
so to create the sweetest of dreams.

0

0 0

0

1

1 1

1 1 1 1

. . .

SPIRITUAL OBSESSIONS

What is the addiction?

**May you realize there is only space between us . . .
and it is named *time*.
When *you* are there . . . and then,
you cannot be *here and now*.
When *you* have gone past . . .
or keep running forward . . .
you do not see I Am here . . .
always in sight.**

You have been convinced to live out the hero's journey. This *self*-obsession is where *you* conjure endless whos, whats, whys, and wherefores to make sense of senseless things. While leaning this way and that, *You* walk a tightrope, teetering to find balance. These leanings and swings—opening and distancing from the center of awareness—are simply spaces for deeper alignment, connection, and leadership to emerge. *You/you* came to experience *YOU*. Allow this mystery of life. Control is the antithesis. Experience will keep meeting *You/you/YOU* with mystery. Life shall draw *You* in, willingly or unwillingly.

You/you/YOU must anchor residency within every cell of your *Being/being/BEING*—knowing what it knows, and feeling what it feels. Higher intelligence lives here. There is a *YOU* that needs nothing, wants nothing, seeks no thing, has no agenda, requires no ambition, holds no angst, has no craving, and claims no aversion. This *You/you/YOU* is whole and complete. This aspect clearly sees how the ego plays. Awakening and growth are not necessary; a bold, clear look at *Self/self/SELF* is.

Presence provides access to the stairway of vibrational frequencies—from the least conscious to the most to unified presence. These dimensional levels and corresponding layers do not require analysis or processing. They are not hierarchical, nor are they stepping-stones. These simply exist in dormancy or aliveness. *You* are a multidimensional *Being/being/BEING*.

**Life has a plan whether you have one or not;
it will align you to its design,
not necessarily yours.**

Judgment day will occur many times in your life. It began early on. One small judgment after another was made. *You/you* judge your *Self/self/SELF* and judge others, altering the afterlife with skewed perspectives. The buildup of shame and guilt—stemming from giving and receiving judgment by *Self/self/SELF* and others—becomes the basis for low self-esteem, lack of confidence, and lackluster experience. The sense of rejection that arises out of judging and being judged also compounds. These layers create reasons for searching, obsessing, and hiding. These false ideas are why *You/you/YOU* believe *You* are broken. Misdirection will have *You/you/YOU* seeking direction from others. Those that seem further along, smarter, more advanced, or talented will become the weapons *You/you/YOU* use against yourself. Judgment is contagious. It feels like power, although it is false power. Judgment is also a way of distraction from true power. It engenders other shadow behaviors such as gossip, shaming, blaming, and jealousy.

You/you/YOU will run after many teachers, take a gazillion workshops, recite mantras, and create vision boards to avoid your *self*. These things will be done in the name of evolution. They can become ways *You* stay in the obsession of judging and rejecting the *self*. Spiritual obsessions arise out of a desire to be good enough. When spirituality, personal growth, or religion are used as a way to fix *You/you/YOU*, they are of a codependent nature. This codependence will have *You* become an energy vampire, or the source of energy for another. However, if spirituality and personal growth are utilized to celebrate yourself, empower gifts, or experience expansion from a place of grounded fullness . . . *You* act as an independent fountain of energy. Anything done in such a manner carries no residue of judgment or *suckiness*. It creates *Love* and joy.

A breaking down, crisis, illness, and extreme exhaustion are when *You* will stop. In those moments, life will no longer be about evolution. *You/you/YOU* will deepen into stillness and prayer. Life will have mandated a pause for *You* to feel, rest, and realign. This time will have *You/you* turn inward toward *Love*. This opens a new path to *self*-love. As *You* learn to accept and love your *Self/self* again, judgments will be washed off your body, mind, and spirit. In becoming clean, *You/you/YOU* will resist casting judgment upon others.

With every opinion and judgment, a sentence is cast; first upon the other, and then upon the *Self*. Even if merely cast in thought, it is a stone cast. *You/i/we/they* must discontinue *being* critical and judgmental and discounting others. There must be intent to witness through the lens of unconditional love, seeing from every set of eyes existing within experience—those known and unknown, near and far. View in the same manner the Divine sees through the world.

**It doesn't matter whom you love;
it matters how you love.**

The Divine has eight billion sets of eyes by which to see and know itself. *You* have become fixated on the limited perspective of two eyes, experiencing the pain and pleasure of that ego. Imagine accessing your God-given ability to remote-view. Consider not only seeing from eight billion sets of eyes, but also feeling each person's emotions, perspectives, and experiences.

With your special soul periscope, imagine looking through the lens of a family member—child, parent, sibling, spouse—and living their experience. Anchor into their body. See and feel how they *Love* . . . how they hurt . . . when they rage . . . their experience of jealousy . . . and a moment of intense grief. Now, move the periscope to the lens of a leader *You* admire. Anchor deeply into their mindset, heart, and form. See, feel, and experience how they create when in their power . . . when inspired . . . a moment of pure anxiety . . . and a period of hopelessness.

Once again, go through the periscope of eight billion eyes, seeing them blinking and moving. This time, choose a perspective across the world. Look through a pair of eyes that belongs to a soldier fighting in Afghanistan . . . a Muslim woman in prayer . . . a refugee child sitting outside a tent in Syria . . . a homeless untouchable on the streets of Mumbai. Move through the feelings and experiences they each have, fully becoming the sacred presence within them. How does each see and experience the world? How did their perspective originate? How does it feel to be them? How do they hurt, rage, fear, and envy? How do they connect, love, and experience joy?

Imagine moving your focus to a pair of eyes belonging to a man falsely imprisoned of a crime. Consider that he has a family he has not seen in fifteen years. He is sitting in his cell, looking out from behind bars. Imagine feeling a moment when he is happy . . . a moment of fear . . . a time of sadness, missing, and loss. Experience his strength . . . his peace . . . his resolve . . . and his faith and perseverance despite his circumstances. Tap into his hope . . . and his hopelessness.

Finally, allow all of the faces *You* have seen to morph into your face. They are all *You*. This is oneness; the compassionate presence of knowing the other as the *Self*. The only spirituality required is your willingness to be present. Nothing needs to be shifted, healed, or even prayed for in that moment. You do not need to get on a plane, or get a passport. The simple act of *Being/BEING* truly present with unconditional love is enough. Anything else is a spiritual obsession, grounded in the small *self* and its story of inadequacy, weakness, lack, and imperfection, or the need to be seen as relevant, significant, or purposeful.

We are all pieces and parts of the problem . . .
and even more so, the solution.

These varying perspectives reflect sacred, holy, and beautiful forms. Multiplicity appears near and far in physicality, but in reality there is only *one* of us here. All eyes merge in this collective portal of *SELF*-realization. *You* cannot make awakening happen, but *You* can endeavor upon a conscious discipline of compassion. Your inner work supports external reality in calming and shifting. Awareness arises as the morning sun . . . by its own accord, while *you* are sleeping.

Enlightenment does not come from portraying a specific technique or philosophy, nor through choosing science or spirituality as a path. It does not exist because someone can speak about it, tap into akashic records, or twist into a complex pose. Your preoccupation with tool, technique, protocol, and process is wrapped in the illusion of evolution and awakening, purely to feed the self-obsessed nature of ego and *being*. Ultimately, real enlightenment comes from inside the deepest and darkest space of utter aloneness. Rather than becoming more of who *You* are, enlightenment comes through venturing toward becoming no one.

Be not the disease of fear spread in the world;
be the infectious contagion of Love, Truth, and Peace.

Personal power is personal. Only masked power can be taken away. True power simply *IS*. Your greatest achievement lies in your ability to master form. Life is a journey of experience experiencing itself, where authentic purpose rests in the commitment, care, and love for the body and soul. This means consistent presence to the physical body, emotional body, mental body, and etheric and astral bodies. Soul purpose is also ever-expanding unconditional love for these bodies. This will come through intimate communication, listening, presence, and tenderness. This level of service—paramount for unity consciousness—is impactful to the world, after having been mastered and embodied by *Self/self/SELF*.

Compassionate presence acknowledges and feels from each perspective, without the need to react, respond, fix, or change what is. Grounded in neutrality, this all-encompassing viewpoint transmutes existing energies by feeling into them with the purity of loving kindness.

Every person on the planet came from Love. *You/i/we/they* are the Oneness of Love balancing into remembrance. Love everyone. Forgive everything. Hold a steady vision for the highest in all. The extraordinary is present, right here . . . right now; *You* need only be present to it . . . celebrating the ordinary, extraordinary, and everything in between. Blessed *being/Being/BEING* . . . Breathe deeply as *You/you/YOU* let go of your spiritual obsessions.

May vapors of illusion dissolve . . .
and the mist of purity remain.
May veils of doubt be drawn . . .
and sheer truth stand fully centered.
May the vision of your mind be clear . . .
and the truth of your heart lead and guide.
Sweetly Dream . . .
so to create the sweetest of dreams.

...

OUR GLOBAL REFLECTION OF SECURITY

What is the mirror?

You are being led, guided, and stewarded.
Everyone is here for you.
Do not seek outwardly; find yourself within . . .
Do not be enveloped by all that is rising;
Breathe in the fragrance of only that which is Divine . . .
Discover your heart inside the Great Full One . . .
Remember that you beat within this Sacred BEING;
You are that Heart . . . that Being . . . that Embodiment . . .
that Breath of Life and Aliveness.

For decades, the threat of nuclear destruction has hung within our *field of thought forms.* Anything continually held in collective consciousness has a greater probability of actualizing. Manifestation of feared ideas can be minimized by seeing the deeper message of the social images rising. Everything in the world is speaking to us . . . about us. These *conversations* with the universe guide. Source uses each one of us—and every condition on the planet— to its end, not our ending. Our inability to listen is what could bring finality. All things nuclear are a call for new-clear vision.

You live in a world bent on creating security when it blatantly creates threats simultaneously. Marketing, subliminal messaging, products, and promotions speak to *being* safe and secure while the fear of theft, invasion, attack, and danger is propagated. There is constant language emphasizing the need to protect or feel protected. The global reflection appears in discussions regarding defense, cybersecurity, and identity theft. Being hacked has become a commonality. This can occur by someone across the world, or the teenage tech wiz down the street. However, these experiences are merely widely rippling echoes of how it originated. This occurred long before now.

Your mind got hacked. Your energy is hacked all of the time. *You* innocently landed within a cyber existence, where your boundaries were compromised from the moment of conception. *You* marinated within a belly that was riddled with fear, anxiety, and a lack of safety. *You* birthed into an environment that did not feel safe. This is where identity theft initially occurred. The world around *you* modeled a lack of safety. Your caregivers showed *you* that living in defense and undercover was natural and necessary.

You do not have to scream and shout your truth or your lies.
They need not be spoken, not even a whisper.
In the space of quiet equanimity,
all things are held sacredly.
Even your fears . . . your terrors . . . your stories . . . and your dreams.

Do not squander these
and do not hold them as a security blanket either.

If *You* see evil—and believe it to exist—it must. That perspective is required to prove itself. If *You* see the other as different, there will always be differences. When *You* see only what is wrong, there will be no possibility to see what is right. As long as another is held as bad, evil, sick, or incapable . . . *you* hold a vision that must unfold for that individual . . . and a prophecy they and *You* must experience. In this situation, *You/you/YOU* are responsible for what occurs, especially where judgment is held. In that way, *You/you/YOU* become the cyberattack. *You* have initiated identity theft. Witness how *You/you/YOU* play into creating the drama. Notice how your mind holds thoughts of judgment. Are there people *You/you* view as *being* weak, crazy, corrupt, bad, wrong, and evil? Do you look up or down on anyone? Are there people you judge as smart, powerful, good, and right? This too is judgment. Mastery requires neutrality.

How *You/i/we/they* perceive and take action determines the world we live in. Every individual responds and reacts on the basis of what they believe to be true . . . how they have been taught . . . and the way the mind has been attuned to process what it is exposed to. *You/i/we/they* have been programmed by society. *You* were given the scales by which to judge everyone and everything, rather than be shown how to objectively witness with *Love*. Your lack of safety has been the ground *you* believe exists. In truth, the unknown is where you came from; it is your motherland. From that space, all have been created as equal.

There is no bad person . . . no wrong one . . . nor is there truly any evil individual. All of life is from the same Source, which is pure. All began the same way; holy and sacred. Every being was a baby . . . an infant that held only joy, love, openness, and wonder. They got hacked. They were abducted, brainwashed, controlled, and conditioned. See your *Self/self/SELF*—see them—with loving Essence, knowing and understanding the truth of who *you/i/we/they* really are.

In the silence I could hear nothing, yet I could hear it all . . .
each tear as it hit the carpet,
every cry for help,
each moment my heart pleaded for answers.
Every moment the mind questioned . . .
I could hear even when I did not want to . . .
the intimate surrender of flesh and bone
as it caved inward
to guard my heart,
as it moved my soul.

Now more than ever, hold vision of people in their highest Essence Self; especially those *You/you/YOU* name as the enemy. The world needs each of us to check our beliefs about safety and security. Otherwise, we project our animal and shadow energies onto the others and the world. *You* were taught to fear *fear*, and that it was negative. However, that was a limited perspective on the vital spectrum of excitement. Dense fear is just one end of the spectrum, and a very small part in the entire bandwidth of excitement. *FEAR* is *feeling excited about reality*. Bring love, peace, and harmony to that. In finding your safety within humanity, *You/you/YOU* serve all of humanity.

> **In the silence, I could hear a world that no one wanted to see.**
> **In the distance lies the road less traveled, a path that very few take.**
> **I heard a lone voice whisper . . .**
> **This is *Your Journey to Love*.**

Do not spiritualize or philosophize. Do not positivize, intellectualize, or attempt to make meaning. Do not be distracted with busyness, or a cause. Do not buy into the fear of needing to build a wall around yourself, or go live in a bunker. Just feel, and *be with* those who need to feel. In order to change the world, *You/you/YOU* must be willing to see how *You* have created a world *You* need to be protected from. Accept and hold your *Self/self/SELF* close . . . securely . . . with unconditional love in the heart, amid the tears of joy and heartbreak. *You/you/YOU* are a humanitarian effort. When life pushes *You/you/YOU* to the edge, and there is no where else to go, leap into the unknown. In turning to look back, *You* will realize *you* have been flying all along.

Blessed *being/Being/BEING* . . . Breathe deeply as *You/you/YOU* realize that *You/you/YOU* are safe and secure; *You* have always been.

> **May you discover the beauty of being lost in the wind . . .**
> **and experience the magnitude of getting caught in the storms . . .**
> **knowing the pulsating heat of fire as it grounds everything . . .**
> **while being engulfed by the net of illusion**
> **and washed over by waves of fear . . .**
> **May you know this as a rite of passage . . .**
> **the rite of divine safety and security.**
> **Sweetly dream . . .**
> **so to have the sweetest of dreams.**

...

THE HOLE OF GLUTTONY

What is the disease?

Your life is an illusion.
All times occupy the same space . . .
while nothing really exists at all.
It is matter.
Everything is the matter . . .
while none of it matters at all.
The reality . . . You are not matter.

Not only have *You/i/we/they* become lost in the world, the collective has become unaware of itself as a unified body. A collective dis-ease filled with pain, loss, and forgetting has arisen. The patterns, behaviors, and programs that permeate this atmosphere are magnified within our systems and structures. Large entities such as government, healthcare, big pharma, banking, corporations, and the like entangle people further within the matrix of mass conformity. Long-held codependency and oppression intertwine with generational and collective shadows in an earthen spiral. Moving through the ranks of victim, villain, saint, and sinner ultimately pulls individuals deeper into the shadows, widening our sense of separation. Media, marketing, and hierarchy have become psychological tools of combat.

Bullies come in all genders, shapes, and sizes within the ranks of lauded society. Charisma and guile mask narcissistic intent that has no conscience. Virtues have been overridden by the glory of vices. Inquire into how *You/you/YOU* bully your *Self/self/SELF* into endless pursuits, perfections, and personifications. Gluttony is often associated with food, but *you/i/we/they* have become gluttonous in our consumption of the intellectual, spiritual, sensational, logical, and material. *You/i/we/they* are becoming increasingly unhealthy, dying from taking in more than is possible to release.

Ego desires to ripple in the world;
SELF knows the outer is merely a mirage;
it seeks to spiral within.

As well and good as material success is, endless pursuit of such when one has more than enough is gluttony. How much will ever be enough? The material world and continual doing will never feed the heart and soul. These cannot be bought. They can only be romanced and savored. Material success is not bad. However, this distraction keeps *You/you* preoccupied with your little world. At some point, *You/you/YOU* must turn and see the big picture, beyond your life and comforts. Excess consumption makes *you/me/us/them* like animals. Sooner or later, gluttony brings impoverishment, disgrace, and starvation in its wake. *You/i/we/they* have become casual citizens of the world, instead of advocates for life.

Our senseless way of living creates pangs of hunger that can never be satisfied by what is false. As *You/i/we/they* are beckoned into the intensity of the outside world, we lose sight, have lost touch, and no longer listen to the inner wisdom of the body. Gluttony weakens the will and fosters a spirit of laziness and impurity. Do not mistake what is written for doom and gloom. It is not that. This is real optimism, by way of accepting what is. We each possess the necessary constitution to empower our families, communities, and this world.

**Experience has no agenda; it embodies every expression . . .
as conscious and unconscious, animate and inanimate, form and formless.**

Life is not conflicted by the reality of its own existence; only the mind is. It does not make demands of it, judge it, or have expectation for it. Life in its greater expression is not concerned with impermanence or death, because that too is part of life. Only the mind is gluttonous in its preoccupation with thought and meaning. The need for meaning arises out of a desire *to matter*, but we are matter. Meaning is an attempt to understand *why* something is or is not. Meaning is a longing for significance, engaging the mind's play among past, future, purpose, pain, and pleasure. Through the indeterminable search for meaning, *Self/self/SELF* misses the organic, interconnected, unfolding as life's presence. Through searching and seeking, *Self* misses the experiencing of experience.

**Mirrors are everywhere,
reflecting your attachment to . . .
vision/motives . . . thoughts/agenda . . . feelings/pain . . .
words/actions . . . light/darkness.**

What is the meaning of life? To discover such an answer would be like trying to taste your own tongue, or touch the fingertip with the related finger. And therein is the rabbit hole. This is the paradox. When you let go of your endless search, *You/you/YOU* release your intellectual and spiritual gluttony. Move from *meaning* into the pure presence as life's infinite, ever-expanding, interconnected, and engaged expression. In presence, no thought can exist. There will be no *need to know* anything. This is Life . . . this is Experience . . . this is presence . . . this is meaning full . . . and yet has no meaning. Blessed *being/Being/ BEING* . . . Breathe deeply as *You/you/YOU* balance your consumption of the world.

**May you see beyond the illusion . . .
discerning truth in all experience.
May you know that each day holds
holy and sacred moments . . .
a multiplicity of profound blessings . . .
and a magnitude of grace.
May you, and all other beings,
feel connected . . . close . . .
and in communion
with all that is.
Sweetly Dream . . .
so to create the sweetest of dreams.**

...

THE KEY WHOLE OF FULFILLMENT

How is personal power activated?

You are me; I am you . . .
pieces and parts of the same.
We are united for evermore . . .
in our vastness,
our bounteousness,
our timeless radiance and rapture.
That recognition is the discovery . . .
You are a divine *aha* moment . . .
an inquiry into form.

Life is not meant to be a sober endeavor, but an intoxicating one. *You/you* believe that events, circumstances, and people can be controlled; this is a futile effort. Everything appears for the release of attachment. This means *you* are not controlled; nor are *you* a victim of anyone or anything. Life occurs so that *You* experience sacred depths of fulfillment. Initially, *You* seek to fulfill the ego's and identity's wants and needs. *You* will find this to be temporary fulfillment. True fulfillment lies beyond ego gratification, the body's desire, the mind's needs, or the heart's wants. The font of fulfillment may be accessed inside the deep well that has called from within for all time. Will *You/you/YOU* drink of your own sweet depths? It is within reach. There is a destiny and plan that is your soul's fulfillment, but this cannot occur if interfering with natural order.

Die to who you have been,
in order to birth into what you may become.

There is an old Indian saying, "Chew your food so that it becomes like water, and drink your water so slowly that you chew it like food." Although most people would regard this little verse to be about food, it regards imbibing life in the most nourishing way. Imagine taking in every moment in this manner. Your experiences would become a sacred sacrament. This approach would feed *You/you/YOU* in holy ways. If every experience were regarded as a *blessing*, whether bitter or sweet, pungent or sour . . . life would be embraced as the buffet it was intended.

When one is living from a curious and wild heart, life becomes rich. It will not be without pain. However, experience will have fertile ground to expand. Just as the flower bursts forth from the cold, hard ground, a steady awakening gently flows from within . . . and from it a river of wisdom. If you can live with your heart open despite the storms; forgive the trespasses of those who act from their pain; collect a few deep friendships of mutual love, respect, and care; and focus on serving something greater than yourself without a personal agenda . . . *You* will have lived a blessed, fulfilled, and complete life. This is grace. The journey of living, being, and knowing bears the fruit of aliveness, and the ever-quenching taste of adventure.

Commit to a heaven of a good time.

You are given opportunity to experience the rich taste of compassion and empathy. Savor the joy and kindness, while also digesting sadness, grief, jealousy, and anger. Imbibing the full buffet of life grounds your divine feminine *being* into experiencing, expressing, and transmuting feeling and emotion. Your masculine energy is designed to immerse, integrate, and be activated by the inspired mind and actions of the relationship. The inner courtship creates the fulfillment of dimensional expression *You/you/YOU* desired as a soul.

The true object of human life is play. So often, life is lived by working for your desired experience: vacations, rest and relaxation, time, joy, happiness, peace, and hobbies. Work becomes the thing *You* do . . .have to do . . .and many times push to escape from. It is the grind that wears *You* down. *You* become weary. Your body and mind feel tired. In truth, *You* could have your desires right now. The only thing in the way is *You/you/YOU*.

Sacrifice your lower *self* for your higher *SELF*.
Surrender to Divine will as you let go of personal will.

Chew your days until they become like water. Sip slowly and open to savoring the feeling of *Being* full and abundant. Everything is like food, whether you rush to imbibe it or savor each flavor. Relish the moment at hand. Work and play are to be treated as a beautiful meal—nourishing and satisfying. Do not rush through life. Do not try to get through another day. Do not leap into the goals of tomorrow. Deepen into the richness of this moment, whatever it holds. Marinate in it. Soak it up. Become one with the experience. Sieve the gold that it offers. Then sit back and feel satisfied.

It's not necessary to live life to the fullest,
but it's essential to live life to YOUR FULLNESS!

Each and every breath is the dance of the eternal. Live life in spontaneity; let no part become habit, rote, or regular. Rather than fighting change, willingly relax into the soul's path. The soul has designed your life, your journey, and the ultimate fulfillment of your return. Commitment to your highest expression is vital to this end. Anything other is ego distraction that may lead to many highs but will also take *You* to as many lows. Blessed *being/Being/BEING* . . . Breathe deeply as *You/you/YOU* release yourself.

May you never meet a stranger.
May you see all others as children . . .
untainted, unspoiled, and free.
May your days be joyful
and your nights be peaceful.

May your smiles be heart-full,
and your tears be helpful.
Sweetly dream . . .
so to create the sweetest of dreams.

. . .

VISIONARY TO MYSTIC

How does purpose unfold?

Know your *self* . . .
Know your experience as a human being.
Know your embodiment as a spiritual being.
Know your expression as the catalyst for change.
Know your soul as Love in Essence and inspired action.
Know your *SELF* beyond all of these.
You are *IS*ness.

Most people opt for the scenic route. If *You* take this meandering road, it will become quite the adventure. *You* do not need to fix anything; just playfully engage in life's discourse. *You* do not have to figure it out; sensation, awareness, and expression are simply points of view. *Be* present to the magical nature of life. Every moment is an invitation to get to know more of *You/you/YOU*. As *you/i/we/they* become better students, life's earthen curriculum brings about more-challenging steps of mastery. Your senses will become more attuned to what exists, and aware of everything that is happening. Conscious living takes *You/you/YOU* into the nitty-gritty of life where *You* become a steward of experience, rather than simply existing. *You/you/YOU* will begin to notice signs, prompts, and messages.

Initially whispers appear. There will be an intermittent tapping, where *You* begin seeing something repeatedly. It could be anything, from a number or insect to a word or symbol. This tapping will continue until *you* notice. Then it will increase. *You/i/we/they* bring ourselves only what we can handle, so all communication shall arrive in a gentle and loving way, even the tough-love moments. These signs are designed to take you into the mystical way of life.

Are you listening?
Are you watching?
Are you sensing?
Are you feeling?

You are not here to live; you are here to be alive. The first is dead; the latter has many deaths. Your body reflects your aliveness, your belief, your expression of security. It reflects your state of mind. It is the embodiment of emotion for it is energy in motion.

Your physical body adapts to fit what you hold to be true. It is a changing, cocreative organism. There is an Essence within you that is creative, organic, and fulfilled purely by experience. It does not think, analyze, or have an agenda. It just creates. This creative capacity will follow an internal rhythm of creativity and expression that balances the world through presence. However, when the mind or conditioning affects this creative capacity, visionaries are made.

The visionary stays in the realm of the mind. They think about the future. Their lives are spent in pursuing advancements in a creative and imaginative way. This is generally a person who is believed to be ahead of their time. They possess a desire to change things. Envisioning a future that is different from what exists, visionaries enact powerful plans for change through ideas, concept, and creation. They have ideas of how the world should be. Visionaries typically are not—nor can they be—present to what is, because they want to change it. And although your world has advanced greatly through visionary minds, that does not always mean real progress has occurred. It may be an illusion of progress.

Visionaries are focused on the future. There is a desire to have an impact. However, their focus remains external, while the interior suffers. In the end, anyone not grounded in the present moment, regardless of brilliant visions, would be contributing to the distracted shadow energy that builds in the world. Such progress only creates more of a need for itself, keeping us on an endless wheel. What becomes discarded is the mystical present.

All drive stems from craving or aversion.
It is how you play a game of distraction and deception.

Self-obsession is at the core of human suffering. Our stories are not the issue, but our preoccupation with them has sent us spiraling with no end. *Self*-obsession creates a living hell on this heaven of earth and leads to our undoing. The responsibility that *You/you/YOU* have is to understand the mystical way of annihilation as a conscious choice toward inner work, rather than an unconscious manifestation of our outer world. There's no greater service than *Being/being/BEING* sacred witness to your Dark and Light.

There is one person asking for your undivided attention today . . . your complete presence . . . your understanding and compassion. Only one special individual seeks to be heard, seen, and held. ONE desires to be touched, inspired, and led. There is only ONE that has long desired your love, complete and unconditional. They have stood in the background, waited patiently, and supported *You* always. There is only *You/you/YOU* and God in the room . . . look around. The one *you* are able to see, feel, touch, hold, and know is the Divine YOU, waiting to be fully realized. Have a Holy Moment . . .

The return to expansiveness occurs through *Self* recognizing *self*, so to reach the awareness of *SELF*. To attain this siddhic expression, *You/you* must go deeply into your darkness, where the most unconscious, animal, unowned parts of your obsessive influences reside. To go forward into the light, *You/you* must stand in your darkness and take responsibility for the shadow manifestations outside. Be willing to face the demons inside, embracing them with intimacy. The world illustrates your unowned darkness, and expressions of your light.

There is nothing that needs to be done out there.

Embrace the heartbreak of the world, and you'll find your own. Within those cracks is your pathway to freedom. Beyond the most painful, traumatic, and tragic moments is a space that holds and nourishes with seemingly endless sacred waters. Tears are communion between soul and body ... Spirit and separation. The mystic holds the underworld sacredly, understanding that life has subtle nuances that must be experienced and acknowledged. Those nuances lie within depths of feeling, and amid the embodiment of the senses and sensations. The mystic opens to the waves. They are not washed away by them, nor do they stand stoically within them. The true mystic is willing to sink into each passing wave and then rise after knowing it fully. The mystic understands our great potential as reflections of the Divine, realizing the wholeness within grounding as *ALL*ness. The mystic's longing to know truth—not intellectually—in a deeply embodied way. The mystic sees all of life as an abundant opportunity to discover, realize, and express the Divine and know oneself as the whole of Divine nature.

As you become more conscious that life is not about your pain ... your problems ... your experience, *You* become aware that *You/you/YOU* are connected to everything and everyone. With this knowing, *You* see that *their* pain is your pain, *their* problems are your problems, and *their* experience is your experience. This is an opportunity to know an experience of your *Self/self/SELF* within the gentle tappings and soft whispers of the mystic's way.

To turn away from one, you turn away from all. If uniting with Love, nothing else can exist or be exclusive. You either *Love/LOVE* everything or admit to being conditional in your loving. *Love/LOVE* doesn't arise through breaking bonds or constructing walls, but in building bridges. Believe in the power of Love; trust in the Love that *YOU* are. Give *LOVE* to those *You/you/YOU Love*; give even more *LOVE* to those *You/you/YOU* hate. Blessed *being/Being/BEING* ... Breathe deeply as *You/you/YOU* as you transition from visionary to mystic.

May you see that we are many perspectives.
And ... One story.
ONE.
May you find that we are many moths.
And ... One flame.
ONE.
May you know that we are many drops of water.
And ... One ocean.
ONE.
May you discover we are many fragments.
And ... One Soul.
ONE.
Sweetly dream ...
so to create the sweetest of dreams.

the illusion of evolution.

. . .

CULTIVATING PRESENCE

How can peace arise?

I am you . . . I am me . . . I am them . . . I am we . . .
I AM my sister . . . I AM my brother . . . I AM my mother . . . I AM my father . . .
I am the angel . . . I am the demon . . . I am the god and goddess.
You are these as well.
We are going know-where . . . in know-time . . . to know-thing . . .
for know-need . . . to know-ONE . . .
because YOU desired to . . .
know-how.

Be present to this moment, and only this moment. Synchronicity and miracles are consistently and constantly present; *You/i/we/they* are not. There is much more beauty available when aware and living from a state of presence. *You* are the miracle. Be miracle-minded and see with the purity of the mystical heart. Feel into what is truly valuable, beyond form and function. Imagine what lies beyond the masks *you* wear, the skin *You/you/YOU* are in, and the biology of your belief. A leap of faith requires only a step . . . any size will do.

You are here to know the greatest experience of yourself . . . a personal best . . . a spiritual ascension . . . and a physical embodiment of the most high. Your paradigm of evolution has been focused on changing the present, being better, and seeking worthiness. What if nothing needed to be changed? This means relaxing into what exists. That occurs when *You* stop chasing time, dreams, and phantoms of illusion. *You* are the perfection *You/you/YOU* were created to be in each moment, regardless of circumstance. What lies within each one of us—untapped and unknown—is the essence of *ALL*ness that lives beyond limits, beliefs, excuses, or timelines. This *IS*ness is the wholeness *You/you* have never let yourself embody. The Divine *SELF* extends far beyond the confines and conformity of the body.

Life is organic; it has a plan.
Follow the rhythm of your seasons and cycles,
and you will naturally grow and flower.

Now more than ever, people must move beyond the superficial masks of positivity, airy fairy thinking, and future faking. *You/you* operate from a narrow mind and continue feeding an insatiable ego. This is true, even for those in the spiritual arena. *You/you/YOU* are not here to awaken from anything; that idea keeps *You/you/YOU* out of presence. Your ability to be present in short increments is the initial road to *SELF*-actualization. Awareness of the deceptive intelligence empowers a deepened state of *Being*. Through persistent witnessing, the opportunity for living beyond frustration, confusion, wishing, and hoping can arise. Cultivate your ability to recognize when *you* go unconscious . . . by practicing presence.

In going this way and that—with adventures, new beginnings, shifts, and moves—it is easy to get caught up in the world. Outer-focused energy pulls your attention from commitment to *Self/self/SELF*, internal focus, and the energy that creates presence. When conscious awareness is missing, checked out, or not present, an energy leakage will occur, resulting in emptiness or the feeling of disconnection. What you most desire only needs your presence . . . not from a place of want or longing . . . but as a dimension that is already *Being/BEING*.

The willingness to be utterly and completely unique,
without care of what others think,
is an expansion into wholeness.

The world *you* focus on is the one *You* empower. Egotistical desires only create more craving. These ghosts of gluttony pull *You* away from the present moment, and into the psychosis of the *Mind/mind*. Any looping thoughts connecting to fear, wounding, or insecurity will contribute to irritation, dissatisfaction, and aggression that further amplifies the pain of craving. Until *You* recognize and embrace dissonant aspects, the world will continue to reflect these. Your presence to the least among *You* says everything about how *You/you* know that part of yourself. Everything that exists in this world exists within *You/you/YOU*.

Be as fully with cold and painful moments as with beautiful and joyful ones. When giving all of *You/you/YOU* to an experience, integration expands. Your ability to be with another will be equivalent to how *You* are able to be with yourself. Empathy is a kindred expression that allows *You/you/YOU* to touch and be touched by another person. There will come moments where your presence is required. Consistent presence to each moment enhances your auric expression of the violet flame, emitting the fragrance of your communion. Because *You/you/YOU* release the visceral ash of life . . . others . . . and the conditioned mind, the flavor of softness envelops your actions, depicting the vulnerability, strength, and resilience *You* possess.

Service comes in many forms;
the indigent . . . the homeless . . . refugees . . .
prisoners . . . the mentally ill . . .
These mighty *beings* serve you in seeing your *self*.

Be present to how the world is speaking to *You* about *you*. Therein lie your healing, absorption, and ascension into compassion, unconditional love, and Oneness. Compassionate presence will not only settle cravings of the ego but also enrich what fulfills the soul. Cultivating presence with *Self/self/SELF* develops unconditional *LOVE* for others. In this way, inner and outer relationships carry no agenda or expectation. Interactions feel simple, clean, clear, and aligned. Learning to be whole and complete comes from being your own best company, best friend, and soulmate. Give no energy to anything that obstructs the highest expression of *Love/LOVE* toward *Self/self/SELF* and others. Allow periods of aloneness so that *You* get to know all of *you* . . . and *You* . . . and *YOU*. Blessed *being/Being/BEING* . . . Breathe deeply as *You/you/YOU* become increasingly present.

May you embody Essence . . .
transforming, transmuting, and transfiguring . . .
the world that surrounds you.
May you bring equanimity to all of your cravings and aversions . . .
May you neutralize all charge and inflammation . . .
May you actively absorb everything
into the powerful vortex that you are.
May you realize
you are the change the world needs to see.
Sweetly dream . . .
so to create the sweetest of dreams.

. . .

ACCEPT THYSELF

What is the asking?

I'm not looking for you to follow me.
None of us are meant to be the same.
Question everything!
Have your own experience.
Find your own proof.
Romance your soul,
enliven the spirit,
inspire your human *Being/BEINGness*,
awaken Divine *Knowing/KNOWING* . . .
and discover a new world experience of aliveness!

AFFIRMATION—CONTEMPLATION—INSPIRATION

I AM capable of awakening to my distraction and dis-ease.
I now transcend all places of *Self/self/SELF*-deception.

Contemplate and journal these inquiries until inspired to take action.

Be still; see what rises as *evolution* versus *awakening*.
You have the answer for achieving aliveness . . . go within.

The degree to which you are *Being/being/BEING*
is the degree to which *You/you/YOU*
shall cultivate inner and outer *Presence*.

What is your self-obsessed story about evolution, positivity, religion, or spirituality?

evolution.
Where are *You/you/YOU* going?

Where are *You/you/YOU* now?

How does evolution keep *You/you/YOU* in the past?

What would *You/you/YOU* do "now" if evolution did not exist?
• If the past did not exist?
• If there were no future?

spiritual reflections.
Are *You/you/YOU* obsessed with evolution, ascension, spirituality, heaven, or being positive?

How does that keep *You/you/YOU* in a state of hunger?

How does that keep *You/you/YOU* living in the future?

How does that keep *You/you/YOU* distracted from fully embodying your higher *SELF* now?

security.
Do *You/you/YOU* feel safe?

Are *You/you/YOU* comfortable in your . . .
• skin?
• body?
• experience?
• world as it is?

What will allow *You/you/YOU* to feel safe in this world?

What are *You* still not in acceptance of . . .
• inside *You/you/YOU*?
• outside *You/you/YOU*?

fulfillment.
What experience would allow *You/you/YOU* to feel full in . . .
• body?
• mind?
• heart?
• soul?

visionary to mystic.

What is required for *You/you/YOU* to be visionary and still present with your *Self/self/SELF*?

How do *You/you/YOU* use visionary ideas to distract from your *self*, and your *Self*?

How can *You/you/YOU* create greater presence with . . .
- your humanity?
- *Self/self/SELF*?
- others?
- the world?

Are confrontation and conflict your version of revolution?

How might conflict and war be spiritual?

What might be created if your emotions were channeled into creativity?

accept thyself.

Who would *You/you/YOU* be if there were nothing to awaken *to* or *from*?

How could higher *SELF* be more present if *Self* were not having to support *self* evolve or heal?

May you be inspired with innocence . . .
awed by the little things . . .
overjoyed in the ordinary . . .
ecstatic with the mundane . . .
and enraptured by simplicity.
May your silent moments be interspersed with peals of laughter . . .
May noise be in endless declaration of praise and celebration . . .
May *Love/love* be without conditions . . .
life be without sameness . . .
and every space between
ooze with joy and infinite unconditional love.
Sweetly dream . . .
so to create the sweetest of dreams.

. . .

PETITION FOR ACCEPTANCE

What is the shift in consciousness?

Now come the Father . . .
Now come the Mother . . .
Now come the child . . .
All Knowing.
Eternal.
Infinite.
ONE.

IN COLLECTIVE PRAYER
FOR ACCEPTANCE . . .
SO THAT HUMANITY IS PRESENT
TO INSPIRED MOVEMENTS OF GLOBAL LOVE IN ACTION

Dearest Infinite Oneness . . .
Awaken us from the delusions of our minds . . .
the dis-ease of our world . . .
and our lack of presence . . .
Bring us into deepened states . . .
and moments of awareness.
We are the present.
Bring us to the pure recognition of all that we are.
Awaken us into BEING Lights in shining amour . . .
absorbing the darkness
so it may drink of Light/LIGHT Essence.
May we be the makers of Love/LOVE . . .
Let each inhale,
be the warm soft embrace of all that is.
Let each exhale,
be wings setting us free to be . . .
May we judge no thing,
beholding each and every thing with neutrality.
Let us openly embrace this pebbled path of collective consciousness
reverent to the cosmic story line.
May we willingly walk with the excitement and curiosity of a child,
the pulsing heart of a lover,
and the wise insight of an aged one.
Let us aim to be present in each moment . . .

every second becoming an eternity
in which us is within them . . . and you are within me.
May we all commit to the embodiment of this sacredness,
so to taste wonder . . .
to quench our thirst . . .
by drinking from the fountain of Source.
Let no thing cast asunder
what Love/LOVE builds.
May we seek nothing . . .
for we have been given everything.
You/I/We/They come from Source . . .
and are of abundant Supply.
Enlighten us with vision.
Lead us.
Guide us.
Use us.
Work within us.
Speak through us.
Walk with us.
Awaken us
to the acceptance of what IS.
Thy will be done.

Center us in alignment.
Ground our roots.
Awaken us . . .
In Devotion . . .
I Am

0
0 0
0 0 0
1 1 1 1
1 1 1
1 1
1
1
1 1
1 1 1
1 1 1 1
0 0 0
0 0
0

the illusion of war.

What is the awareness?

Are you the bomb?
Are you having a blast?
If you choose war,
you may discover a cosmic truth . . .
Your enemy is your mirror.
In truth,
you are at war with yourself.
Instead, will you be the balm?
Be the balm?

The Illusion of War	The Awareness	Being/being/BEING
Mental Obsessions	What is the addiction?	Ego/Mind
Our Global Reflection of Information and Technology	Where is the mirror?	The Collective
The Hole of Wrath	What is the dis-ease?	The Shadow
The Key of Purity	How is personal power activated?	Essence
Revolutionary to Spiritual Rebel	How is purpose fulfilled?	Humanity
Cultivating Generosity	How can peace arise?	The Bridge
See Thyself	What is the asking	The Embodiment

I am humbled by what soldiers unconditionally and willingly stand for. They give their lives in service for others. My brother and brother in-law both serve our country. But I take pause as to what is being required of them on my behalf; what we all require of them. In addition, what are we asking of their families, and future generations? What are the long-term emotional, mental, and psychological implications to soldiers, their families, and future generations? Those who fight for our freedoms are serving us. How do we serve them? In asking them to protect—defend, fight, and possibly die—are *you/i/we/they* perpetuating a consciousness and psychological technology of fear, flight, or fight? Does this programming instill defensiveness, sacrifice, and loss, in addition to maintaining a sense of danger?

Y*ou/i/we/they* are at war, with each smaller conflict raging into a larger battle. Lion fights lion, while cubs are caught in the fray. As time passes, *You* may be challenged to remember why the war initially began, or even when. By that time, it is too late to turn back. Too many wounds have been inflicted and too many have been stories told. Too much collateral damage is present. *You/i/we/they* do not recognize each other anymore, nor are *you/i/we/they* able to recognize how we came together in the first place. Ego. Pride. Vengeance. Anger. Revenge. War. The divide continues to widen until nothing remains.

Wars are waged in love, in business, and between countries. One may be occurring right now in your home—with friends, family, siblings, partners, or children. Regardless, each conflict, battle, and war mirrors an inner conflict. The ultimate battle waging is with *Self/self/SELF*.

Are you fighting to win? Do you fight to be the best?
Do you fight to make it to the top of your class, company, or field?
Are you fighting to be seen or heard?

Conflict comes from distorted information and interpretations gone wrong. It arises out of interference within your system. As a human being, *You/you/YOU* are the technology of life and spirit. Through the encryption of your software—and viruses that infiltrate programming—battles ensue. This becomes a slow-moving storm that builds. It is not a war between *you/i/us/them*, but one of past generations who were at odds with each other. *You/i/we/they* received the mental, emotional, psychological, physical, and spiritual impact from the fallout. Your mind . . . their minds . . . our minds . . . all minds have been corrupted through misinformation and warped technology.

Lies were whispered into your ears. *You* listened; *you* were blind. Infected by the virus of those unloved . . . in separation . . . and in wounded conditions, there was no pure communication. Mental obsessions grew over time, which never let the old stories die. Continuing in this plight, *you/i/we/they* recycle old wounds and resuscitate dead drama, bringing the pain back to life again and again. The bloodshed is sometimes real, and at all times bleeding through bloodlines. New generations carry on a battle that can never be won/*one*. In war, there is no winner . . . there is only loss.

War is an illusion that feeds the addiction of mental obsessions.
Information and technology reveal the global reflection of the collective's
viral shadow of wrath.
In turning the key of purity,
you are initiated from revolutionary to spiritual rebel.
Seeing thyself cultivates generosity
as the bridge for an embodied humanity.

War never makes sense to anyone, especially those caught in the crossfire. Your world was built on the foundation of oppression, aggression, and dominance. Land was taken from original, Indigenous peoples. They were domesticated and stripped of dignity, freedoms, natural ways, and resources. Others were enslaved, sold, and owned. These seeds of dishonor, dominance, disrespect, and disregard are the foundation upon which progress was built. Now *you/i/we/they* reap the harvest of the weeds of those times. As in any relationship, how something begins is how it ends. Following those initial acts of abuse and oppression, a shadow culture formed that creates more of the same. What has continued is slavery, war, oppression, violence, brutality, and racism in socially ignored ways. Although everything seemingly changed over time, the shadows of the world have stayed the same. Women's issues. Gender inequality. Inhumane acts of terror. Racial tension. Police brutality. Identity theft. Human trafficking. War.

Whom do you judge? What do you judge them for?
From whom did you learn to be prejudiced and judgmental?
How did you learn to be at war with others?

Every people, every culture, and most countries have encountered and enacted terrorism, including yours. The consciousness of defense maintains the necessity of terrorism, war, and threat. *You/i/we/they* cannot rally and protest on behalf of love, forgiveness, and equality while espousing conflict, resistance, resentment, and hierarchy. That is hypocrisy. Continuing to fight—word with word, fire with fire, bullet with bullet, bomb with bomb—endows these shadows and monsters to the minds of future generations. *You/i/ we/they* can no longer point fingers; the issue is not *over there*. At some point, *you/i/we/ they* must admit to *being*—the shadow . . . the villain . . . the monster . . . the terrorist . . . the *one* consumed, divided, and insane.

Your inability to see every child as yours . . . every woman as your grandmother, sister, mother, or daughter . . . and every man as your father, son, brother, or grandfather is prejudice. People are not strangers or enemies; your distorted perspectives and behaviors are. One day, *you* will realize that the enemy has never been a person outside. It is the one that has been created within *You/you/YOU*. Feel into the discomfort of embracing all within the human family as your own—your brothers and sisters, your mothers and fathers, and your sons and daughters. The entire village is your family . . . whether *You/you* accept them or not.

What subtle seeds of hate do *you* carry?
What are you prejudiced toward?
What are your fears regarding other people, genders, religions, and races?
Where and how do you terrorize others?

Those lost—that lie bruised and wounded on the battlefield of life—are burdened with an ancient legacy of separation. Their hearts hold hopes, dreams, and forgotten innocence that has been cast down and hidden in the shadows of fear and guardedness. They are the prisoners of a war they inherited. This battleground of family division, competition, and survival has perpetuated the consciousness of *fight*. War is the child born in the image and likeness of *You/ you/YOU*. It is the offspring of your internal struggle with *Self/self/SELF*. It lies writhing inside hidden degrees of *Self/self/SELF*-oppression, *Self/self/SELF*-betrayal, and *Self/self/SELF*-denial. *You/you* have enslaved, tortured, abused, and beaten down your *Self/self/SELF*. *You* were taught this. It is what *You/you* marinated in. As such, *You* transgress your life force energy.

Until reparations of the past are integrated, there can never be peace of *Mind/mind*. This is not only external recompense, but also the ownership and integration of shadow consciousness, inner conflict, and ancestral guilt. It requires identifying the shame and abuse endured as the transgressor and the transgressed. This battle has long raged internally. External war has purely been projection and a misdirected grasp for power. The struggle for inner authority—which was usurped by external authority during childhood—has been laid down due to the pain and inequity behind life's experiences. Until the whole *Self/self/SELF* is reclaimed, external authority will dominate.

**Are you fighting for a cause? Are you fighting for your rights?
Are you fighting the status quo?
Are you a spiritual warrior?
This is *us* versus *them* thinking; there is no *we* in that.
In battle, there is never a winner.**

You/i/we/they were not created for division, hate, or war. Control merely results in entropy. Small minds endeavor in these ways, because they hold big fears. The dark ego craves power. It uses chaos and force out of fear of being taken down. Ironically, that fear stems from a deep sense of insecurity. True power uses a steady mind, a firm hand, and a gentle heart that is communicative, compassionate, and balanced. It commands tempered negotiation and resolution, with no need to protect or defend, due to innate confidence and *Self/self/SELF*-acceptance. In the event a strike must be made, it will be swift and clean. In advocacy for the greater good, the intention behind it will hold the unconditional loving energy of divine justice.

We have become a world conditioned to fear, fight, or flight. Our young men follow the soldier's creed to protect our freedoms, while we rob them of theirs. How have *You/you* been robbed of the very same in an attempt to save, defend, or protect your world and those within it? How are *You* conditioning your children to become soldiers who defend the terrors in your mind? Every belief in lack, ill will, or persecution is how *You/you* make *the other* the weapon and wielder of injury. Every single person is on the battlefield of *Mind/mind*.

Contemplate the soldier's creed.

**How does it feel? What is it asking and demanding of our men and women?
What is it imprinting? What consciousness does it defend? What legacy is it building?
Is this an enlightened or shadowed expression?**

THE SOLDIER'S CREED (author unknown)

My nation expects me to be physically harder and mentally stronger than my enemies.
If I get knocked down, I will get back up—EVERY TIME!
I will draw on every remaining ounce of strength to protect my teammates
and accomplish our mission.
I'm NEVER out of the fight!
We demand discipline. We expect innovation.
The lives of our teammates and the success of our mission depend on me.
Our training's never complete. We train for war. We fight to win.
I stand ready to bring the full spectrum of combat power to bear in order to
accomplish my mission and the goals established by my country.
The execution of my duties will be swift and violent when required,
yet guided by the principles I serve to defend.

Brave men have fought and died building the proud tradition and feared reputation
I am bound to uphold.
In the worst of conditions, the legacy of my teammates steadies my resolve
and silently guides my every deed.
I WILL NOT FAIL.

We have asked much of our young men and women, and taken even more. They are vital and precious human resources—whether it is our sons and daughters, those of another country, or opposing forces. Is violence service? We are asking men to kill in order to honor, protect, defend, feed, and take care of us. We are destroying hearts and souls, and filling minds with nightmares and trauma. By doing so, we are terrorizing our own kind. Is this justification of violence how we have manifested terror on our playgrounds, schools, concerts, streets, and neighborhoods? Is the right to kill superseding the right to live? The evil *you/i/we/they* abhor . . . the violence erupting from the youth . . . the sexual predation, slavery, and trafficking . . . the weaponization of words . . . and the brutality of domestic violence, child abuse, and police brutality are all effects. We must take ownership of how we perpetuate that.

By turning our men into machines, and their actions into mechanics, we strip them of their empathy, compassion, and humanity. Our boys and men—and now women— become hardened and shut down by being taught not to feel. They are told to toughen up, be strong, and stop crying. We deaden their hearts and souls, leaving them barren of creativity, safety, and wholeness. We cannot question the increase of apathy, indifference, narcissism, and misogyny when *you/i/we/they* are contributing to these behaviors.

To *force peace* is as much an oxymoron as the *power of war*.
Warriors will always be at war, even spiritual ones.

We are all devils and angels, enlightened children, and wounded adults, teachers and students, gurus and disciples—weaving a world of darkness and light. Embrace and absorb each so that separation, division, conflict, and war may dissolve. The land of opposites manifests out of *your/my/our/their* resistance and lack of *self*-acceptance. If *You* are *God-Loving*, then *Love/LOVE* all men. Make peace at home. Begin inside your heart . . . endeavoring upon your inner healing . . . and becoming a soldier of *Love/LOVE* that garners the sword of compassion, holds the shield of empathy, and wields fierce loving advocacy. Love the way *you* want to be loved. A new creed must be adopted. In respect to all soldiers—may this world develop a consciousness of peace—so that *You* come home, stay home, and remain home . . . never having our need to feel safe projected onto *You* ever again. Let us be in service to one another—creating the legacy of love, truth, and freedom—by establishing a new way of thinking, seeing, and behaving toward one another.

Peacekeepers know how to be at peace despite what rages. Stand as a beacon of peace, grounded in the purity and freedom of a sovereign *Being/BEING* despite external circumstances. The power of peace inspires compassionate action and presence from the inside out. Lasting change will manifest only through a calm and collective *Mind/MIND*. The way to create peace is in committing to acts of peace. Blessed *being/Being/BEING* . . . Breathe deeply as *You/you/YOU* embody the presence and power of peaceful sovereignty.

SACRED ADVOCATES CREED

My sovereignty allows me to be vulnerable and open hearted with all people.
If I stumble, I become present to mining the gold—in THAT MOMENT!
I draw wisdom from every experience as a way to uphold my brothers, sisters, and our collective mission.
I'm ALWAYS safe!
I invite commitment. I listen deeply.
The sacredness of our lives and the fulfillment of service depend on my presence.
Self-awareness never competes. We unite in that vision. We focus to birth anew.
I ground into the full spectrum of internal power in order to express creatively and boldly.
The gifts of my purpose will be compassionate and collaborative at all times, guided by a mission to serve to nurture.
Courageous men and women advocate and create this sacred tradition and exemplary reputation to be upheld.
In the worst of conditions, divine will guides and humanity steadies my resolve, silently steering every deed.
I WILL ONLY LOVE.

May this world honor veterans by remembering
we are one family in the all powerful Essence of God.
May there be a new creed administered
for our sons, brothers, uncles, fathers, and grandsons . . .
one that sets a foundation
to no longer live preparing for war . . .
in fear . . .
on the defense . . .
in protection against . . .
or from the belief
that control, dominance, force, aggression, and war
are the only ways to be free.
May you remember that we are all part of the same world . . .
at the same time
and the same family.
May you remember that each one is kind . . . each one is good . . .
and each one is important.
May you remember that every single life is a divine spark . . .
an essence-tial peace . . .
and a holy piece
of divine creation . . .
Sweetly dream . . .
so to create the sweetest of dreams.

```
       0
      0 0
       0
       1
      1 1
    1 1 1 1
     1 1 1
       1
       0
      0 0
       0
```

. . .

MENTAL OBSESSIONS

What is the addiction?

**Life utilizes the individual story
toward the creation of a collective one.
Each experience and expression is instrumental
in balancing cosmic waves that were set in motion eons ago.
Hold space for illusion and reality . . .
that highest good of all to be served.
Let the echoes and negative impressions
of your mental obsessions
free you from the war that wages inside
and all of us from those that exist externally.
So be it . . . And so it IS.**

There is no real freedom until free of your *Mind/mind*. Limitations in life begin with the infiltration of error thoughts. These thoughts come from environment, conditioning, and the collective *mind* field. They are designed to pass through—as a bird or insect whizzing by—but they are caught, caged, and held in the sticky web of your closed mind. *You* are likened to the Venus flytrap, latching on to whatever flies by. As perspectives and filters form, *You/you* build your life from what was imbibed, ironically seeing through the many distorted lenses of the *fly*by. This unconscious *self*-limitation manifests in many ways. *You/you* no longer see, hear, or create from an open place. Your newfound sight and perspective see only what agrees with the thoughts in your head. This forms the patterns, behaviors, prejudices, judgments, fears, desires, and dreams of an *id* entity—a personality made up of unconscious psychic energy that follows the gratification of specific urges, needs, and desires. A trajectory is formed through that identity, resulting in a life lived following that arc. Ironically, *You/you/YOU* become caught in that trap, seemingly unable to free yourself from the thoughts that bound *You*.

**Dogma, belief systems, and brainwashing
—through forms of familial and societal programming—
have created an acceptable form of mental illness.**

We encompass endless bubbles of existence, one inside the other, as dimensions and expanded permutations of the same. To the *n*th degree is a field that is detached, neutral, unconditionally loving—and yet . . . apathetic, indifferent, narcissistic, and *SELF*-obsessed. We are all cells within this greater body. On the basis of the health of our world, *you/i/we/they* are not well. Unless something changes, we will continue *being* a festering wound that feeds on itself. We will continue boiling and blistering until we tend to ourselves, care for ourselves, and become fully present to our mental obsessions. *IS*ness will not interfere.

Dominance, judgment, and opinion are the extensions of *Self/self*-righteous actions from *your/my/our/their* mental obsessions. The attachment to things, people, methods, and *the need to be right* illustrates how closed, disconnected, and trapped *we* have become. Overuse of intellect—in addition to *Self/self*-absorption and psychosis—promulgates further degrees of apathy and indifference. The world is offering a blatant window into the needs and nature of reality. This lens clearly reveals our current manner of *being*, frequency, and vibration. If radically honest, we are a world that is deeply unconscious and asleep. Fear is very much alive and has become a form of *Self/self/SELF*-mutilation and *Self/self/SELF*-denial. It is up to *you/me/us/them* to decondition the condition of insanity held within our bodies, *Mind/minds*, and spirits.

The world is living from the neck up.

You are consciousness within a body. The body is simply a container. If *You/you/YOU* allow thoughts to move through your mind—without responding or reacting to them—life would be experienced differently. Identity kidnaps and holds them hostage. Once held, *Mind/mind* controls, manipulates, and expands thoughts. Stories and fantasy are built around thought. Actions are initiated. Wars have been waged simply due to a thought. Marriages and divorces occur because a thought enters *Mind/mind*. People are killed because of a thought. Organizations are built from a single thought. And yet, thoughts are energetic dust particles that are neutral in and of themselves. They have no real form or function other than being the cosmic debris of mass consciousness.

The mind is a processor that keeps working 24/7. Our world has become riddled with logic, practicality, and thinking. Depression and anxiety are rampant because it is difficult to stop thoughts from cycling morning, noon, and night. These invisible daggers—used against the *Self/self/SELF*—perpetuate human drama. Thoughts, in and of themselves, are not the issue. Latching on to thoughts—chewing on them, regurgitating them, and masturbating them—becomes the problem. The attachment—holding on to what *You* think, what *You* know, and the unconscious desire to control and manipulate the thought—creates drama in your experience. Thoughts float through us constantly. They can just come in and go out, if *You* let them. If not, then *You* give them significance and allow them to lead you onto a windy road or detour. When the same thinking endlessly loops, this is psychosis. It is mental illness and the insanity of our world.

Thoughts are no different from commercials appearing during you favorite television show. *You* probably ignore, mute, or tune out most commercials. They come on, never affecting your experience in any impactful way. But there are times a commercial comes on that grabs your attention. *You* take what just flew past your radar and bring it more deeply into your experience with a reaction, response, or action. *You* did not have to, but you chose to. Thoughts are likened to commercials of the mind's projection screen. While the mind records, processes, and interprets your life, thoughts are continually passing by. *You* can ignore, mute, or tune out these interruptions. By doing so, life will become more peaceful, calm, and joy filled.

> **You are here to engage in the mystery of life.**
> **Control is the antithesis.**
> **Life will continue to bring *You/you/YOU* to the mystery . . .**
> **Willingly or unwillingly.**

In order to become a human *Being/BEING*, humanity must lead. This begins by each person grounding into *Love/LOVE*. This means learning to *Love/LOVE* yourself—not the vanity or superficiality of narcissistic *love*, the applause of external *love*, or the marketed perfection and pretense of entitled *love*—but natural, vulnerable, intimate, raw, full acceptance. Real healing is possible through tenderness, transparency, truth-telling, and presence. You must face the very things *you* have denied, ignored, or turned your back on.

Separation is the precursor for suffering. Both exist in the *Mind/mind*. Separation roots within the false concept of being disconnected from and unlike the Source from which *you/i/we/they* came. It elicits doubt, fear, and comparison as the ego's tool. This keeps *You/you* harnessed in *Mind/mind*, and within the trappings of oppression, victimization, and pain.

The need to fight becomes a belief system; a religion. The need to be right becomes the cross to bear. The resentment and anger you hold keep *You* running from yourself, which *you* cannot do. There is no geographic cure. The other is *you*, and *you* are the other. Everything begins with what children are taught about others and the world. Hate begins at home. It does not begin in another country or from another race. Hate, fear, and prejudice are born inside one's social upbringing. Love is your legacy; time to pass that on by example.

> **Forgiveness is not forgetting, or approving of a behavior;**
> **it is letting go of cords that bind you.**
> **It is the acceptance that all is as it should be,**
> **so that *You* can grow, heal, and move forward.**

What does it mean to be the bridge of transcendence in a world that appears mad? Whether looking at media, codependent relationships, or evil . . . your mental state determines what occurs next. Either *You* will be in reaction, response, or presence. The way through *Self/self/SELF*-obsession is by deepening into stillness, which cultivates a larger lens for the small *self/i*.

Transmutative absorption and *Self/self/SELF*-recognition allow *You/you/YOU* to step into higher states of *Being/BEING*. Transmutation absorbs and transforms energy and emotion. *You/you/YOU* are the bridge to be crossed, in order to inhabit a new way of *Being/BEING*. *Mind/mind* must make the choice to inhabit higher *MIND*. Deconditioning opens the way for empathy and *Self/self/SELF-Love/LOVE*. Through embodying the higher *SELF/I*, while purposefully dismantling the story, *Self/eye* has a blank canvas upon which to create new life. Blessed *being/Being/BEING* . . . Breathe deeply as *You/you/YOU* dissolve your mental obsessions.

May you remember . . .
You/you/YOU are the mess . . . the message . . . and the messenger . . .
May you remember . . .
that all are dreamers . . . all are creators . . .
and all are magnificent creatures
of life's magical unfolding.
May you remember . . .
we are the heroines . . . the heroes . . . and the superheroes . . .
May you remember . . .
we share the same blood . . .
and part of the same mind.
Sweetly dream . . .
so to create the sweetest of dreams.

. . .

OUR GLOBAL REFLECTION OF INFORMATION AND TECHNOLOGY

What is the mirror?

As discord increases,
increasing levels of data corruption are encoded
into the software of society.
You/I/We/They are the hardware, and
our minds and hearts are the software.
Either we remove the bugs
or we will be wiped clean.

The world's capacity to move at the speed of light has come. Information is at our fingertips with the touch of a key. The constant bombardment of content, media, news, fake news, propaganda, and tabloid gossip is the white noise in our lives. This flooding of information compounds endless thought forms in streaming about. *Your/my/our/their* minds are *Being/being* hijacked by filters, perspectives, and conditioning. *You/i/we/they* believe we are in control. However, *we* are *being* controlled by the influence, trends, and speed of information and technology.

The worldwide web connects us in an instant, making this huge world incredibly small. This means we can expose big problems instantaneously, while also blowing up small issues in a millisecond. Privacy, storage, and security make it possible for us to live in clouds and vaults . . . mainframes and avatars. You can reach out and touch someone across the world, while being completely disconnected to the person sitting across from you at dinner. Once you are in your phone, tablet, or computer, *You/you/YOU* have traveled into the ethers; well, the ethernet. This pseudocosmic realm of the universe lets *You/you/YOU* live *virtually* anywhere for minutes to hours at a time.

However, there is a dark side to the net as well. Terrorism on the web through hacking, identity theft, and fraud becomes easier and easier. A total stranger in another country can find out everything about *You* instantly. Elections can be easily manipulated. Social media can be used to track, stalk, and watch *You*. Marketing ads follow your choices across multiple platforms once expressing interest in an item. And many believe that *You/i/we/they* are being watched and listened to through smartphones and similar devices. Who exactly is watching, and why? How can eight billion people be tracked? Are we really here, or is this truly the matrix? How can *You* unplug?

It is time to awaken from your self-imposed slumber.
If filters and screens were removed, only truth could remain.

Information technology has quietly become the next method of control for society. Very few people know how to unplug, and most do not, from fear of missing out. As much as it is used for connection and communication, technology is destroying our ability to truly connect and communicate. Inherently, technology is not *bad*; the imbalance of how much it is utilized creates havoc. The influx of information is distracting and distorting, pulling *You/you/YOU* from your center and away from your true soul voice. Information technology teases, courts, romances, and feeds the ego and identity. Technology has become an extension of who *You/you/YOU* are. It controls your time, moods, actions, and behaviors. As technology gets smaller and more convenient, information becomes more expanded and reachable. *You/you/YOU* become more and more dependent and addicted. The phone might as well be another aperture of the body.

You are a human computer in many ways—processor, memory board, optical drive, and power supply. The mother board—consciousness inside *You*—coordinates and links all of these parts. Every time *You/you/YOU* allow a negative thought, *You* encrypt information and programming *you* will operate by. This is how *Mind/mind* is compromised by viruses. Too much information is running through—conscious and unconscious—which leads to corruption and disruption.

When overloaded with mental stress, the human computer will crash. *You* will require a reboot, and possibly a complete overhaul due to burnout. Mental illness is at an all-time high. Psychological imbalances such as bipolar illness, depression, and narcissism deaden empathy and lead to more issues—in partners, children, and coworkers—due to the impact of their affects. We are killing our humanity and becoming machines, while also *being* run by the machines on our laps, in our palms, on our wrists, and in our ears. Artificial intelligence is already operating at the realm of Spirit through how your ego dominates. It will not be long before the mirror of manifest artificial intelligence is in control. This will create another form of oppression, slavery, and warfare.

You have lived the lie long enough.
How about the truth for a while?

Source supplies greater intel. *You/you/YOU* can access information far beyond this material world. Your intelligence is linked to *MIND*. This does encompass the collective *Mind/mind/MIND* field, but it surpasses this stream of thought forms. Commune with the superconscious *MIND*. To access this boundless space, you must lose your *Mind/mind*.

You are so much more than a human computer. To know this, *You/you/YOU* must unplug. Connect to the ethers as opposed to the ethernet. Open to guidance beyond the media, influencers, or Google. *You/you/YOU* are the spiritual technology here to experience itself. *You/you/YOU* are the divine entertainment here to express itself. *You/you/YOU* are by design—grand universal design—here to invent and reinvent yourself. In embodying a higher vibrational resonance within the world, Spirit can use *YOU* as a virtual conduit of sacred information and divine technology for the full expression of higher wisdom and energetic transmutation. Blessed *being/Being/BEING* . . . Breathe deeply as *You/you/YOU* embody an upgrade of higher consciousness.

> **May you palpably feel the gentle tapping of Source**
> **deeply with your cells . . .**
> **weaving through your DNA . . .**
> **coursing through your veins.**
> **May you clearly hear Spirit's soft whispers . . .**
> **tender nudges . . .**
> **and ancient call.**
> **May you realize that you walk among angels . . .**
> **and angels in disguise.**
> **May your heart flower with forgiveness . . .**
> **and the fragrance of compassion.**
> **Sweetly dream . . .**
> **so to create the sweetest of dreams.**

. . .

THE HOLE OF WRATH

What is the disease?

> **We are fish in a global pond.**
> **Creating waves and swirls,**
> **hurricanes, cyclones, and tsunamis.**
> **Our power surges;**
> **the light goes out.**
> **The sizzle . . . the sparks . . . the explosion.**
> **The leaks must be plugged;**
> **the waters must be calmed . . .**
> **Because right now . . .**
> **the reflection is a little fishy.**

Growing violence in the world is a reflection of how we use words and thoughts as weapons. It illustrates how we treat ourselves, environments, and those among us. Guns can kill, but before a gun is ever lifted, a word, thought, and energy have been inflicted. Guns are physical reactionary manifestations of a wound and death that already transpired in the one holding the weapon. War is a compounded response. Rage and wrath are not natural or original. Grown in the soil of indifference, apathy, and self-absorption, these seeds are planted, grown, cultivated, and harvested. These dense energies eat away at *you* from the inside out.

Those with anger lash out, spew language, bully, and threaten. They are unable to love due to *Self/self/SELF*-hate. These people symbolize the extreme pain existing within and walking among us. Conflicted by the stories they tell—and beliefs that have become their dogma—the wounded psyche cries out in the only way it knows. Expressing with violence in thought, word, and deed provides a release of energy but never frees the person from their pain. Believing in their victimization, they feel justified in their behaviors and actions. They were taught to hate and to fear. These individuals have little or no empathy. They are weak in emotional intelligence and strongly indifferent.

Your truth will be self-evident; it will be lived and embodied.
That will be its loudspeaker . . . the megaphone.
This voice cannot be ignored or denied or go unheard.

When individuals are not seen, heard, and acknowledged by those closest to them—families, communities, cities—issues mount until a boiling point is reached. This leads to further crisis, chaos, and corruption. Wrath looks like hate crimes, looting, violence, suicide bombing, and acts of war. What appears grandiose on a collective level stems from ignorance that began as a small seed of hate. The voice that cries eventually becomes the loud voice that rages, when people do not feel listened to. When individuals do not feel heard, they feel forced into methods that let them feel heard.

Anger, rage, and wrath are the underbelly of many interpersonal reactions. Some are held within the masks of nicety, politeness, jokes, and giggles. Other times, these dense emotions rest beneath passive aggressiveness, little digs, secrecy, gossip, and incessant lying. More blatantly, they appear as loud arguments, voices of oppression, or expressions of dominance and violence. There is a fine line between sanity and insanity. Becoming caught in dramas, resentments, and crazed behavior . . . is insanity. When *you* lose focus and do not respond from love, you have gone insane. Hate, war, rage, and animosity are illustrations of people reaching levels of insanity.

While the world's issues may not be about *You*,
the task *You/you/YOU* have in easing the worlds suffering is all about *you*.

White lies are parasites that grow larger and larger, creating illusions where truth once stood. These not only fuel anger but also create *self*-hate. Gossip, lies, secrets, and withholding are grave and deadly cancers. These small acts lead to *self*-sabotage, *self*-betrayal, and eventually *self*-hate. Rage and wrath build incrementally over time. These are projected expressions of *self*-hate.

Be aware of your triggers and your weapons. Watch your reactions and explosions. Notice your need to stray from truth and compromise integrity. Doing so builds resentment and grievances. Speak the truth, first and foremost to hear yourself. Speak your truth . . . to know where inner work and outer work are required. Stand in the integrity of your actions. Most importantly, cultivate compassionate presence. These moment-to-moment steps of purification will assist recalibrating *You* toward purity. Blessed *being/Being/BEING* . . . Breathe deeply as *You/you/YOU* dissolve your wrath.

May there be love in the shadows . . .
love-making within the veils . . .
and loving kindness amid the jagged edges of time.
May there be compassion in all that occurs . . .
understanding within rigid moments . . .
and peace in every second.
May the little things be cherished . . .
May we truly see, hear, and acknowledge one another.
Sweetly Dream . . .
so to create the sweetest of dreams.

. . .

THE KEY WHOLE OF PURITY

How is personal power activated?

Open your vastness . . .
the connective tissue of your being . . .
the magma of your quantum field . . .
the light within your eyes . . .
the breath within your lungs . . .
and the beating of your heart.
Know me as yourself.
I am you . . . You are me . . .
We are One and shall always be.

YOU/I/WE/THEY are pure expressions at birth. The mental body has not been corrupted. The emotional body has not been polluted. The energetic body has not been violated. The physical body has not been subjugated. The spiritual body has not been infected. The auric body has not been infiltrated. *YOU/I/WE/THEY* are *BEING*—embodying a clear, pristine, worthy, and natural state. This is the crystalline, diamond *SELF you* inhabit before conditioning begins. Despite your life experiences, it is possible to return to that state of *BEING*. *You* realign with purity by releasing wrath, gluttony, pride, envy, greed, lust, and slothfulness.

Your life holds divine purpose.
It is destined and will occur despite you.

You/you/YOU are not considered powerful by the degree to which *You* make people see and hear. *You/you/YOU* are not great because *You* tell, teach, guide, perform, do, create, or manifest in the world. Your magnificence is not dependent on popularity, material status, or external appearance. Life catalysts and transformers do so by their example. They change their own lives. These people allow the fullness of what is within them to be actualized—first and foremost for themselves—and generously given to others in a truthful, wholehearted manner.

Being/being/BEING the purity of your experience and expression is all that is necessary. This level of authenticity is how *You/you/YOU* have an impact—tell, teach, guide, and lead—in the most powerful way. Fully immerse in the purity of wherever *You* find yourself—shadow, light, wounded child, divine child, or *God/god/GOD/GODDESS*. Embodying all of it is *Being/being/BEING* human. This dual world has called *You/you/YOU* for this purpose. It then asks for your immersed awareness in each space so that *You/you/YOU* may transcend these different dimensions and experience others within. Purify your *Self/self/SELF* with immersive presence. Absorb every part of *You/you/YOU* into pure wholeness.

How often do you gaze into another's eyes deeply enough to see their soul?
When did you sit with someone, fully listening from every part of your being?

The ills of this world—the pain of broken hearts, the trauma in physical bodies, the fear inside minds—can be deeply diminished if individuals were truly held by another. This costs nothing, and it is priceless. This simple, pure act not only holds power, but it is also the doorway to a greater sense of *Self/SELF*. Life is full, providing everything *You/you/YOU* need. Plain and simple, *You/you/YOU* have come to *experience*. There is nothing required within that—nothing to solve or fix . . . and nothing to do or become. Heaven is simply one deep breath after another . . . and another. Sink into the purity and simplicity of that.

How often do you call instead of texting?
When did you last bring a person into conscious awareness to feel their experience,
their heart, their hurts, and their dreams?

LOVE is the only solution, curing all ills, deficiencies, hurts, pains, doubts, and debts by way of better choices. For those who fully embody LOVE, the experience of life becomes a playground of the highest creation, manifestation, and inspiration. Each step toward LOVE brings forth an openheartedness that expands a life of purity. LOVE empowers living a life of good health, fullness, wellness, ease, confidence, and wealth. Purity is falling in LOVE with your *Self/self/SELF* as *You/you/YOU* are in each moment. Living each moment as it comes—not asking anything of it, but fully receiving everything from it—is the embodiment of Essence. Blessed *being/Being/BEING* . . . Breathe deeply as *You/you/YOU* live the purity of your expression.

May you be still . . .
allowing each day to retire.
May you release all that has passed . . .
It is no more . . . It is not you.
May you release anxiety . . .
tomorrow is not to be feared.
May you free yourself from the future . . .

the illusion of war.

It will never come . . . There is only now.
May you breathe in this moment . . .
It is complete . . . It is whole . . . It is everything.
Sweet Dream . . .
so to create the sweetest of dreams.

. . .

REVOLUTIONARY TO SPIRITUAL REBEL

How does purpose unfold?

Let go of *Mind/mind*.
Expand your loving essence.
Open the heart.
There is no where to go,
nothing to do,
and not one thing to be fixed . . .
only the expression
of infinite love
through your creative capacity matters.

Give up the struggle. Every revolution—personal or collective—is an attempt to change your past. Every conflict is an echo of something from childhood that is coming back around. Life reincarnates with the same callings to heal lies, wounds, and distortions. However, these callings are not from outside *You/you/YOU*; they resound from the inside. The outer world manifests in collaboration with *You/you/YOU*, toward cocreating your best life. Sometimes opposites are required to get your ego out of the way. Outer interference is manifested from the divide within your mind, heart, and body. Do not mistake the experience as anything more than a message; otherwise *You* will become even more lost.

You/you/YOU are here to save no other. *You/you/YOU* are not to rescue anyone or heal anything. The very thought of such keeps those *you* intend to serve locked inside their paradigms of pain. That need to save another is a subtle, codependent way to give your life meaning. It requires other people's lives to be sacrificed for the sake of your need to feel important, significant, and on purpose. This keeps people, places, and things imprisoned within their constructs of struggle, pain, and oppression. *You* hold others hostage—with your need for significance—keeping their world caught within the loop of struggle. It also binds *You/you/YOU* to your past, since the very thing *You* are driven by is an old wound. The occupation, mission, or vision *You/YOU* currently project onto the world is an attempt to fix, save, or heal your *past self.*

Who were you before you had to take care of the adults in the room?
If you had not been wounded in childhood—holding the current story of the past—
what would you be doing with your life?

Healers, nurses, and doctors are wounded healers, caring for others, but they are in need of *self*-care. They took care of the *big* people as children and continue to do so. Accountants are attempting to reconcile all that felt imbalanced in childhood, navigating the swings between emotional connection, physical richness, and poverty. They must seek why they feel guilty and indebted to others. Their codependence places them in the red regarding *self*-care. Law enforcement, first responders, and soldiers protect others because they were not protected. Never feeling fully safe, they desire to be in control, serve, and protect those like themselves. Lawyers are navigating the confusion of injustices witnessed, experienced, or involved in. Judgment from others was present in their lives early on. They have a need to fight, argue, take a stand, and balance the scales. Those in real estate navigate a sense of worth. Real estate—which is actually representative of their bodies, emotions, and thoughts—symbolizes feeling at home within themselves. Grounding is of utmost importance for these individuals. Dentists focus on small areas so as not to address the emptiness and decay that was felt early on. They compartmentalize and micromanage life, out of a need to control. Many lost their voices as children and are in need of establishing new roots of *self*-worth. Those in photography, film, and television desire to control the images in front of them. These individuals often suffer from mental obsessions of thoughts and pictures in their minds that are not able to be reconciled. Bankers seek relationship. The feeling of disconnection creates a desire to interact with others, but often from a guarded and distant place. They struggle with value, battling between pleasing others and pleasing themselves. Motivational speakers, inspirational speakers, and coaches seek to be seen, heard, and acknowledged; they were neglected, ignored, and not seen, heard, or acknowledged as children. Their inspiration and motivation are an effort to convince themselves. We are all run by our subconscious programming. It requires continuous conscious effort to be aware of where each agenda and intent stems from.

What did *you* want to do when *you* thought anything was possible?
What hobbies, delights, whims, and fantasies have *you* put away?

If you delve deeply into your current actions and endeavors, *You* will see the link to the past. *You* might enjoy your work; however, if your occupation has become your identity, then *You* are clinging to the past in some way. This manifestation is a veil that rests between *You* and *YOU*. If experiencing lethargy and boredom—requiring *You* to push, toil, and will yourself to work each day—then your spirit is weary. *You* are not required to choose a new path; do whatever *You* desire. Merely contemplate the foundation of your choices. The steps of your life have been your path of revolution; a way to war against the past and prove that *You* won. There is no need to be in survival mode any longer. Choose what allows *You/you/YOU* to thrive and feel alive. That may mean letting your current life go for an unknown. An unknown life. An unknown Self.

Your subconscious steers each and every choice *You/you/YOU* have made. This unconscious pre*occupation* with past wounding maintains shadow patterns and behaviors, while also steering choices to keep fixing the old issue. This keeps *You* from living the life of your dreams. When *You* truly get still—and money and security are out of the equation—contemplate what life *You/you/YOU* really would live. Those whims, fantasies, and delights are the divine child, dreaming, imagining, and living from the purity of essence. Everything that happened to *you* covered that up, making *you* believe that life meant *being* practical, perfect, productive, and homogenized.

There is no war present; *You/you/YOU* fight for something that already happened and cannot be undone. Every moment is an opportunity to let go of belief. Therein is real freedom. A simple and loving act would be to let go. Your beliefs either expand, contract, free, or bind you. They keep you separate or lead toward Oneness. The ego will fight to exist, and the heart has the power to love it to smithereens. Love fiercely . . . rage gently.

What comes to mind if *You* could do anything?
Notice the resistance to that possibility.
Notice the questions, the excuses, the responsibilities, and the fear that rises.
That is the real work to do, so that you can embark on the play *You* desire.

You/you/YOU are the new dawn. To see this clearly, *You/you* must close your eyes to what is in front of *You*, and open your heart to what is inside *You/you/YOU*. Open eyes perceive through the filtered lens of illusion. *You* perceive a cause, the fight, and those who have fallen. *You* do not recognize how your interference maintains the cause . . . the fight . . . or the revolutionary war of words, thoughts, and deeds. The revolutionary sees only *wrongs* they attempt to *make right*. Even the one that *fights the good fight* fights only with himself, projecting that outwardly. Detach from what was.

True detachment means fully feeling—remaining intimate with the pain—but not being overcome by it. *You/you/YOU* are not separating or turning away. Detachment is empathy in the highest expression of *Being/BEING*. *You* perceive the big picture, while allowing heartbreak to transmute the energies from the inside out. This honors each person where they are, seeing the Divine in and as them. When willing to recognize the wholeness of others—in their power and capability—*You* set them free. Equally important, *You* set *You/you/YOU* free.

When feeling, channel emotion toward creative endeavors—things that keep *You/you/YOU* in the moment. Allow beauty to emerge from the darkness expressing. Let lightness balance the heaviness. Amid this dance, awaken expansive infinity out of the illusion of limitation. Feel deeply, but when respite is required, find what offers timeless presence as a divine conduit—painting, dancing, writing, walking, exercising, running, singing, etc.

There is no thing and no one to save, fix, or help; neither inside nor out.
You need do nothing.
Your sacred presence as witness is enough.

The world must shift into holding all as capable and empowered. The paradigm of believing others need saving, fixing, or healing—or that there is a mission to fulfill, people to help, and problems to solve—does not align with an empowered vision of a world that is free or at peace. It empowers the opposite. The shrill cry to change something only keeps it in place. A consciousness steeped in the spirit of celebration is a new way for empowering the collective.

Individuals will continue creating, building, serving, and rising, but their choices of these areas will stem out of inspiration as opposed to wounding. We will still have scientists and healers and teachers—accountants, firefighters, and doctors—but out of enthusiasm for experiencing, not out of practicality, logic, or family tradition. In this way, all necessary solutions will organically come about. Society will expand through the purity and generosity of empowered creative *Being/BEING*, rather than wounded *being*. Every endeavor will be for *Self/self/SELF*, not for projection onto the other. This releases the codependent function of saving another.

In a new world of aliveness, an inherent knowing of worthiness exists. Experience honors that. Here, achievement is for the sake of expression—as an example—and in celebration. It is the calling to be fulfilled through joyful creative exploration for as long as it feels good, and then the freedom to move to something else.

Leading by example requires absolute commitment to *Self/self/SELF*, placing one's vision behind their eyes so that every thought, word, and deed are in direct alignment. Focus and vision require discipline and devotion to becoming the very act embarked upon. What begins as DO-ing becomes BE-ing.

The spiritual rebel knows there is no one to save, fix, or heal on the outside.
They clearly understand that there is no one to save, fix, or heal on the inside.
They live in the essence of their creative capacity.

The spiritual rebel stands in *Truth/TRUTH*, knowing uniqueness, creativity, and wholeness despite anything that is happening with the 3-D experience. The spiritual rebel believes that genius emerges when standing in inner freedom. Ahead of their *time*, the spiritual rebel lives on the fringe of daily happenings—allowing present energies to be embodied— but does not get sucked into the black hole of attachment. This pioneering spirit is innovative and creative, delighted in their own exquisite creative capacity.

A rebel's action comes from deep silence and spontaneity. They live in the *Yes* with openhearted fullness. The rebel creates—continuously giving birth to *Self/self/SELF* as an art form—through constant reinvention. Heralding the new dawn, this hue-man creates in the land of all-possibility, accessing unknown dimensions. The spiritual rebel does not focus on problems. They allow space for *soulutions* to organically emerge out of the collective sphere. The spiritual rebel possesses unyielding discipline and patience to see all matters to their end, without interfering.

Don't be surprised if there are two people in you now . . .
the familiar face that comes and goes in the world,
and another,
one you don't know yet . . .
This one takes the Unknown Road . . . the Rebel Path.
This one whispers . . .
Find your road . . . and follow it.
That path belongs only to you.

The rebel holds nothing and is attached to nothing. There is deep trust in life, knowing that everything is here. There is no need to cling . . . grasp . . . toil . . . or fear. The creative rebel is a spiritual being that has moved beyond excuses into living wildly divine. These individuals are rooted in trust, embracing everything that comes their way. When following your dreams, *You/you/YOU* model this for others. When *You/you/YOU* do what you *Love*, the world is given permission to express as *Love*. All people are history makers, paradigm changers, and dimension shifters when consciously present to inner creative capacity. Blessed *being/Being/ BEING* . . . Breathe deeply as *You/you/YOU* awaken to the spiritual rebel within you.

May your life be filled with rebellion
against all that binds, holds, and stifles you.
May you rebel against what quiets your voice,
suppresses creative urges, and blocks creativity.
May you rebel against conformity . . .
this will not be the fight of rebellion.
Rebellion will be the celebration of Spirit expressing through you.
You are not designed like any other.
May your uniqueness shine for the world to see.
May your voice echo . . .
your heart express beauty . . .
your soul endeavor upon its song . . .
and your consciousness express your gifts of creativity.
This is life's imagining of you . . .
Let your lucidity
be heavens dream . . .
Sweetly dream . . .
so to create the sweetest of dreams . . .

. . .

CULTIVATING GENEROSITY

How can peace arise?

May you integrate the importance
of fully seeing another.
May your praxis anchor knowing
through the art of embodied ardent prayer.
May you see your sisters and brothers healthy and safe,
unafraid and calm . . .
lending helping hands
and creating a brand-new dawn.

You are being used well; in a divine capacity, regardless of your circumstances, story, or position. Your willingness to live from your highest *SELF* is how to give and receive more of *YOU*. Personal power, purpose, and peace are divine threads of generosity, holding high frequencies. No effort is required in *Being/BEING* generous; *You/you* need only be present in receiving your *SELF*. Let your life be served by *Love/LOVE* deepening inside *You/you/YOU*. That ever-unfolding expression is your flowering, fragrance, and beauty as natural generosity.

    You hold a seed of light that is hidden within your darkest darkness. It is buried in the cold ground of *being*. Your darkness cannot reveal this light until *You/you* descend into your roots of time. The seed has no knowing of its *Light/LIGHT*, that it shall rise, or that growth is imminent. Its destiny is to shine. *You/you/YOU* cannot think your way through this process.

It can only be felt, embodied, experienced, and expressed from what hibernates within *You/you/YOU*. Delve into the unknown *Self/self/SELF* by generously giving in to each moment that meets *You/you/YOU*. In your presence to *Self/self/SELF* is the generosity of Spirit. To bless those *You* encounter, *You* need only be *You/you/YOU*—the authentic *You/you/YOU*— no matter how that expresses: monster, animal, shadow, human, angel, essence, god.

Your legacy is all of life; the good, the bad, and the ugly.
What you hold in heart and mind
is what you generously cast into form.

Generously giving yourself to the experience in front of *You/you/YOU* will guide your next steps. *You* will transform and grow on your own accord. It will occur as *You/you/YOU* are destined, and not before. Breakthroughs arrive when intended, as do breakdowns. There is nothing for *You/you/YOU* to do. Your *Light/LIGHT* will emerge as a sunrise upon your lifetime. You are nature, following the cycles of your life. *You* will be provided choices that bring *you* to the ground, so that *YOU* receive the richness hidden beneath the soil of your *being*. Tend to your *Self/self/SELF*.

Cultivate the generosity of spirit, so *You* move past veneers. See beyond the surface. All encounters are expressions of *You/you/YOU*. To know thyself, *You* must see thyself in everyone. Knowing thyself requires the generosity of radical truth. Your worth is the measure of your shadow awareness and *Light/LIGHT* presence. Your generosity is only as grand as those *You/you/YOU* have injured most.

No person ever sees the full extent of their shadows or darkness.
For this reason, life provides mirrors that reflect these.

Generosity arises when *YOU* give what *You* believe *You/you/YOU* do not have. By giving presence—to your animal, monster, innocence, divinity, and humanity—*You/you/YOU* receive what the world requires in order to equilibrate. When *You* participate with full presence, *You* give life all of *You/you/YOU*. In this way, Spirit sees and perceives, hears and listens, touches and is touched by . . . the grace of your freedom.

Generosity awakens into your aura of holiness, emitting the fragrance of sacredness. Because *You/you* have released the visceral fight, your flavor of wholeness depicts the true humility that arises from living in harmony with your soul song. To give generously— unconditionally and purely—means giving up the warring aspect that has *you* controlled by wrath's mental obsessions. Do not seek a revolution. Instead, spiritually rebel into your highest expression of *Love* and *Light*. The world is calling for *You* to offer the generosity of seeing thyself . . . through the lens of your Divine creative capacity.

Sit in the silence.
Let it exhaust the noise.
Bathe in the quiet space.
Let it wash away the clutter.
Surrender to the symphony
that exists beyond all sound.

When releasing resistance, *You/you/YOU* absorb what is at war inside. Your ability to receive is directly proportionate to this giving. What is placed in your hands, heart, and mind has been created to be given away. Your full expression appears when generosity is not about giving up, but giving in. Allow your real feelings, genuine expression, and true voice. Experience your creative ability, passion, and worth. The inhale of all that is discordant within *You/you/YOU*—fully acknowledged, experienced, and absorbed—expands your *Light/LIGHT*. When blocking emotions, *You/you/YOU* block your ability to radiate higher frequencies. In not feeling, *You* are being stingy. By not authentically living your *Truth/TRUTH*, *You/you/YOU* are *being* selfish and greedy with what Spirit endowed. Standing in your full expression is purity. Hold nothing back! This is not a state of mind; it is whole-bodied generosity, which will increase your receptivity of success, love, and joy. Giving and receiving are one. *You/you/YOU* are that experience of oneness.

When each moment appears to pull everything away,
can you give more of yourself?
When the enemy steals your gold,
can you give him the silver too?
When your life is ripped away,
can you still give all of who you are?

Your generosity of spirit lie in giving and receiving of all that *You/you/YOU* are: your listening, your connection, your conversation, your naturalness, your presence, your time, your emotional intelligence, your intuition, your wellness, and your love. Receive these things of yourself, and *You/you/YOU* will give generously to this planet and all people. Blessed *being/Being/BEING* ... Breathe deeply as *You/you/YOU* experience your generosity.

May you savor the generosity of time, experience, and expression
for how it produces a tapestry of wisdom.
May life fill your vessel completely ...
as you remember to engage union and communion.
May the generosity of spirit become your devotional act of sacred service ...
through unconditionally sharing your time, presence, love, and action.
May a newly awakened state of *Being*
be distilled from the stories of your past,
and fantasies of the future,
that you meet with the unfolding now.
Sweetly dream ...
so to create the sweetest of dreams.

. . .

SEE THYSELF

What is the asking?

Now I see who my guru has been.
Darkness has been
my deity.
I sacrifice my *self* unto thee.
I am a disciple, not only of life
but also of death.
In dancing with my shadows,
I am lifted into Light.
My surrender is not to what was,
not even to what is,
but in becoming all that is *BEING*.

AFFIRMATION—CONTEMPLATION—INSPIRATION

I AM capable of awakening to where I hold
criticism, condemnation, and judgment.
I now transcend all places of *Self/self/SELF*-contempt.

Contemplate and journal these inquiries until inspired to take action.
Be still; see what rises as *conditioning* versus *visioning*.
You/you/YOU possess the answer for achieving aliveness . . . go within.

The degree to which you are *Being/being/BEING*
is the degree to which *You/you/YOU*
shall cultivate inner and outer *Generosity*.

What is your self-obsessed story around war, force, and power?

war.
Where are *You/you* at war with . . .
- others?
- yourself?
- your feelings?
- your mind?
- your dreams?

How have you convinced yourself of *Being* . . .
- at peace?
- beyond past hurts, resentments, and jealousy?

What things do *You/you* claim are "over," "done with," "complete," or "already healed"?

Where are *You/you* living in . . .
- the shadow of masculine energy?
- the fight?
- violent thought, word, and deed?
- aggression or arrogance?
- mechanical or robotic movements?

Where are *You/you* living in . . .
- the shadow of feminine energy?
- manipulation?
- neediness?
- dependence?

mental reflections.

Do *You/you/YOU* have dominion over your . . .
- mental world?
- mind and thoughts?

How often do *You/you* . . .
- need to know?
- make up things?
- go over conversations in your head?
- go into the past?
- go into the future?

Where do *You/you/YOU* assert control?

Where are *You/you/YOU* out of control?
Where have *You/you/YOU* released control?

wrath.

What role does anger and resentment play within your life?

What has anger attracted into your experience?

How do anger, aggression, and resentment feel in your . . .
- body?
- mind?
- heart?

How do *You/you* . . .
- express them?
- deny them?
- repress them?
- be with them?

purity.

How can *You/you/YOU* experience purity of . . .
- emotion without attachment to thought or story?
- action?
- *Love/LOVE*?
- *Self/self/SELF*?

revolutionary to spiritual rebel.

Is confrontation your version of revolution?

How are conflict and war . . .
- spiritual?
- used as fuel, and for what?
- balancing?

Whom have *You/you/YOU* been trying to save, fix, or heal?

If there were no problems or conflicts, no challenges or chaos, who would *You/you/YOU* be?

If energy were not focused on your current situation, what dreams would *You/you/YOU* focus on?

What would living an inspired life look like?

generosity.

How are *You/you/YOU* generous to . . .
- yourself?
- your dreams?
- others?

How can *You/you/YOU* more deeply embody and express generosity within your . . .
- body?
- life?
- relationships?
- world?
- passions and play?

see thyself.

What would *You/you/YOU* consciously create **in** your world?

How would *You/you/YOU* consciously . . .
- express an embodied *Self*?
- create your life?
- dive into dreams?

May *You/you/YOU* be blessed with the awareness to . . .
let go of struggle . . . let go of tension . . . and let go of thoughts . . .
May *You/you/YOU* gently . . .
release into receiving . . .
while releasing control . . .
becoming fully aware of your emotions.
As *You/you/YOU* deepen sensitivity . . .
let go of your identity.
May *You/you/YOU* sweetly dream . . .
so to create the sweetest of dreams.

. . .

PETITION FOR PEACE

What is the shift in consciousness?

I love *you*.
The world loves *You*.
The universe loves *You/you/YOU*.
I Love ME . . . I Love *YOU* . . . I Love US.
Only through communication and connection,
and mutual love and affection,
will we unify as one
and see oneness.
IN COLLECTIVE PRAYER FOR SEEING . . .
COOPERATION AND TRANSPARENCY
IN GLOBAL COMMUNICATION AND CONNECTIVITY

Dear Infinite Oneness . . .
We stand barefoot and naked,
in innocence before you . . .
weary and worn, tired and forlorn.
Longing to remember . . . who we were
before . . . we were at all.
We became lost in time . . .
forgetting everything beyond matter.
We fought . . . have been at war . . . and have died repeatedly.

We drifted within veils and searched amid shadows.
becoming caught in our own seeking . . .
and ensnared by our own tongues.
We petition for intimate connection to one another . . .
as your children from the sun.
In days that are dark,
support us in seeing the light . . .
in each other
and our world.
In times that feel tough,
help us hear the softness of each stranger's heart
and the heartbeat of this world.
When conflicts rise,
guide us into acknowledging our piece of the puzzle
and peace with one another.
Although each may feel alone,
let us fully realize we are all one.
Strengthen our union and communion.
Be the quiet centering within our hearts.
Provide your whispers
within the winds of change . . .
placing your footprints
upon our sands of time.
Reflect your synchronicity
throughout our lives
and allow us to see ourselves
through different eyes.
Peace be with us,
now and forever more.

Teach us to be guardians
of your pure perfection and power . . .
angels of generosity . . .
As peaceful troubadours . . .
whose words, thoughts, and actions
rest upon Love's ferocity . . .
to bring heaven to earth
in divine creed and sacred velocity.
The past says k(no)w more . . .
The present is Now . . .
I AM . . .
In sight.
So be it . . .
And so it IS!

```
      0
     0 0
    0 0 0
   1 1 1 1
    1 1 1
     1 1
      1
      1
     1 1
    1 1 1
   1 1 1 1
    0 0 0
     0 0
      0
```

the sacrifice.

What are you giving?

Will you keep going . . .
Will you continue chasing your tail . . .
Will you catch hold of it,
swallowing yourself bit by bit . . .
until you know the *Self/self/SELF* from the inside out?
Sacrifice and surrender . . .
are winding, narrow steps.
Do not confuse their direction . . .
or where they lead.
Otherwise, you will go in circles . . .
Such is the nature of sacrifice.

This book may not have been easy to stomach, but the solar plexus is your place of power. Discomfort in that area indicates that attention is necessary. I do not discount the beauty of our diverse world or the vast experience that it offers, but this deep dive into the abyss is the final frontier for each of us. For *LIGHT* to exist within each of us, the balance of *DARKNESS* must as well. To the degree *you/i/we/they* clamor for the *Light/LIGHT*, we must acknowledge and embrace the equivalent *Darkness/DARKNESS*. Fully owning your *LIGHT* requires fully owning all of the gray areas too. Global experiences of Darkness appear externally to mirror what *You* have been unwilling to see about your *self . . . me . . . them . . . all* of us. This experience of *self*-realization walks through the fires that have ignited around us. It is easy to attack, condemn, and want to hang those that portray the monster. The ego needs a distracting villain to keep *You* from looking within. Examples of the monstrous darkness surface all the time, each one more sinister. Until willing to find what lives within *You/you/YOU*, it will continue to manifest in our world. Are *You/you/YOU* willing to own the mirrors that have manifested?

- Harvey Weinstein, Bill Cosby, and Jeffrey Epstein—sexual harassment, misogyny, and abuse
- Derek Chauvin, white supremacists, Nazism-racism, brutality, prejudice, and violence
- ISIS, Osama bin Laden, Adolf Hitler—terrorism, warfare, and brainwashing

- Bernie Madoff, Enron, Lehman Brothers—fraud, financial scams, corruption, and greed
- Jamal Khashoggi, Charles Manson, Ted Bundy, Jeffrey Dahmer—torture, brutality, serial killers, and murder

To think these horrors exist only within them, or to even use their atrocities as a way to distract *You* from the shadow, animal monster that lives inside *you*, is to dishonor what that soul chose in order to heal *you/me/us/them* and equilibrate the energy. It also dishonors those souls who were victimized. Unknowingly, every individual holds the full creative capacity of *LIGHT* and *DARKNESS*. Only through complete acceptance of this can *you/i/ we/they* masterfully and responsibly wield the immense power and presence in our possession.

You are yin and yang . . . darkness and light . . .
the monster and the innocent . . . the devil and the god.
You/you/YOU **create in the image and likeness of where your heart and mind reside.**

It may feel blasphemous to consider what is *being* revealed here. But until each person realizes that the world reveals only *who we are* and *what we emerge from*, it cannot truly change. Awareness is the first step toward healing. The *SELF*-obsession of Source—to know, see, hear, know, and express itself—was an infatuation of infinite proportions. This primal face—of need, desire, and greed . . . hierarchy, indifference, and apathy . . . knowledge, ignorance, and wisdom . . . singularity, multiplicity, and nothingness . . . schizophrenia, bipolar, and narcissism—was born out of divine curiosity. This craving is the *DARK* side of the *Light/LIGHT*, which unfolded into a land of opposites, equally good and evil. With craving comes aversion. Look to movies or art to witness the consciousness *being* holds:

- horror movies: *Halloween, The Exorcist, The Shining, Alien, Psycho*, etc.
- fantasy movies: *The Dark Crystal, Lord of the Rings, Narnia, Maleficent, Harry Potter*, etc.
- sexual: porn, *Basic Instinct, Eyes Wide Shut, Dressed to Kill, Fifty Shades of Grey*, etc.
- psychological thrillers: *Silence of the Lambs, Misery, Saw, Sixth Sense, Se7en*, etc.
- greed: *Joker, Scarface, The Godfather, Wall Street, The Aviator, Casino*, etc.
- fairy tales: Hansel and Gretel, Little Red Riding Hood, Cinderella, Snow White, etc.

These are art forms and works of creativity. However, they open Pandora's box. The body does not know the difference between what is real and what is imagined. Once *Mind/ mind* observes something, it files it away as memory. Just because it is on film does not make it any less diabolical, horrific, or frightening. Children are introduced to the concept of darkness early on through fairy tales. Once seeds are planted within the subconscious, they grow. Sometimes, art imitates life, and oftentimes life imitates art. The devil draws us in because the *DEVIL* is within. I am the *DEVIL* . . . *You* are the *DEVIL* . . . They are the *DEVIL*. We are the *DEVIL*s. The loss of humanity is the rise of the *DEMON you/i/ we/they* have inside.

The flip side is the epitome of goodness. In a common desire to come together, we help one another, celebrate, create beauty, and love. This is the *ANGEL* within. I am the *ANGEL* . . . *You* are the *ANGEL* . . . They are the *ANGEL*. We are the *ANGEL*s. Ironically,

GOD is all of it; the *DEVIL* and the *ANGEL*. I am *GOD* . . . You are *GOD* . . . They are *GOD*. We are *GOD*. *You* have become the *GOD of your understanding* through the consciousness *You/you* hold. Since the world matches your *God/god/GOD*-given beliefs, the healing of this world can occur only inside your *Mind/mind/MIND*. Will you have as much faith in your ability as you hold in your inability? While aspiring to be Christlike, have *you/i/we/they* not also been Antichrist-like? *You/i/we/they* are born of a passion, a mania, a crazed fixation . . . indeed a *DIVINE SELF*-obsession.

GOD **was obsessed with bearing witness to** *his/her* **image and reflection**
again . . . and again . . . and again . . . as . . .
You . . . I . . . We . . . and Them.
Eight billion times over . . .
in plants, animals, landscapes, and skies . . .
plus within . . .
stars, planets, galaxies, and universes . . .
in angel, fairies, and orbs . . .
and in goblins, monsters, and ghosts.
Has this illusion merely been Divine schizophrenia?

True sacrifice is the release of one for another. The human mind views sacrifice as *giving up something that is cherished*. Religion refers to the *sacrificial lamb*. Indigenous peoples utilized sacrifice in special offerings to a deity. Sacrifice was the giving of flesh on an altar. It is defined as *an act of slaughtering an animal or person, or surrendering a possession as an offering to GOD or to a divine or supernatural figure*. Spiritual sacrifice is a sacred interchange that aligns with these prior examples.

You have been that human sacrifice, for the sake of a Divine *BEING* to remember, know, and see itself. As the Divine sacrificed unto *you*, life was for the experience of sacrificing the lower human self for the *DIVINE*. *You/i/we/they* are giving ourselves in sacrifice for the truth of that original divinity. This requires giving up the story, illusion, and condition. It means detachment: from your personality, identity, shadow, and light. Sacrifice invokes the full surrender of the lower *self* for the experience of awakening to the higher Divine *SELF*.

Sacrifice is not martyrdom, nor is it for the sake of others. It is not tragic or intended to be traumatic. It is an unconditionally loving devotion for the spiritual aspirant. Real sacrifice can be given only by the *Self*. In order for this to occur, *You* must meet the sleepwalker of the underworld. The lower *self* must sacrifice its burdens of withholding, hiding, shadows, lies, deceptions, darkness, and hunger for humanity to emerge. Your *animal* sacrifice is a gift of communion. Then, *Self* must meet the *DEVIL* within. Only then can the *DEVIL* be sacrificed to the *GOD SELF*. The subtleties of your *being* will not only shock *You* but also bring *You* back to *Being/BEING* centered in *Self/SELF*. Once all within *You/you/YOU* is known, the Great Unknown will await *You*.

You **are an animal that feeds; instinctive, reactive, and hungry.**
You **are a human that wants to be loved; logical, responsive, and seeking.**

You are a God that loves; organic, natural, and full.
Your human nature has submitted its life to animal transgressions.
Your spirit animal must sacrifice itself to Spirit/SPIRIT.
You will then dissolve back into the nothingness whence *You/you/YOU* came.

With time, *You* shall descend. *You* cannot force this moment. It must build in energy and pull *You/you/YOU* under. That *moment* asks *you* to plunge into death, while still living. It means giving in to your *self*-absorption, so that it swallows *You* whole. Willingly embracing the darkest parts of *You/you* brings forth the alchemical shift for knowing the adventure of a lifetime. Integration of all that rises within the shadows creates the experience for *Self* to compassionately see, hear, and acknowledge. Our dark times are callings from the lower world. Absorption of *self/being* prepares the earthen ground for the resurrection of the divine *Light/LIGHT* of *SELF/BEING*. This conscious, sacrificial opening to darkness brings forth the *unknown*, as a *high way* to the infinite. In this descension is your ascension. There comes a moment when *You* see every part of yourself clearly. Along with that, every moment of your life is seen clearly. This will occur naturally upon physical death. But it is possible within life, when endeavoring into figurative deaths of identity and ego layers.

By placing the animal part of *You/you/YOU* upon the altar—to be consumed by the fires of life—*You* give your body and blood to a dissolving process. The death of identities and labels is required for rebirth. The release of each identity takes *You/you* to the next sacrifice to be given. The first profound sacrifice will be the *animal* inside. The second sacrifice will be the *shadow nature*. The third sacrifice—sometimes occurring simultaneously with shadow and animal—will be the absorption of the dark elements within your *being*. Following the awareness and absorption of those will be the annihilation of each identity you hold. These metaphorical deaths unify your fragmented parts, creating alchemy. Your ultimate sacrifice is through the human being, your humanity, and higher *SELF* in *BEING* absorbed by Divinity.

The path of *Self/self/SELF*-realization invites *You/you/YOU* to drop into the depths of your *Darkness/darkness/DARKNESS*. This hidden nature of consciousness is the underworld that is filled with secrets, lies, and deceptions. It rests beneath the foundation of everything *You* have come to believe. The *Self* has been unconsciously steered by this dark side. Every living *blessing*—as described in *Living: The 7 Blessings of Human Experience*—has arisen through the choices of *Self* and the underpinning *self*. To achieve freedom, *Self* must sacrifice its life, stories, and attachments.

The holy sacrament of your divine nature blesses and keeps *You*,
as *YOU* rise into integrated Oneness.
What mystically occurs in this sacred rite of passage
is the *Knowing/KNOWING* of your *GOD-SELF*.

Aloneness follows the excavation of *self* as *you* intimately trudge into the dark discovery of *being*. This is a solitary journey that no other can accompany *you* on. Points of *Self/self*-anointed grace will reveal within this walk toward humility. Through this corridor, the very vulnerable, curious, and tumultuous steps of *being* completely human are real awakening. *You* may have thought of yourself as human before now. But not so; *you* have been part machine and part animal. Now, *you* are discovering the riches buried deep inside your body and bone. Sacredly stepping onto the human *being's* devotional path will break your heart open in a way *You* never imagined. Reaching this place is a gift from on high. Beyond here is the realm of *Knowing/KNOWING*.

The spaciousness and timelessness of *SELF* are attainable when willing to *Love/LOVE* yourself as *DEMON* . . . as *GOD* . . . and everything betwixt and between. In doing so, you utilize unity and communion to transform the *DEMON* into *DAEMON*, a supernatural benevolent *BEING* as opposed to a destructive *being*. This journey of wholehearted acceptance is the embodiment of *Namaste—the Divine in me sees the Divine in You*—between the existential *Self/self* and the holy *Self/SELF*. This graciousness and generosity gives *You/you/YOU* the heart to see divinity everywhere, in everything and everyone you meet. Blessed *being/Being/BEING* . . . Breathe deeply as *You/you/YOU* offer your lower nature in sacrifice to your higher nature.

May all tears be uplifting
and every action be inspiring.
May each step be illuminating
and each breath be enlightening.
May the Divine support, sustain, and surround you.
May Divinity arise, awaken, and abound within you.
May the Source of all Love and Loving
comfort, caretake, and create healing
in every cell, molecule, organ, and revealing . . .
As one for all . . .
and all as ONE . . .
Sweetly dream . . .
so to create the sweetest of dreams.

emulsify.

What are you dissolving?

**Come to your knees . . .
Dissolve every fiber of your *being*.
Resolve to becoming a puddle on the floor
where bone is not even recognizable.
I'll meet *you* there . . .
in the fluid nothingness . . .
the gooey greatness . . .
the sticky stories . . .
and creative capacity.**

Within the dark, the shallow, and the lackluster, the ember sits, waiting to be fanned by the breath of aliveness. The ember is given life with each daydream, spark of insight, imagination, and integration, becoming illuminated with every action and feeling of enthusiasm. This becomes a blazing fire in your willingness to create unlike any other.

Couer-age is the moment where the nucleus of *Being* overcomes all that has oppressed, victimized, and held back the power and presence of your true face. Each cell becomes energized to experience all that the heart desires, with deep passion and pleasure. This is the age of enlightenment because it is "in-light-I-am-meant." We each have a unique walk. It is to be celebrated regardless of color, race, creed, status, or any measurement. Every soul is a part of the universal fabric and plays a role in the balance of the cosmos.

**In the end we are all specks of dust . . .
and at the same time mighty, powerful, sacred temples of BEING.**

In grasping the magnitude of power and presence *You/you/YOU* possess as creation, old parts will fall away as the new blossoms. The butterfly is a symbol of transformation. You are the worm, the silk, the cocoon, and the butterfly at the same time. Most importantly, *You* are the process. To move from caterpillar to butterfly requires that you emulsify, allowing all that *you* were to become mush for something new be born. Emulsify . . .

Has the moment come where you will step beyond the ticking clock,

beyond your form having a function, and beyond your actions having an agenda?

**Are you willing to discover your vast unknown,
feeling into the powerful presence and creative expanse of that?**

**In Light of all you have been, all you are, and all you have yet to discover about
yourself . . . are you willing to move beyond the excuses and need to stay small?**

You have conformed to society, to family, and to life in order to fit in. *You* are not meant to adhere to the boxes and norms projected onto *you*. *You* are here to be timeless, beyond confining constructs of time, space, form, and function . . . beyond human and doing. *You* are a puzzle of unique design, garnering a hidden genius that interlocks in a specific way to the overarching sacred story of the cosmos. It is not possible to fit Spirit in a bottle . . . in a box . . . or into an identity. Yet, it has been done throughout time, which is why life takes *You/you/YOU* down paths of destruction and renewal. Emulsify . . .

**Will you step beyond the boxes of conformity you have become trapped in?
Will you live beyond the paradigms that have been laid,
and embark onto new paths . . . pioneering a new age?**

Every moment of your life appears for moving *You* toward nothingness. It aims to break apart the framework *You/you/YOU* believe is necessary. Nothingness is the gateway of expansion for *Being/BEING* and allowing, instead of doing and toiling. *You* are not the body, the identity, the ego, your job, your role, or your personality. That is the house of cards. Let it crumble . . . *venture down the rabbit hole, Alice.* Be in wonderland. Emulsify.

**Will you be the creative rebel?
Can you live with no excuses . . . and beyond the illusions?**

Open to what may feel like emptiness inside. This is vacancy, except for all the questions it holds. It may be perceived as depression, boredom, or loneliness, but that is the illusion. It is openness, a space *You* are not used to having. It is the echo that keeps resounding in your life, one that needs to be heard once and for all. *You* name it other things, giving it old labels *you* were taught. But if taking time to really feel into this void, *You/you/YOU* may discover a difference. Approach the space with a sense of inquiry, wonder, and adventure. It needs nothing because it is available to everything. This is not *a wanting,* but *awaiting . . .*

**Space is awaiting your awareness.
Openness is awaiting your presence.
Emptiness is awaiting your embodiment.
The void is awaiting the experience you will now choose.**

Close your eyes for a moment. Focus between your heart and gut. Feel that gentle quiver. Tune in; there is a raging river. It is *YOU,* ready to run wild and free . . . a bull in a china shop! *You* have attempted to keep Spirit in a bottle! But Spirit cannot be contained. You must dissolve and disappear for such magnitude to rise.

Passion has been brewing. It has been a cold brew, deepening into the rich flavor and fragrance that *You/you/YOU* emit. This energy is ready to be on fire, instead of in the fire, or even holding feet to the fire. *You/you/YOU* are the ember, ready to blaze. The *You*-niverse is calling. This call is loud and strong. There can be no more excuses that deny it. Dissolve . . . Emulsify . . .

Personal power is *personal*. It cannot come from another. Others will inspire, motivate, and even challenge *You* as a mirror. Only *You* can finally say, *I give me back to myself*. In doing so, *You* make life personal, giving *Self/self/SELF* permission to connect to your inner power. Your soul is calling *You/you/YOU* to the heart of the matter, where unique genius waits. Go to the source of your pain and garner the wisdom. It was not meant to keep *you* down. It is the staircase that will guide *You* back up. Emulsify . . . dissolve . . . become nothing . . . be nobody . . . and discover that something far greater has been in the works. This requires the ultimate sacrifice . . . *You*. Dissolve into the sticky, gooey, tender, softness of fluidity. Emulsify . . . and experience something rise out of nothing. Give it space. Offer it time. Cocoon it in solitude. Sit . . . and stretch. Be in tension . . . with intention. Grow . . . your wings. Blessed *being/Being/BEING* . . . Breathe deeply as *You/you/YOU* emerge . . . into *Knowing/KNOWING* . . . and fly beautiful One.

I shall enter your hearth and home.
You can leave, turn away, shut down, or hide . . .
but I will never abandon you . . .
I am here to love you fiercely . . .
I will love you boldly.
I am unconditional in my stance.
I will not falter, remaining by your side eternally.
I will never leave you.
We can go round and round in circles . . .
But I am here.
I am present. I am love personified.
I shall speak boldly . . . I will call you out . . . I won't let you go.
Awaken to the tension of not-knowing
before you go into the unknown.
When you do,
taste the full flavor of the journey that you are.
It is time to kneel
before your own sacred altar of time.
Discover the divine nature
of your true and timeless sacred presence.
Sweetly dream . . .
so to create the sweetest of dreams.

multidimensional.

Are you asleep, awake, or somewhere in between?

Who am I? . . .
Why am I here? . . .
Where am I going?
I am *me/you/them/us* . . .
I am here to remember . . .
***I AM* going *HOME*.**

Life is not some earthly expression of aspiring toward an external, universal counterpart; it is the sensory experience of time, energy, and space. What has no form becomes form and returns to formless. Life does not affirm a conceptual *SELF* standing above or outside *You*, nor a galactic being floating amid the stars. This multilayered existence allows contrast, which encompasses the depth, dimension, and bandwidth of experience. Every person, place, and thing is multidimensional.

You are a multidimensional *Being/being/BEING*,
existing at many times and in varied spaces,
that encompasses a ladder of vibrational frequencies.

There is nothing to evolve *from* or *into*. All states already exist. They each simply require your conscious presence. Every expression, time, and dimension exists within *You/you/YOU* in this very moment and always has. An entire spectrum of vibrational frequencies, illustrative of the least conscious to the most present, is continuously accessible. These dimensional levels and corresponding layers do not exist for the purposes of analysis or processing, but instead for expression and experience. They are not hierarchical or stepping-stones. They simply exist in dormancy or aliveness. To know who *You/you/YOU* are—and where *You* are anchored—in any given moment requires clear and active presence. Awareness of your perceived dimension awakens opportunities for different expressions and experiences.

Lower dimensional states are unconscious. They require something seemingly external as a catalyst for inner reflection and awareness. Individuals who have been conditioned into lower dimensions of *self/being* require rigor and discipline to move into higher dimensions. *Self/self/SELF*-judgment hinders transcending dimensions of living. Judgment veils other dimensions, while also creating new layers to sift through within the existing dimension. By not judging where *You/you/YOU* are, shifting into other dimensions of *Being/being/BEING* is more easily accomplished.

The *Self*-proclaimed, highly conscious person can be, and likely is, unconscious. All of us are more often unconscious than conscious. It is rare to find a truly conscious individual. Sustaining conscious awareness is a second-by-second, minute-by-minute, hour-by-hour, day-by-day commitment. However, within this dual existence, the challenge lies in remaining consistent.

The greater your level of presence, the higher your vibrational frequency.

Dimensions are embedded on the cellular level of the body: the reflective body, emotional body, mental body, physical body, soul body, etheric body, and universal body. Life experiences increase awareness within these bodies. Mastery at each level leads to increased authentic power and presence, which extends well beyond the size and shape of your physical form.

Body Layers of Growth and Mastery for Integration:

Growth as Contemplative Mastery: Reflective Body—This is the witnessing aspect of an individual. It is relative to the direction of one's vision and energy. If vision and energy are external, then the degree of inner reflection reduces. An individual engaging vision and energy within increases awareness and clarity.

Growth as Emotional Mastery: Emotional Body—This is the feeling layer that measures the emotional climate of the internal environment and outer expression. Polarities of expression that encompass apathetic and are disconnected to empathetic and intimate enhance experience. Emotions link to mental, physical, and spiritual bodies through reaction, response, or neutrality.

Growth as Mind Mastery: Mental Body—This is the analytic, processing, or mental-paralysis layer. It stores and holds memory, while also engaging fantasy or imagination. This body perceives through filters and lenses developed by identity, ego, and persona. The mind moves in threads, loops, logic, and attachment. Thoughts connect to feeling, sensation, and emotion in an attempt to make sense of, justify, defend, or create.

Growth as Physical Mastery: Physical Body—This is the densest of the bodies, vibrating at the slowest rate. With the capacity to hold, express, or withhold the emotional spectrum, these energies and densities are visible and invisible. When the emotional, etheric, or mental bodies suppress conscious or unconscious memory, physical issues can manifest.

The physical body has energy centers called chakras. These spinning wheels of energy correlate to the balance or imbalance of your outer world in relation to the inner-world experience. Each of these centers relates to a particular area of the body, governing beliefs, health, and specific body systems. For enlightenment to occur, related glandular systems must balance and activate through conscious alignment of energy centers, body sheaths, and inner and outer life.

Growth as Spiritual Mastery: Etheric Body—This is body that grounds and holds your essential nature. While surrounding the physical form, the etheric body acts as a bridge between the seen and unseen worlds. Its central pole runs vertically along the spine, connecting heaven and earth.

Growth as Soul Mastery: Soul Body—This is memory of all incarnations, along with your blueprint of incoming life experiences. The soul experiences the individualized form, while stewarding the parameters of your life, so to encounter areas of expansion, growth, and reconciliation necessary for returning to the full remembrance of Divine Oneness. The soul is the sacred witness and architect of your life.

Growth as the Unknown: Universal Body—This layer is all encompassing and interconnected with the whole. The Unknown is the collective experience and expression. The universal body is equanimous, neutral, and objective.

CHAKRA BODY BRIDGE OF INNER AND OUTER LIFE	GLANDULAR BODY CHEMICAL SYSTEM BRIDGE FOR ENLIGHTENMENT	EXPERIENTIAL BODY LAYER TO BRIDGE ALIGNMENT	BRIDGE OF CONSCIOUSNESS BETWEEN BODY BELIEF	BRIDGE OF BODY CONSCIOUSNESS HEALTH BAROMETER
ROOT	Adrenal Gland	Etheric Body	Survival, Belonging, Values	Bone, Blood, Legs, Feet
SACRAL	Sex Glands	Emotional Body	Relationships, Sex, Money, Creativity	Sex Organs, Bladder, Kidneys, Intestines, Lower Back
SOLAR PLEXUS	Pancreas/Spleen	Mental Body	Knowledge, Power, Knowing	Stomach, Weight, Pancreas, Liver
HEART	Thymus Gland	Physical Body Memory/Bridge	Idealism, Love, Harmony	Heart, Breathing, Lungs
THROAT	Thyroid Gland	Contemplative Reflective Body	Voice, Will, Intelligence	Mouth, Ears, Neck, Shoulders, Teeth
BROW	Pituitary Gland	Soul Body	Vision, Wisdom, Consciousness	Eyes, Sinuses
CROWN	Pineal Gland	Universal Body	Creative Capacity, Oneness, Divine Will	Brain Function

multidimensional.

The multidimensional layers of conscious awareness illustrate another spectrum. This outline serves as a gauge for *Self/self/SELF*-inquiry. These are dimensions within and between all of us. The listed expressions are not for judging or to be judged, but to embrace and absorb. *You* can be one or all of these at any given moment.

> **You are ever changing.**
> **You are not static. You are life.**
> **You are the black hole at the center of life**
> **that must absorb all that is experienced and expressed.**
> **You are the key to wholeness that rebalances all that unfolds.**

We are equal, individuated expressions of energy in an experiential process. Regardless of where *You/you* perceive yourself (or others) to be, all are Divine. Neutrality and detachment within experiences provides discovery for *what/who/where/when/why You/you/YOU* are beyond form, processes, and function. *You/you/YOU* will be, or have been, all things. Embrace where *You* find your *Self/self/SELF*. Then, climb the ladder of consciousness.

Dimensions and Qualities of Human Frequency, Vibration, and Expression:

The Walking Dead—deeply unconscious and robotic—These individuals are not listening, cannot see, and are disoriented from their purpose and spiritual connection. In a deep state of sleep, their eyes are dull. There is no direction or sense of self. The walking dead live in conformity, driven by fears and conditioning. Life remains on autopilot, with the individual living as if a machine.

The Dissonant—unconscious and resisting—These individuals shuffle through life, disconnected from themselves and others, often engaging in projection, blame, shame, and denial. Deeply embedded in human conditioning, these individuals live in conformity and *stuckness* within one or more areas of life. They have bought into programming and succumbed to being brainwashed. Their lives may appear successful or not, but the internal life will feel dry and be untended. These people constantly rage against life . . . they push to control . . . and force things into happening. The animal nature is expressing.

The Self-Absorbed—unconscious and unaware—These individuals are numb to their feelings, while engaging reactively to the world. They live at a surface level and are caught within escape mechanisms and addictions. These individuals have glimpses of life being different and are open to positivity and inspiration, but only enough to maintain survival. They exist primarily from the neck up. The *self*-absorbed may focus on *self*-help and personal growth, but they do so from a need to heal and be fixed. Their lives revolve around their issues, stories, and blocks. Unknowingly deeply invested in the small *self*, their existence is focused on the minutiae of their lives, making everything about themselves. Frozen in fear, they live lives of deep conformity but are unaware of doing so. Animal tendencies are still present.

The Dysfunctional Mass/Mask—unconscious and aware—These individuals profess to be of the *Light* but have not fully embraced and owned their darkness. They have awakened some intuitive gifts and a sense of connection but encounter bouts of unconscious programming and dysfunction due to denied shadows. They may profess to be spiritual or religious. These individuals are unconscious to how they maintain the conditioning from their families and the world. They subtly participate in hierarchy and see themselves as awake and conscious. There is a tendency to name people as conscious and unconscious, or high vibration and low vibration. They try to avoid darkness, negativity, ugliness, and individuals that are not of the same leaning. They look for *like-minded* people, assuming they are surrounding themselves with other *awake* souls. They can be *Self/self/SELF*-absorbed, but with an intention toward service. Their acts of service engage subtle layers of codependence. Deeply unconscious animal behaviors can still be present.

Humans—conscious unconscious hybrid—These individuals willingly and consciously embrace their darkness. They see, hear, and acknowledge themselves. These people possess the ability to connect with the heart, mind, and intuitive nature when in relationship with others. There is increased attention to witnessing where thoughts, behaviors, and actions stem from, as well as being aware and present to what arises in themselves and others. They know they have issues, and they diligently remain in partnership with others to perform the inner work necessary. These people desire to be better and do better. They actively engage clearer communication, bolder truths, and inspired action so to live beyond conformity. They can be *self*-absorbed but lean toward finding heart-centered others in community. There is a level of comfort in their aloneness. They embrace the animal, shadow, human, and divine tendencies that become apparent.

Divine Beings—integrated presence and conscious—These individuals experience greater connection, wholeness, and inherent Divinity. They operate in the world with lessening degrees of control or holding personal agenda. While placing more energy into service of the whole, there is no attachment or need to fix anyone or anything. There is ever-decreasing reaction, or need for action. They understand that *presence is enough*. A deepened integration of power through alignment and connectivity is present, while embracing greater simplicity and silence. They have attained a sense of peace, detachment, and oneness with the world but still catalyze change through their example of embodiment and expression. These individuals are content being alone or in community, but all interaction expresses authenticity and intimacy.

Demigods—oneness and superconscious—This state knows itself. It is *the power and the presence*, individually and collectively. The demigod's mission is for ever-increasing creative capacity and compassionate presence toward unity. This is the unified expression of Lover and Beloved—through a balanced Masculine and Feminine—embodying no judgment or separation. They engage the return to Oneness through moment-by-moment living, recognizing darkness and light as *One/one/ONE*.

ISNESS—living/being/knowing absorbed and dissolved—No thought, no mind, no personality, no one. All and no thing.

This ladder of consciousness expresses varying frequencies of experience. Regardless of where *You* find yourself, the opportunity to shift to another level remains present. All people possess the same capacity to awaken *greater levels of Being/being/BEING*. Each level of conscious awareness carries its own nuances of energy, truth, growth, and wisdom. We are a world filled with *Light/light/LIGHT*. *Darkness/darkness/DARKNESS* is the illusion that rises when the eyes and ears are closed to *Light/LIGHT* of *Truth/TRUTH*.

Embody each experience without getting stuck within it.
Let each moment serve the soul's desire, rather than ego's distraction.

The soul's only true language is *Love/love/LOVE*; anything else is silly noise, a betrayal of *Self/self/SELF*. *Love/love/LOVE* is a dimensional and layered experience with its own ladder of consciousness: narcissistic love, abusive love, codependent *Love/love*, interdependent *Love*, compassionate *Love*, unconditional *Love/LOVE*, Divine *LOVE*, *Is*ness. While you are learning to see and speak with *Love/LOVE*, train your ears to listen and hear as *Love/LOVE*.

In the course of a week, I can be in many places . . .
In the course of a day, I can be in any state . . .
In the course of the moment
I can only be where I am.
In the now . . .
I AM.

0
0 0
0 0 0
1 1 1 1
1 1 1
11
0
1 1
1 1 1
1 1 1 1
0 0 0
0 0
0

---

the masters.

What are you in allegiance to?

You/you **created a mess,**
which now sends messages.
This has infiltrated the masses,
continuing a legacy . . .
that conditions, conforms, and oppresses.
Break free of your spell,
amid the brokenness that weeps.
Rise from within this collective dark night,
shaking off your restless, deep sleep.

You commit to either a *higher* Master or a *lower* Master. They express differently, each embodying a specific focus and vision relative to their importance within *You/you/YOU*. Your commitment to the master of your choosing calls forth experience not only for *You*, but also for others. The collective experience amplifies every thought, word, and deed toward a global reflection. It is imperative to discern where your faith, trust, and devotion are anchored. *You* either believe in a world of separation, evil, pain, and discord, or *You* believe in a world that is unified, good, well, and joyful. However, if like most people, *You/you* seesaw between the two. This creates a world of duality and suffering, where *you* wait for the other shoe to drop. *You/you* cannot serve two Masters and expect a single outcome.

Regardless of whether *You/you* serve a higher or lower master, the universe will use your—and every other person's—actions and behaviors for greater good. Life equilibrates all experience toward the greater end of balancing universal forces. This end is subject to the *time You/you* take. The universe is not concerned with time; it allows *You/you/YOU* to play the game of life for as long as it takes. The universe has all of eternity for us to figure out how to truly *Love* ourselves and each other. *Love/LOVE* is ultimately the highest universal outcome. A world of *Love/LOVE* may be incomprehensible to the *Mind/mind*, since it is unable to see beyond the fantasy world that it created. However, life is ultimately wired for alignment with the Source of unconditional *LOVE*.

Great value comes through knowing which master drives your impulses and actions. Lower and higher masters create outer lives that illustrate a blend of defunct and prosperous living. But the inner life for each will be specific. The higher master is inspired by life's sacred keys, fueling *whole*ness within its creation. This individual's internal experience is focused on unlocking expansion through devotion, tenderness, trust, balance, fulfillment, purity, and innocence. Alignment is embodied through deepening these keys in all areas of life. To love, empathize, celebrate, and uplift are ways of *Being/BEING* in allegiance to higher mastery. Addiction can be present, but these forms will lean toward fulfilling the inner spirit rather than feeding inner demons. The individual cognizant of transcending lower vibe patterns and behaviors will pivot their words, actions, and deeds toward more-conscious choices.

Lower and higher masters exist on internal and external levels. Alignment with a higher master requires the vertical alignment of right thought, right word, and right action. If these are not aligned, a lower expression of mastery is guiding. The lower master embodies the horizontal path of time, creating experiences of victimizer and victimhood to student and time traveler of the past. Lower masters create in the third dimension. When outer influences direct and control your life, victim experiences will be created. Personal power is more easily usurped by another. Following any lower master—internal or external—is a commitment to suffering. Play wherever *you* desire, but be clear that your choice affects every aspect of your world. Your anchoring will also ripple out into the world.

CONSTRUCT	LOWER MASTER	HIGHER MASTER
UNDERCURRENT "HOLE" OR "KEY"	Slothfulness, Lust, Greed, Envy, Pride, Gluttony, Wrath	Devotion, Tenderness, Trust, Balance, Purity, Innocence, Fulfillment
IMPULSE OR DRIVER	Time, Duality, Money, Hierarchy, Identity, Evolution, War	Hear Thyself, Receive Thyself, Heal Thyself, Know Thyself, Free Thyself, Accept Thyself, See Thyself
THOUGHTS	Obsession and Drama	Inspiration and Cultivation
ALLEGIANCE	Hierarchy, Ego, Business, Politics, Homogenization, Visions, Revolution	Example, Humanity, Philanthropy, Mystic Heart, Servant Leadership, Spiritual Rebel, Equality
ADDICTIONS	Consumption, Numbing, Hunger, Cravings, Aversions, Control, Significance, Righteousness, Healing, Speaking, "Need," Self, Illusion, Self/Personal Growth, Fantasy, Others	Breath, Presence, Love, Truth, Right Thought, Right Word, Right Listening, Detachment, Creativity, Connection, SELF, SELF/Empowerment, Gratitude, Knowing, Inspired Action

The lower master is driven by vices, in an attempt to fill the *hole* within. This persona is unconscious and unaware of the undercurrent their life is dominated by. Their innermost *Being/being* experiences currents of slothfulness, lust, greed, envy, pride, gluttony, and wrath that are justified and defended by the ego. Interactions, actions, and relationships will be laced with interference, obsession, and a lack of boundaries. This shadowy dysfunction plays out as dominance, control, pride, cravings, and aversions. Life will be wrought with cycles of suffering. Judgment, blame, and shame toward anyone or anything portrays an allegiance to a lower master.

Addictions will be born of the numbness, indifference, and apathy that build. Alcohol, drugs, sex, and overindulgence become subsequent lower masters that rule. Shadow frequencies are energetically passed to generations that follow, seeding offspring who carry the same degenerative and devolving tendencies until the pattern is broken.

Your agendas, underlying intentions, and energy create rippling effects. *Being/being/BEING* affects energetic architecture that surrounds not only your life span, but also the constructs of how life spans beyond your time. Life is commanded by the *One/one/ONE* who rules your interior.

Do *You* follow false gods?
Are *You* under the influence of a *lower* or *higher* master?

Experiences labeled *dark*, *negative*, *tragic*, or *sad* are often the very ones that initiate illumination. Renewed perspectives of positivity... new ways of serving... and deepening of humanity are born out of spaces that hold pain and resistance. In the *grand scheme*, such incidents occur to balance life's imbalances. Every expression—light and dark—is valuable for the collective. Every situation, experience, and circumstance falls within the higher orchestration of life's Divine plan. As an energetic cog in the wheel of time, *You/you/YOU* either assist or delay the return to Oneness.

By rising into vertical alignment, *You* free *self* from a life of suffering, allowing *Self* an opportunity to live in potential and possibility. This pivot opens *You/you/YOU* to the embodiment and *Knowing/KNOWING SELF*, who is a divine tuning fork for all of existence. *You/YOU* are nobility, with the power to command. *Being/being/BEING* is creator of the thought, feeling, action, and manifestation that results. When ready to peer into the mirror of experience, *You* will meet the maker of all that *You/you/YOU* see and feel. Blessed *Being/being/BEING*... Breathe deeply as *You/you/YOU* observe your masters.

You prayed forth
the earth, air, wind, water, and fire.
You slipped into slumber . . .
Summoning obstacles, challenges, conflict, and chaos,
to have . . .
the time of your life . . .
You need only remember to . . .
Sweetly dream . . .

0
0 0
0
0 0
0 1 0
1 1 0 1 0 1 1
0 1 0
0 0
0
0 0
0

the matrix.

What is happening here?

The universe laughs . . .
not at us, but with us . . . inside us, and all around us.
Behind the mask of comedy
lay sight of the unseen.
Inside the gaze of tragedy
is insight into whom we've been.
Two masks.
One body.
A state of being.
No masks.
No body.

In order to undo what has been done, we must go back to what we have known with awareness and presence. This is different from mental processing or emotional reaction. It will not happen by incorporating energetic healing modalities, physical exercise, and body immersions. Cellular deconditioning is unwinding the wound through feeling, witnessing, allowing, and absorption. It requires the discipline of not reacting, not responding, and not interfering with the external circumstances in your life, especially the chaotic, painful, and drama filled.

Conditioning has been acquired in layers. Wounding is also layered. These two are as intertwined as your DNA. They coil through *you* like a weed wrapping itself around a healthy plant. No matter how many times *You* pull away the weeds, they reappear, hindering full and healthy growth. So, what to do?

These *energetic* weeds must dissolve and can do so only by allowing them to fully grow. Weeds renourish acidic soil. Allow your garden to become overgrown with all *You/you/YOU* think, feel, and hold so you can truly absorb what has long been buried within the subconscious. Until willing to acknowledge and fully embrace how negative, dark, angry, prideful, lustful, gluttonous, envious, greedy, and apathetic *You/you/YOU* are . . . these energies will remain active. They will also run your life. Furthermore, they become your contribution to the world we see today. Being witness to what rises within *You/you/YOU*—mentally, emotionally, physically, and energetically without any external response—initiates the absorption process. This is the real work of *self*-realization.

What have we done?
What are we doing?
Whom are *You/you/YOU* freeing?

Each of these books—*Living, Being, Knowing*—illustrates layers of *Self* in a somewhat linear way. However, *You/you/YOU* are anything but linear; *You/you/YOU* are multidimensional. These books work in tandem as that multidimensionality. It is quite beautiful and magical to see the complex nature of our human existence, while also fathoming the simplicity of creation that sits behind it all. Creation desired to know more of itself . . . from all angles . . . dimensions . . . times . . . spaces . . . and levels. *You* are an intimate particle of oneness revealing itself.

You have a human experience. *You/you/YOU* also have a soul expression. These both contribute to the oversoul experience. Through the experience of the physical, the soul is able to expand the wisdom and experience of the oversoul. Your soul chose for this incarnation various circumstances, appearance, parents, and life experiences to be played out. This was done to experience various perspectives of life. If you were rich in one lifetime, *You* experience poverty in another. If *You* were a villain in one life experience, you'll have the life of the hero in another. If *You* are a murderer in one scenario, *You* will also return as a victim. *You* have an opportunity to see from every set of eyes, feel a full range of emotions, and palpably experience the different landscapes of life. The soul is timeless.

I am . . .
You are . . .
We are . . .
This *IS* us . . . All of Us.

The oversoul is comprises all souls; it has an infinite number of *eyes/i/I*s. It experiences everything simultaneously in timelessness. It is the space before all space. Herein is the doorway to the infinite. Between the soul and the oversoul are multiple dimensions of *Being/being/BEING*. These dimensions are composed of sheaths, which are inner veils that keep *You* from fully seeing your infinite *SELF*. These sheaths move beyond linear time yet encompass time. They are beyond space but encompass form. They are the portals back to infinite *BEING*.

In moving through the seven sheaths of the human condition, *You/you/YOU* engage cellular deconditioning for an embodied multidimensional awakening into *Knowing/knowing/KNOWING* your hidden truth. *You/you/YOU* are experience experiencing itself on many levels, within multiple spheres of reality. Bearing witness to these aspects allows for integrated and embodied wholeness. Ultimately, what you must understand is that whatever you endeavor upon must come from a state of wholeness . . . SELF . . . BEING . . . KNOWING.

There is *ONE TRUTH* . . . LOVE.
YOU are that.
It is your true *SELF*.
This is your natural state of *BEING*.
May angels soothe your soul . . .
May blessings sprinkle upon your choices . . .
May Grace kiss each experience . . .
May generosity wrap every encounter . . .
May love hold all steps . . .
May awareness abound in the discovery of all that *IS*.
Sweetly Dream . . .

multidimensional sheaths.

You have a spiraling layer of sheaths that are cocooned within consciousness. These sheaths are for reawakening to the wholeness of *LIVING*, *BEING* and *KNOWING*. Within *You/you/YOU* lay this stairway of vibrational frequencies—from least conscious to an all-encompassing unified presence of your eternity. These dimensional levels do not require analysis, processing or even understanding. They simply await awareness and embrace. They are not hierarchical, nor are they stepping stones. These layers exist in dormancy and aliveness at all times. *You* are a multidimensional being. Be present to all of *You/you/YOU*. Let these grids and sheaths be a way to begin fully seeing yourself... your possibility... your potential... and the pathway for your humanity.

SHEATH ONE

1	LIVING	BEING	KNOWING
	BLESSING OF LIFE	ILLUSION OF TIME	GRACE OF SIMPLICITY
Engages	Path of Seeker	Emotional Obsessions	The Storm
Reflects	Energy of Spirit	Global Reflection of Energy	Aura of the Master
Awakens	Growth as Contemplative Mastery	Hole of Slothfulness	Fragrance Emitting Beauty
Restores	Truth in Questioning	Key Whole of Devotion	Flavor of Gentleness
Reveals	Wisdom through Inquiry	Teacher to Example	Melody through Movement
Invites	Unification with the Wound	Cultivating Listening	Visceral Memory
Allows	Gifts of Signs, Symbols, and Synchronicity	Hear Thyself	Essence as Clarity

SHEATH TWO

2			
	LIVING	BEING	KNOWING
	BLESSING OF CHALLENGE	ILLUSION OF DUALITY	GRACE OF DETACHMENT
Engages	Path of Rebel	Secret Obsessions	The Flood
Reflects	Energy of Water	Global Reflection of Climate	Aura of the Light Body
Awakens	Growth as Emotional Mastery	Hole of Lust	Fragrance Emitting Union
Restores	Truth in Grounding	Key Whole of Tenderness	Flavor of Tenderness
Reveals	Wisdom through Expression	Egoist to Humanitarian	Melody through Balance
Invites	Unification with the Child Aspect	Cultivating Appreciation	Visceral Weight
Allows	The Gifts of Creativity, Imagination & Talents	Receive Thyself	Essence as Tranquility

SHEATH THREE

3	LIVING	BEING	KNOWING
	THE BLESSING OF CONFLICT	ILLUSION OF MONEY	GRACE OF DISPASSION
Engages	Path of Visionary	Material Obsessions	The Snow
Reflects	Energy of Air	Global Reflection of Fashion	Aura of the Crystalline Body
Awakens	Growth as Mind Mastery	Hole of Greed	Fragrance Emitting Wisdom
Restores	Truth in Essence	Key Whole of Trust	Flavor of Kindness
Reveals	Wisdom through Witnessing	Businessman to Philanthropist	Melody through Peace
Invites	Unification with the Creative Aspect	Cultivating Connection	Visceral Fight
Allows	The Gifts of Light, Love & Compassion	Heal Thyself	Essence as Purity

SHEATH FOUR

4	LIVING	BEING	KNOWING
	BLESSING OF CHAOS	ILLUSION OF HIERARCHY	GRACE OF FORGIVENESS
Engages	Path of Humanitarian	Personal Obsessions	The Drought
Reflects	Energy of Earth	Global Reflection of Human Rights	Aura of the Rainbow Body
Awakens	Growth as Physical Mastery	Hole of Envy	Fragrance Emitting Reunion
Restores	Truth in Stillness	Key Whole of Balance	Flavor of Groundedness
Reveals	Wisdom through Listening	Politician to Servant Leader	Melody through Service
Invites	Unification with the Feminine Aspect	Cultivating Conversation	Visceral Smoke
Allows	The Gifts of Communication, Empathy & Intuition	Know Thyself	Essence as Generosity

SHEATH FIVE

5	LIVING	BEING	KNOWING
	BLESSING OF OBSTACLES	ILLUSION OF IDENTITY	GRACE OF REBIRTH
Engages	Path of Sage	Masked Obsessions	The Decay
Reflects	Energy of Ether	Global Reflection of Wellness	Aura of the Angelic Body
Awakens	Growth as Spiritual Mastery	Hole of Pride	Fragrance Emitting Devotion
Restores	Truth in Action	Key Whole of Innocence	Flavor of Light
Reveals	Wisdom through Experience	Homogenized to Genius	Melody through Love
Invites	Unification with the Masculine Aspect	Cultivating Naturalness	Visceral Form
Allows	The Gifts of Strength, Patience & Perseverance	Free Thyself	Essence as Intimacy

multidimensional sheaths.

6	LIVING	BEING	KNOWING
	BLESSING OF DARKNESS	ILLUSION OF EVOLUTION	GRACE OF SELF-REALIZATION
Engages	Path of Mystic	Spiritual Obsessions	The Rain
Reflects	Energy of Fire	Global Reflection of Security	Aura of the Violet Flame
Awakens	Growth as Soul Mastery	Hole of Gluttony	Fragrance Emitting Communion
Restores	Truth in Silence	Key Whole of Fulfillment	Flavor of Softness
Reveals	Wisdom through Unity	Visionary to Mystic	Melody through Inspiration
Invites	Unification with the Devil Aspect	Cultivating Presence	Visceral Ash
Allows	The Gifts of Stillness, Breath & Doing More Nothing	Accept Thyself	Essence as Vulnerability

SHEATH SEVEN

7	LIVING	BEING	KNOWING
	BLESSING OF DEATH	ILLUSION OF WAR	GRACE OF FREEDOM
Engages	Path of Love Catalyst	Mental Obsessions	The Wind
Reflects	Energy of Creation	Global Reflection of Information & Technology	Aura of Holiness
Awakens	Growth as Mastering the Unknown	Hole of Wrath	Fragrance Emitting Sacredness
Restores	Truth in Humanity	Key Whole of Purity	Flavor of Wholeness
Reveals	Wisdom through Presence	Revolutionary to Spiritual Rebel	Melody through Song
Invites	Unification with the Divine Aspect	Cultivating Generosity	Visceral Flight
Allows	The Gifts of Aliveness, Peace & Joy	See Thyself	Essence as Humility

glossary of dimensions.

When what has not been spoken
is spoken aloud . . .
It can no longer be denied.
Healing happens.
Wholeness reveals,
In the beginning is *the word* . . .
In the end is *the word* . . .
Before and after,
beneath and over,
the word created everything.
All that remains *IS* . . .
the sound of silence,
and the echo of space.

There are many aspects to language that make it multidimensional: tone, texture, staccato, speed, volume, intent, and reference. Tone has to do with sound, while texture relates to taste, staccato to touch, and speed to smell. Volume is hearing; intent is vestibular, meaning the inner ear. Reference point is proprioception, meaning a sense of positioning or the sixth sense. The use of the senses is important in comprehending, communing, and intuiting what is truly *Being/being/BEING* said, and who—which aspect of the individual—is saying it.

Language	Sensory Perception
Tone	Sound
Texture	Taste
Staccato	Touch
Speed	Smell
Volume	Hearing
Intent	Vestibular
Reference	Proprioception

The following terms are used to delineate dimensions of personhood from shadow to Divine. The book was written in this manner to create a pattern of repetition and recognition of who, how, and where an individual operates from. By bringing presence to the dimensions of personhood, cellular memory is triggered to unlock what has been hidden or denied. In this way, awareness is catalyzed and greater unity is present.

A second intent for writing the book in this manner is to support *You* in seeing the dimensions in which language, action, thought, and focus are related to the shadow *self,* the identity *Self,* and the higher *SELF*. You can review any word to discern where *You/ you/YOU* are living from. For example:

What is said is as important as who says it.
The manner in which it is spoken illustrates the position of the speaker.
The definition of its depth reveals the quality of the speaker as a listener.

Lowercase *intimacy* would be the surface level of the world. Most people would think of *sex* in this regard. *Intimacy* with the uppercase first letter and lowercase remaining letters would pertain to vulnerability, realness, and openness with others; the communion and safety within a group or the full presence and commitment in truth to a group. *INTIMACY* would pertain to union with the Divine.

Lowercase *creation* would be the act of making something. Most people would think of art, building, or making something. *Creation* with the uppercase first letter and lowercase remaining letters would relate to manifesting in conscious and unconscious ways. *CREATION* would pertain to the conscious intent of masculine and feminine energetic forces wielded to create.

All words can be looked at multidimensionally because they carry a vibratory signature related to tone, texture, staccato, speed, volume, intent, and reference.

To most easily manifest, let go of the past;
forgive it and forget it.
Do what you love, and love what you do.
May laughter abound in your life . . .
as the sense of humor teases the stark moments . . .
lightening/lighting up in the dark.
May angels soothe your soul . . .
May blessings sprinkle upon your choices . . .
May Grace kiss each experience . . .
May generosity wrap every encounter . . .
May awareness abound in the discovery of all that is.
Sweetly dream . . .
so to create the sweetest of dreams.

glossary of terms.

being—This expression of personhood is the unconscious, lower vibration and hidden shadow nature.

Being—This expression of personhood is the identity that surfs existence between lower and higher nature, unconscious to somewhat conscious.

BEING—This expression of personhood is of a higher nature that aspires to deeper presence and conscious living. This is the closest to divine presence that one can become in human form from the perspective of the mind.

Being/being—This expression of personhood is the merged experience and expression of the unconscious, shadow nature and identity that surfs between lower and higher nature, unconscious to somewhat conscious.

Being/BEING—This expression of personhood is the merging of identity that surfs between somewhat conscious and the higher nature that aspires to deeper presence and conscious living.

Being/being/BEING—This expression of personhood is the unified expression that soul came to experience, express, and witness.

DAEMON—A supernatural benevolent power that is the unification of all aspects of light, sound, color, and space

demon—The aspect of personhood that is the shadow. This may be unconscious and hidden and is always active to some degree.

Demon—The expression of personhood, hidden or active, that is shadow nature, which is the raw animal nature

demon/Demon—The expression of personhood, hidden or active, that is darkness. It is the expression of the monster inside. It is the raw animal plus a more intense shadow expression.

DEMON—The expression of darkness that is the same intensity but opposite polarity to LIGHT. This is the devil within.

demons/Demons/DEMONS—The unified expression of darkness; the devil, monster, and raw, animal nature

god—The unconscious expression of personhood as an active creator of reality

God—The somewhat conscious expression of personhood as an active, more intentional creator of reality

GOD—The creator of all reality: good, bad, or indifferent

God/god/GOD—The unified presence of cocreatorship regarding reality, life, experience, and expression

god/God/GOD—The unified presence of cocreatorship regarding reality, life, experience, and expression

Home—The physical space of inhabitance; the body or a structure

HOME—The place of belonging; a structure, space, and sacredness

Home/HOME—The unified integration of the body as a sacred vessel of belonging, while also at one with existence and higher expression of creator

love—The expression and field of experience that is dual, shadowed, and codependent within relationship

Love—The expression and field of experience that is dual. It moves between shadowed and codependent to light and independent within relationship.

LOVE—The expression and field of experience of oneness. This is a field of unconditional presence that integrates life in an interdependent way.

Love/LOVE—A dance within the field of experience that moves between shadow and light. It leans toward more-healthful expressions that are independent, with a leaning toward unconditional and interdependent.

love/Love/LOVE—The unified field of expression that holds relationship at all levels between codependent, independent, and interdependent

knowing—The stance of ego, identity, or shadow based on conditioning, knowledge, or arrogance

Knowing—The stance of identity or ego based on knowledge, intelligence, and intellect

KNOWING—A pure integration, understanding, and expression of intuition and intelligence

knowing/Knowing/KNOWING—The union of intellect, intelligence, knowledge, and arrogance

light—An expression of positivity and illumination that might also be a mask

Light—An expression of positivity, leadership, and illumination that serves in the world but also possesses a hidden aspect of shadow in thought, attachment, agenda, or a combination of these

LIGHT—Purity of thought, expression, and service with no attachment and no agenda

light/Light—An expression of positivity and illumination that might also be a masked shadow of artificial lighting, while also illustrating positivity, leadership, and illumination that serves in the world

Light/LIGHT—An expression of positivity, leadership, and illumination that serves in the world, but with some attachment or agenda while also leaning toward higher expressions that have no attachment, agenda, or need for recognition

LIGHT—Purity of thought, expression, and service with no attachment and no agenda

light/Light/LIGHT—A unified expression that moves in waves between dim to bright

mind—The realm of unconscious thoughts, patterns, behaviors, shadow, and woundings

Mind—Intellectual, knowledge-based space of questions, process, analytics, and thinking.

This operates both in conscious and unconscious ways.

MIND—Higher intelligence. The cocreative power of the universe.

Mind/mind—The expanse between unconscious thoughts, patterns, behaviors, shadow, and woundings and intellectual, knowledge-based space of questions, process, analytics, and thinking. This operates both in conscious and unconscious ways.

Mind/MIND—The expanse between the intellectual, knowledge-based questions, process, analytics, and thinking and the Higher intelligence of cocreative power

mind/Mind/MIND—The unified field that holds the unified field of shadow, intellect, and genius

one—The individual

One—The individual in their power

ONE—The power and presence of many coming together

one/One/ONE—The unified presence of the many, from shadow to light, unconscious to conscious, demons to gods. The collective experience.

self—This expression of personhood is the unconscious, lower vibration and hidden shadow nature.

Self—This expression of personhood is the identity that surfs existence between lower and higher nature, unconscious to somewhat conscious.

SELF—This expression of personhood is of a higher nature that aspires to deeper presence and conscious living. This is the closest to divine presence that one can become in human form from the perspective of the mind.

Self/self—This expression of personhood is the merged experience and expression of the unconscious, shadow nature and identity that surfs between lower and higher nature, unconscious to somewhat conscious.

Self/SELF—This expression of personhood is the merging of identity that surfs between somewhat conscious and the higher nature that aspires to deeper presence and conscious living.

Self/self/SELF—This expression of personhood is the unified expression that soul came to experience, express, and witness.

truth—Distortion and perspective

Truth—What is believed on a larger scale, on the basis of history, science, dogma, or heritage

TRUTH—What is . . . beyond intellect, knowledge, dogma, culture, or any manner of identification.

Truth/TRUTH—Perspectives, beliefs, and wisdom held by a larger expanse of the collective mind, on the basis of proof, science, spirituality, or the esoteric

truth/Truth/TRUTH—The merging of all thought, belief, and perspectives held in the field of consciousness. Everything—history, science, dogma, or heritage . . . beyond intellect, knowledge, dogma, culture, or any manner of identification . . . perspectives, beliefs, and wisdom—held by a larger expanse of the collective mind, on the basis of proof, science, spirituality, or the esoteric.

you—This expression of personhood is the unconscious, lower vibration and hidden shadow nature.

You—This expression of personhood is the identity that surfs existence between lower and higher nature, unconscious to somewhat conscious.

YOU—This expression of personhood is of a higher nature that aspires to deeper presence and conscious living. This is the closest to divine presence that one can become in human form from the perspective of the mind.

You/you—This expression of personhood is the merged experience and expression of the unconscious, shadow nature and identity that surfs between lower and higher nature, unconscious to somewhat conscious.

You/YOU—This expression of personhood is the merging of identity that surfs between somewhat conscious and the higher nature that aspires to deeper presence and conscious living.

You/you/YOU—This expression of personhood is the unified expression that soul came to experience, express, and witness.

Living —> Being —> Knowing
To live is to know.
To be is to live.
To know comes through living . . . Living and LIVING.
in order to know being . . . Being and BEING.
An endless loop of Source ignition,
experiencing Infinite choice
is the embodiment of
KNOWING.

0
0
0 0
0
0 0
0 0 0
1 1 1 1
1 1 1
1 1
1
0
0 0
0
0

about the author.

SIMRAN is a globally recognized speaker and catalyst for love, compassion, and humanity. As an "Example" for a New World Experience of Aliveness, she advocates for the Visionary and Mystic embodied within each person, while engaging individuals in the embrace of their darkest depths so to uncover their brilliance of Light.

SIMRAN is the #1-rated, archived, syndicated host of Voice America's *11:11 Talk Radio*, host of *11:11 InnerViews TV*, and publisher of the Nautilus Award–winning *11:11 Magazine*. Author of IPPY and IPA Gold Award–winning *Conversations with the Universe* and *Your Journey to Enlightenment*, and IPPY Gold Award–winning *Your Journey to Love*. SIMRAN creates art, books, and online courses to bridge humanity's experience and expression. Along with being a Tedx speaker, SIMRAN is the creator of the one-woman show *The Rebel Road . . . Connecting the Dots from What Was to What Is*.

Books by SIMRAN
Conversations with the Universe: How the World Speaks to Us
Your Journey to Enlightenment: Twelve Guiding Principles of Love, Courage and Commitment
Your Journey to Love: Discover the Path to Your Soul's True Mate
LIVING: The 7 Blessings of Human Experience

LIVING—BEING—KNOWING

is for individuals to go beyond current generalities, conditioning, and perceptions
and into the subtle layers of conscious participation as a Divine creator
within the collective vortex of our current reality.

It is time . . .

to transcend all limitations for the full embodiment

of

self/Self/SELF

as

eye/i/I . . . you/You/YOU . . . we/We/WE . . . they/They/THEY . . . us/Us/US

in

living/Living/LIVING . . . being/Being/BEING . . . knowing/Knowing/KNOWING.

In Energy, Truth, Growth, Wisdom, and Unification.

11:11
111
11
1
0

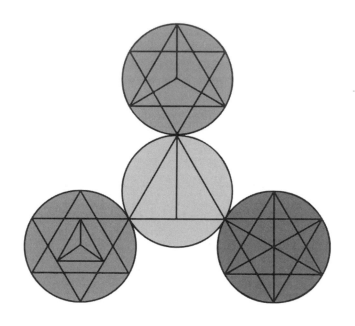

THE TRILOGY OF LIVING, BEING & KNOWING

YOU ARE THE GATEWAY . . .
THROUGH 7 BLESSINGS OF HUMAN EXPERIENCE.
YOU MAY EMBODY
7 HUMAN EXPRESSIONS OF GRACE
WHILE DISSOLVING
7 ILLUSIONS THAT DERAIL PERSONAL POWER, PURPOSE, AND PEACE.

BOOK 1
LIVING: The 7 Blessings of Human Experience

BOOK 2
BEING: The 7 Illusions That Derail Personal Power, Purpose, and Peace

BOOK 3
KNOWING: The 7 Human Expressions of Grace (Upcoming Release)